FORGOTTEN LADIES

BY RICHARDSON WRIGHT

HAWKERS AND WALKERS
IN EARLY AMERICA

"A veritable encyclopaedia of vagabondage. I do not see how anyone could read it without some twinges of envy both of the author for having thought of it and of the vagabonds he describes. There is hardly a page without its curious fact or fancy. A delightful and informing book—one not only to read but to dream over."—ATLANTIC MONTHLY.

THE PRACTICAL BOOK
OF OUTDOOR FLOWERS

"Tells of the culture of flowers with a frankness and thoroughness that give the confidence that might be expected only from a personal chat with an expert horticulturist. Many an amateur grower's problems are anticipated and answered."
—BOSTON TRANSCRIPT.

DEBORAH SAMPSON.

Published by H. Mann, 1797.

DISGUISED AS A MAN, DEBORAH SAMPSON FOUGHT IN THE REVO-
LUTIONARY ARMY WITHOUT REVEALING HER SEX. ALSO, HER
BIOGRAPHER ASSURES US, SHE "PRESERVED HER CHASTITY
INVIOLATE"

FORGOTTEN LADIES

NINE PORTRAITS FROM THE
AMERICAN FAMILY ALBUM

BY

RICHARDSON WRIGHT

Author of
"HAWKERS AND WALKERS IN EARLY AMERICA," ETC.
EDITOR OF "HOUSE AND GARDEN"

With 32 Illustrations

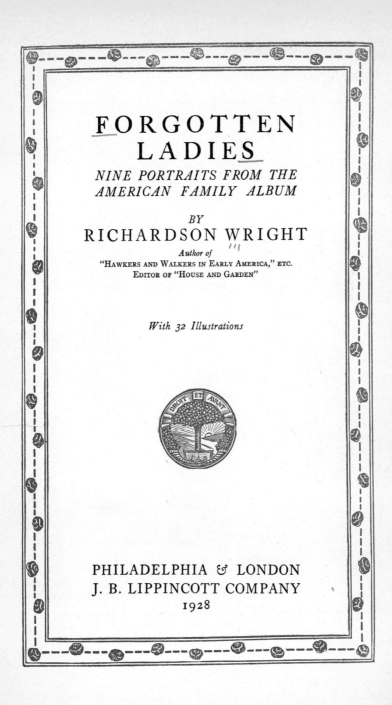

PHILADELPHIA & LONDON
J. B. LIPPINCOTT COMPANY
1928

FIRST EDITION

TO ANNE

Foreword

ON MANY a romance dust lies thick. Its glitter tarnishes like an old silver buckle. Its laughter is forgotten with last June's roses. Its beauty lost in the pale twilight of unremembered dusks.

Time brings this fate alike to the just and the unjust, to valiant endeavor and ignoble ambition, to tawdry scandal and gay romance. Out of the teeming hordes of the past only a few figures remain; the others—

> And they are gone; aye, ages long ago
> These lovers fled away into the storm.

Yet such time as they lived to be the playthings of Destiny many of these that are now obscure and forgotten made passing fair names for themselves and influenced their generation. And although their names may have been merely local reputations, their stories—piquant and romantic, evil or good—were products of their eras. However insistently Fate dogged their footsteps, it played its game according to the rules of their time and place. To reconstruct their lives one needs must reconstruct the *milieu* in which the comedy of those lives was played. The process presents a phase of their epoch.

Such is the purpose of this book: to select from the women of America's past a few whose lives show the diverse workings of Destiny, to set them against the backdrop of their times, to make them once more strut through the awkward, romantic, gay, ambitious, adventuresome and "sweet enforcement" of Fate.

They have been selected in this manner: as though, turning over the pages of an American family album, one encountered a face that stood out from the rest. "Somehow," you remark, "that woman must have had a past, must have lived life to the full, must have made a name for herself!" Yes, she did. And here are several of her kind—Forgotten Ladies!

RICHARDSON WRIGHT

SILVER MINE
CONNECTICUT
1 March, 1928

Contents

CONTENTS

Illustrations

FORGOTTEN LADIES

CHAPTER I

THE PRINCESS WHOSE STAYS PINCHED

AGAINST THE BACKGROUND OF COLONIAL LOUISIANA AND THE COURT OF LOUIS XV MOVES "THE SAVAGE MAID" TO HER ROMANTIC END

I

IT IS about time someone rewrote our nursery jingles and fairy tales, brought them up to date for the sophisticated youth of this era.

An Einstein, for example, might well trace, in words of one syllable, the astral trajectory that the vaulting cow followed when it jumped over the moon. Or a dietician give us his ultimate opinion on the gastronomic consequences of Jack Horner's having consumed that Christmas pie and its prize plum. And there are numberless pious people, self-elected pontiffs of the morals of the world, who could tell us in no uncertain terms the evil effects of old King Cole's pipe and bowl.

But of all these fantasies the one that has distressed us most is the story of Cinderella. We can accept her poverty and the fact that she wasn't invited to the ball; we know countless desirable young women who experience both of these disappointments. We can accept her rags being turned to rich silks and her sandals to glass and the pumpkin coach that took her to the party; science performs

even more wonderful miracles than these every day.
But we have often wondered how she ever managed
to dance in those glass slippers. What a relief, on
fleeing down the stairs at midnight, when she lost one
of them!

Meanwhile harken to another Cinderella yarn as
it is spun together from the slim threads of musty
old documents and legends. For here is the story
of a Princess whose rude garments were actually
turned to rich damask, who was gaily entertained by
a Court and its King, who won her Prince Charming
without a struggle, and should have lived happily
ever after.

II

Fr. Beaubois was ordered home. Being a good
huntsman for the Heavenly Kingdom, it was natural
that he would return with spoils.

This Jesuit missionary—Nicolas Ignace de
Beaubois—came out to Louisiana in 1720 and took
his post at the French village adjacent to Fort
Chartres up the Mississippi, not far from the Indian
settlement of Kaskaskia near where Chester is today. Missionaries had been working with the Indians
there since 1667, had converted vast numbers of the
Illinois and won their allegiance to France. For five
years Fr. Beaubois labored at his post and then,
being called back to France, he cast around him for
proofs of his labors.

The same suave, earnest appeals that won Indians

thereabouts to his banner and his cross soon convinced the tribes that when Fr. Beaubois returned, some of them should go with him. From the Illinois, the Osage and the Otoplata warriors were chosen chieftains who would undertake the long and perilous journey to France. With them went along a young Indian maiden. By what method she was selected out of all the Indian beauties of these tribes we are not informed. Nor are we told her name. In the quaint old chronicles she is referred to as "The Savage Maid." Perhaps the "Black Gown," as they called their Jesuit leader, superintended the selection. (¹)

The first ship on which they embarked came to grief. "One of our chiefs died by the way," the chronicle says, "and others were left on the Sea Shore." Fully a year passed before they landed in France. The priceless skins and the handicrafts of their wives, those fantastic garments woven of a fine glossy stuff made from buffalo hair and dyed, intended as presents for the King and the Court, were lost in this shipwreck.

Landed in France, they were taken straight to Paris. Here they saw, to their amazement, tall buildings—"five cabins, one on top of another." They "took rides in movable leather cabins," and visited cabins full of sick people where surgeons performed miracles. Years later, when Chicagou, the chieftain of the Illinois delegation, wanted to boast,

(1) Notes will be found beginning on page 295.

he would tell his people of the time he had visited Paris where the Frenchmen in that great village were as thick as leaves on the trees or mosquitoes in the woods.

Unaccustomed to the pomp and circumstance of Court life, these chiefs evidently thought that one walked straight in on a King, sent in the calumet as a calling card and the King came out smoking it. Here they found him hedged about with frustrating circumstances.   Chicagou earnestly protested:

"I am come hither to see the King in the Name of my Nation and my young people. When shall I see him? All the fine things I see are nothing if I do not see the King, our true Father and yours, and if I do not hear His Words to report them to my young people."

The Comptroller General answered this speech with a dignity befitting the occasion, and to each chieftain he gave a copy of his reply that they might take back to their people. After the manner of diplomats, he promised them everything under the beautiful shining blue of Heaven and then, to show that he really meant it, began passing out gifts.

Their *au naturel* costume evidently was a bit too scanty even for a Frenchman of the Regency. The gifts implied a hint directly pointed at their robust nudity. To each chief was given "a Habit completely French, being a blue coat with silver buttons, red breeches and hose, silver Lac'd hats, some with red and others with blue feathers, six ruffled shirts, six necks, etc. A Savage Habit, consisting of a Cloth Wrapper, five Quarters wide, with Silver Lace two inches above the List, which is left there because the Savages reckon it an ornament, a Broquet, which is a quarter of an Ell of scarlet cloth adorned with silver lace above the selvage. This they make use of to cover their Nudities. And a pair of Mitose, which are Cloth Stockings half blue and half red, which come up to the thighs, and are ty'd with Ribbons to their Sashes."

While all this palaver was going on, and while the chiefs were getting into their blue coats with silver buttons, their red pants and silver-laced, be-feathered hats, the Savage Maid was sitting modestly by. When her turn came, it was to dazzle even the most envious. Her dress was "a Damask Gown of Flame Colour, with gold flowers, an under petticoat of the same, a Panier, two pairs of Boddice, six lac'd Shifts, and Ribbonds of Gold and Silver, and a pair of Silk Stockings."

Some one of taste must have chosen that flame-colored damask gown, some early *couturier* with an eye to beauty; who else could have selected so becoming a color for a bronze-skinned maiden? Her difficulty in handling the panier, her reluctant and piquant awkwardness in getting into the bodice and laced shifts and the silk stockings we can leave to the imagination. It must have been a trying ordeal; indeed, she seems never entirely to have mastered them.

In this costume the Savage Maid was destined to write as pretty a page of romance as anyone could wish. And from this point on, splendidly arrayed in her flaming damask paniered gown, she begins to dominate the story.

III

In the expedition that left New Orleans was a young French sergeant by the name of Dubois, who had evidently accounted well for himself and merited this furlough home. Being susceptible, his fancy was captured by the charms of the Savage Maid.

This wasn't the sort of thing the French frowned upon just then, although Bienville lamented the scarcity of women for wives and complained that his men were running into the woods after Indian girls. In those primitive and dangerous days of the colony it was not unusual for young men to take wives from the Indian maidens. (²) It assured a certain degree of security against attack—for even a new son-in-law has some influence in the family circle—and, besides, it was better for lusty young men not to dwell alone. Then, too, such unions were not eternally binding, for the Indians of the near-by tribes seemed reluctant to form marriages for life. They were the first advocates, if we might inject a very modern term, of the companionate marriage. All these quaint affairs happened, of course, before the lovely *Filles a la Cassette* came to New Orleans, to lay the foundation of Louisiana's aristocracy. Consequently, when Sergeant Dubois was smitten, the good Fr. Beaubois conveniently looked the other way.

Having been entertained and properly clothed by the Comptroller General and his gentlemen of the Company of the West, the next move was to take this savage troupe, chaperoned by Fr. Beaubois, to Fontainebleau. On November twenty-second, they set out for the place, and two days later began a hectic series of visits to the Princes and Princesses and other Lords and Ladies of the Court who—"were fond to see Savages whom (a quaint touch!) to their Surprise they found to have as much Spirit and Good Sense as other Men."

They evidently made a vivid impression, for that night they topped off a busy day by being presented to the Duke of Bourbon. Indeed, they must have been pretty tired and hungry; in those days dinner at Versailles wasn't served till 10:30. Once more Chicagou, doubtless uncomfortable in his new finery, arose and made another flattering address.

Thus by slow stages they were surmounting the barriers that surrounded His Majesty. One step more, and they would enter into the Presence. It was a skilfully managed ascent, this approach of the Illinois, the Osage and the Otoplata Chiefs and their Savage Maid to the imperial throne. With a graciousness that only a courtier could extend, His Serene Highness promised to present them the next day to the King as he came from hunting.

Louis XV at this time, 1725, had reached the

impressionable age of 22. Already he had had his fill of blue coats with silver buttons and vermilion pants and silver-laced hats. He was always bored, this King, bored from the day he opened his eyes to the day he closed them. He "had a cold contempt of all mankind" we read, and the only thing that aroused his interest was the chase. Consequently, when these deer-hunting savages appeared, he roused himself sufficiently to demand his Indians wild. And no red damask skirts on that Savage Maid, either!

In which one of the many lovely ante-chambers of Fontainebleau they divested themselves of their finery, history does not record, but when Fr. Beaubois marshalled them into the presence of the King and his assembled cabinet, they were clothed with as little as they usually wore when they sauntered around the forests and rude huts of Kaskaskia. The good Father presented them in a flowery speech, after the manner of the times, and led Chicagou, war paint and all, up to the King. These ceremonies over, the fun commenced.

War dances! Dances of seed-sowing and harvest! The gyrations of mourning! The rhythmic exultations of conquest! Even a deer hunt was staged in the Bois du Boulogne. With such a strange olio did the chieftains entertain the Court. And quite a sight these savages must have been—naked to the waist, their chins and eyes lurid with Chinese vermilion, their shell necklaces rattling like seeds in a gourd, their bead-hoop earrings hopping at each step and their plaited pigtails, tipped with silver disks and vulture's feathers, swinging half a yard long behind them. Before the architectural and classical background of French sophistication, in the midst of all the elegant toilettes, visualize this wantoning of savagery! How strangely did their grunts and noisy inhalations lend a basso to the crisp and brittle chatter of the French tongue! And yet their luridly painted faces could not have seemed so strange to this Court, for in no other era of French history did the élite use such appalling quantities of rouge.

In all these fantastical and colorful games the Savage Maid gave delight to the jaded eyes of the Court. A little woman, lithe and quick of movement, she conducted herself in their presence with politeness and gentility. After the style of her tribe, her costume was more elaborate than the men's. She wore her hair parted in the crown, the line of the part streaked with vermilion. When occasion came for laughter she seized it, like French women. Who could resist her allure?

> Her limbs were straighter than the mountain pine,
> Her hair far blacker than the raven's wing,
> Beauty had lent her form the waving line,
> Her breath gave fragrance to the balmy spring.
>
> Each bright perfection opened on her face,
> Her flowing garments wantoned in the breeze,
> Her slender feet the glistening sandals grace,
> Her look was dignity, her movement ease.   (3)

Upon her the Court showered its generous attentions and its lavish gifts. She caused a furor!

She was *à la mode!* They called her a Princess. To entertain her became *chic!* Among the statuary in the gardens at Versailles stands a figure of an Indian girl that may well have been inspired by this Venus from Kaskaskia.

But to delight a pleasure-wearied Court and be a figure of esteem on which to pour rich presents was only a small part of the rôle the Savage Maid was destined to play. The moment had now come in this pretty game of romance for Fr. Beaubois to lay down his queen!

When all things were ready, Sergeant Dubois was raised from non-commission obscurity to a captain's rank and given command of the Illinois district. The Savage Maid, having proven by her docile attendance on Church services that she could be as good a Christian as any at the Court, was converted to Christianity and baptized at Notre Dame. Thus was she prepared for the inevitable consequence of her desirability. A short time afterward in the Royal Chapel, surrounded by a glittering Court and showered with the abundant blessings of the Church, Captain Dubois took the Savage Maid for his bride.

IV

The home-coming of this Indian expedition was made one of the unforgettable days in New Orleans's history. Quite a crowd debouched from their ship to the shore. Having been made superior of the missions, Fr. Beaubois brought seven other missionaries with him—non-Jesuits, by the way, since the Company of the Indies did not permit Jesuits to administer to French colonists. There were the Indian chieftains, of course, and Captain and Madame Dubois.

Everyone in New Orleans turned out to greet them. There was great feasting and many speeches and much display of the finery given them in France. So attached to French ways had Chicagou become that he lingered in New Orleans fully three weeks before starting up the river for home. But such blissful days must end, and life eventually assume its commonplace gait.

Fr. Beaubois settled down in New Orleans and soon became engrossed in the manifold duties of his office. Thanks to his persuasive endeavors while in France, there soon arrived in New Orleans a company of Ursuline nuns from Rouen, who founded the first convent in the United States. From that day, 1727, to this, they have continued without cessation their noble work of educating children, nursing the sick, comforting the sorrowful and holding up the arms that are wearied. Through many and varied regimes, in devastating wars and under conquering foes, through flood, pestilence, famine, fire, through poverty and the assaults of the world, these women have gone about their work unhindered, unruffled, courageous and devoted beyond measure.

When Chicagou arrived home in Kaskaskia he had great things to tell his tribe: all about those buildings in Paris that were five cabins high, and the King who received him, and the Court, and the marriage of Captain Dubois to their maiden. Regard this noble chief as he struts between the cabins in his blue coat with its silver buttons and his red trousers and his harlequin hose giddy with ribbons and the silver-laced cocked hat sprouting feathers! How the others must have envied him! How the lads must have sat, speechless and wide-eyed far into the night, listening to his tales of wonder! None of them ever forgot; indeed, his great-grandson vowed then and there that some day he would go to France—and he lived to keep his vow. [4]

Chicagou had the presents, too, to display. So many were these mementoes and so jealously did he guard them, that his relatives and friends were skeptical of his loyalty to the tribe. They really suspected the old man of having been bribed in Paris. Such treasuring of possessions was not the habit of the Red Indian in those times. He usually soon tired of what he owned and passionately desired whatever he saw but did not own. Chicagou, however, had a bag expressly made for the purpose, in which he kept the magnificent snuff-box the Duchess d'Orleans gave him at Versailles, and no amount of offers and bribes could induce him to part with it.

In good time the bride and groom took the station in the colony's life that their experience and rank merited. Boats, rowers, and an escort of soldiers conducted Captain Dubois and his wife up the Mississippi to the fort that was to be his command. Then they settled down into what might have been blissful rusticity.

Of course, at such an isolated station, there really were very few occasions when a girl could wear a flame-colored damask gown with paniers and gold ribbons, and if she went walking in those silk stockings the bushes and briers were certain to start a run! However, they *were* the latest models from Paris, and she was the only woman for miles who had anything like them. If she was a good wife, she doubtless copied all this finery in cheaper goods and saved the best for Sundays.

V

It is a great pity that this idyll cannot go on indefinitely. What fun it would be to trace back through the wilderness files the genealogy of this captain and his Indian bride, their children and grandchildren and great-grandchildren, and all the spreading branches of the aristocracy that sprang from them! Facts are unrelenting, however, and facts interpose an exciting and tragic finale.

Not all the Indians were so docile as Chicagou and his companions had been in France and since they came home. The constant and increasing invasion of their lands began to make bad feeling among Indians up the river, especially among the Natchez and such smaller groups as the Allibamons, the Chitimaches, and the Chicassas.

The tribes immediately around New Orleans had

been pacified with gifts. Bienville, the Governor, was as alive to the efficacy of gentle bribes as were William Penn and his followers, who had a fund set aside for that purpose. (⁵) The Tunicas, who lived near the Red River, he kept in good humor with presents of food that often proved embarrassing to the colonists. Many a time the French went without so that the natives might be fed, doubtless, on the principle that a good meal a day kept the Indian away. As soon as the French called a halt on this wholesale catering, the Indians transferred their allegiance to English traders who were deadly rivals of the French. Bienville also saw that their chief was given with due ceremony the loud-sounding title of "Brigadier of the Red Armies," and through him the King bestowed upon this warrior a gold-headed cane and a medal on a blue ribbon. (What in the name of sanity did this Tunica overlord do with that gold-headed cane? Lead dances with it? Or just strut?) The other tribes, however, suspected those bearing gifts, especially when they took the form of solid, business-like, lethal shot.

The French from Canada understood their Indians, but the French fresh from France seemed to lack this subtle comprehension. While the natives of the lower Mississippi were apparently being kept on peaceful terms with the settlers, those of the upper reaches showed open hostility. Much of this was due to the panic that possessed planters newly come to the colony. They lived in constant fear of Indian

attack and foresaw the day when their negro slaves
would join forces with the natives to exterminate the
whites. This living with one's nerves on edge caused
several groundless alarms and eventually led to a
bitter Indian warfare. Unsuccessful in handling these
Indians even with gifts, Bienville attempted to solve
the problem by bribing their enemies to attack them:
he offered handsome bounties for scalps of the Allibamons and Chitimaches. Due to this attrition,
many tribes that early explorers had known were
killed off or made nomadic within a generation after
the French came to Louisiana.

In 1728, a cabal having succeeded in unseating
him, Bienville was called to France, his lands confiscated and himself disgraced; this, after giving his
youth and manhood to the colony. In his stead
Perier ruled Louisiana, and Perier's novel scheme
for handling the savage Indian was to keep him sub-
dued by a campaign of terror. He armed the negroes
of the plantations and promised them freedom if they
dispatched whatever Indians came their way. Four
braves and two squaws of the Natchez were captured
and publicly burned on the levee before New Orleans.
Then he summoned troops from all parts of the colony, sent word to France for reinforcements, and set
out to slaughter the Natchez. But these savages
were too quick for him—they fled and took shelter
with the Chickasaws up the Red River.

Perier's failure was the failure of the Company of
the West. It returned its charter to the King and

the affairs of the colony were turned over to a board of three commissioners. Bienville was once more put in the saddle. His first step—doubtless spurred into sanguine activity by the failure of his precedessor —was to turn New Orleans into an armed camp, and such it was for the next seven years while he was leading his expedition against the Natchez and Chickasaws. October to December 1729 saw the Indians pillaging and massacring with fury. Life on the river became desperately unsafe.

During these times of terror, those who could, fled to the safety of New Orleans; those whose duty kept them in the Indian country, carried their lives in their hands. Among the latter was the new commandant of the department of the Illinois in his little stockaded fort far up the river. Of the few remaining white people in that territory perhaps he could enjoy the most satisfaction as having had the most enviable past. Paris was a long way off, and it had been many, many moons since he and his bride stood up before the Court and plighted their troth. What happy days! What splendid recollections! Anyhow, no one could take that from him! His immediate future, however, was rather uncertain, and the cause for uncertainty lay very near home.

The situation grew tense. No Indian was above suspicion. This proved extremely embarrassing to Captain Dubois. He knew his wife was loyal, but were the others at the fort so sure of it? How could

anyone suspect her of treachery? She had been to
France, she had enjoyed the hospitality of the French,
even at that moment her *armorie* was filled with the
gowns they had given her; could she be disloyal
to them? She was a Christian; would she dream of
helping his enemies? The idea of treachery was
unthinkable. Nevertheless he noticed that she began going off into the woods more than usual—going
off at strange times, always alone and always on
unexplained errands. Her disappearances became
pronounced. She began to have a different air about
her, too—independent, silent, insolent. Finally she
went off one day—and didn't come back.

Worry enough he had without this! Each courier
who dashed in through the stockade gate brought dis-
quieting rumors. Bienville was having a stiff time
of it. Refugees poured into New Orleans with their
tales of horror. On all sides the Indians had armed.
What chance had they if the Indians came, way up
there, far from reinforcements or help?

No news from his wife. She had left behind her
all those treasured gowns and all that finery that
women love. Surely she had not done this of her
own accord. Had she intended to desert him she
would have managed somehow to take them with
her. Of this Dubois was certain. He knew her too
well for that. There wasn't the slightest doubt in
his mind but that someone had caught her unawares
in the forest—some of her tribesmen, angered by her
loyalty to him and the French had dispatched her

out of hand and without mercy. And that was the end of it!

But the end came soon enough. One night the sentries sounded the alarm. The forest was alive with Indians. They crept nearer. Their arrows filled the air. With a wild yell they swarmed over the stockade. Thinned at each step, the garrison retreated before them. Dubois, his back to the wall, fought like a madman. For the leader of the Indians was his wife!

Some may say, "That's the way with Indians, always treacherous!" And the knowing ones will nod gravely and remark, "Ah, the poor thing had her head turned." They always say that sort of thing about a woman who has enjoyed her crowded hour of glory and then changed her mind about it.... Her head turned? Rubbish! Her stays—as did Cinderella's glass slippers—probably pinched her!

CHAPTER II
OUR EARLIEST "SISTER ACT"

*IN TELLING OF THE THREE STORER SISTERS AND THEIR AMOROUS AFFAIRS
WITH JOHN HENRY WE MANAGE TO TAKE A GLIMPSE AT THE THEATRE IN
EARLY AMERICA*

I

L IKE the poor, the mothers of actresses will always
be with us.

From that first performance when a Restoration
maiden faced popular disfavor by presuming to play
a woman's rôle, from that far-off day to this, the
wings of the theatre have been cluttered by adoring,
hopeful, hovering, protecting mothers intent on seeing their stage-struck offspring climb to stardom.

Living vicariously on echoed applause; by dint
of wit, quick tongue and ingenuity managing to
make ends meet; tawdry and overdressed themselves
and their brats prettified, simpering, bold, self-
conscious; enduring the rigors of the "road" and the
tragomasculous miasma of dressing rooms; meeting
with humility or hauteur the rebuffs and blandishments of managers and stage hands; bearing the
scorn or worship of stars; amiably dabbling in the
stale waters of sentimentality—such are the Niobes
of the theatre who sacrifice their children on the altar
of popular amusement. Some of them, contriving
and deceitful hussies, live through a lurid era of false
prosperity—of smart clothes and expensive eating

31

and the costly baubles of the luxurious—and eventually pass down into that sordid obscurity whence they sprang. Others, hoarders and long-headed, make hay while the sun of their children's popularity shines, gathering it into safe barns against the winters of their unpopularity and unemployment. Still others—alas, they are numbered!—grace their time and place with charming and abundant personality, women beloved for themselves alone, sprightly, amusing, rich in enduring talents.

Into this latter and estimable category fall many of those mothers of actresses who, themselves, are of the stage. The exactions of theatrical life seem to forge in them a different sort of fibre than is found in the ordinary woman whom chance has made a mother in Thespia.

Into this class of supple-fibred stage mothers we would presume to place Miss Clark of Covent Garden who, as Mrs. Storer, gave abundantly of her offspring to the beginnings of the American theatre. Her story and theirs is intimately entwined with that colorful and primitive raising of the curtain on Colonial America.

In 1763, Miss Clark, fresh from honors and applause at the Covent Garden Theatre, came to Jamaica, the British colony that was the birthplace of the legitimate American stage. She had recommended herself by "her amiable person, good nature and excellent sweet harmonious manner in singing."

Being a valiant mother of the stage, Miss Clark

brought to Jamaica her four daughters: one whose
name is not recorded, Ann, Fanny, and Maria, and
there superintended their acting and taught them
music.

In the same company at Kingston was a handsome
Irishman by the name of John Henry, a well-educated
lad out of Dublin, who had made his début at the
Drury Lane under the elder Sheridan. Here Henry
became a leading man, and his charms soon captivated the eldest of the Storer sisters. Unfortunately
their romance and her career met with a sudden end;
she was burned to death in a fire on the ship coming
up from Jamaica. The captain, the crew and the
other passengers managed to escape.

Having thus tragically disposed of the first of
these famous and amorous sisters, we can continue
tracing the development of the theatre in America.

II

In the latter part of 1766 David Douglass, manager
of the Jamaica Theatrical Company, ventured on a
tour of the American continent—came from Jamaica
to Charleston ([6]) where he played a season. Here he
was able to recruit some more members for his troupe,
"particularly in the singing way," among them Mr.
Woolls and Mr. Walls, both from London. The
latter was teaching the guitar to the genteel of
Charleston at the time and the former became the
leading male singer of the cast. Among the attractions Douglass put on between acts was George

Alexander Stevens's lecture on "Heads," which became very popular. Having completed the Charleston run, he went to Philadelphia to superintend the building of the new Southwark Theatre, a pretentious affair for the times, since it was built partly of brick. Here he managed to pursue quite a successful and remunerative season. Later he went to London to purchase scenery.

Accompanying Douglass from Jamaica came the remaining three Storer sisters—Ann, Fanny, and Maria, and during this Philadelphia run of 1766–67 all three made their débuts. Ann, or Nancy, as she was known to some, first appeared as *Biddy Belair* in "Miss In Her Teens," being advertised as "from the Theatre in Jamaica." Fanny, the next oldest sister, also made her first appearance, as did the youngest, Maria, then a mere child.

Whether or not Mrs. Storer sat in the wings and watched their first performances we do not know. Mrs. Storer fades from the records after her arrival in Jamaica. She did enough, however, in contributing these three daughters to the delight of American audiences.

The youngest daughter, Maria, was led on between the acts to lisp her childish songs, a fitting start for one destined to become the most popular singer of early America. Now and then she was entrusted with a simple child rôle. Her first appearance was in a ballad at the end of "The Gamester" on January 8, 1767. With this encouragement she be-

gan assiduously cultivating her talents and by the
end of the season she had won her way to celebrity.

The company moved on to New York. On
December 7, it opened the famous John Street Theatre, which was to serve as the centre of New York's
theatrical life during the next thirty years. It was
located on the north side of John Street a few doors
from Broadway—about numbers 17 to 21. The
premier at this house was the comedy of "The
Stratagem" with an "occasional epilogue" by Mrs.
Douglass and followed by the dramatic satire "Lethe."

As theatres are built today, this John Street house
was a ramshackle affair, a characteristic in which it
differed little from theatres built at that time.
Temporary structures, they were easily run up and
as easily pulled down, not unlike the "tabernacles"
built in country towns today for revivals. An idea
of what they were like can be gathered from the fact
that the predecessor of this building, the Beekman
Street Theatre, cost only $1625 to build and equip.

Properties and scenery were negligible. On the
road the scenery was rolled up and stuffed in the
trunks with the costumes. A row of candles furnished
the footlights, and the lighting of the auditorium was
by sconces which attendants replenished during the
evening. If the theatre was really first class, it
might boast a rude wooden chandelier. The heating
of these primitive theatres was accomplished by one
large stove, but the wise play-goer always brought
along her foot-warmer.

Such were the conditions at John Street. Constructed principally of wood, painted barn red—the favorite color for theatres of the time—and standing sixty feet back from the street, it was far from imposing. A rough, wooden, covered way gave entrance to it from the pavement. It had a large stage, beneath which the dressing rooms were located. After the Revolution these were placed in a shed wing added for the purpose of housing them. The auditorium accommodated the usual pit, two rows of boxes and a gallery. Completely filled, the "house" was worth $800, no mean sum in those days. However, devoted New York patrons of the stage paid lightly for their amusement: boxes, eight shillings; pit, five; gallery, three. The curtain rose at six o'clock, and it was customary to send one's servants at four to hold the seats.

From contemporary accounts one gathers that our early American audiences behaved themselves pretty badly. Hissing and rude shouting were commonplace—audiences and actors alike got used to them, but when ancient eggs and *Stalkus Cabbagiensis* began showering down from the gallery, Douglass felt it incumbent on him to complain of them. Fortunately they missed the stage, but they spattered the fine clothes of those in the pit and boxes. In Charleston when displeased play-goers expressed their feelings, they "shied" bottles across the foot-lights.

Nor were there any such fire regulations as safeguard the theatre today, no choosing of exits as soon

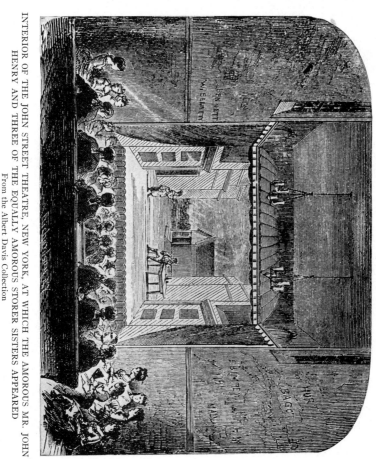

INTERIOR OF THE JOHN STREET THEATRE, NEW YORK, AT WHICH THE AMOROUS MR. JOHN HENRY AND THREE OF THE EQUALLY AMOROUS STORER SISTERS APPEARED

From the Albert Davis Collection

as one takes his seat. The young blades were accustomed to invade the stage itself and view the play from the wings. Often they interrupted the players and cut in on their lines with rude remarks. This became so troublesome that the manager was forced to put down his foot: No more Stage Johnnies! "No Person on any account whatsoever will be admitted at the Stage Door," Mr. Douglass announced, "And he is well assured that after this Representation, no Gentleman will insist upon it." Thus was instituted the regulation that is still enforced today.

This John Street Theatre under Douglass's management and with John Henry playing the second lead to his first, proved immensely popular. So great became the traffic of coaches that the management was obliged to ask their patrons to enter John Street by the Broadway end and leave by the other—either Nassau Street or Cart and Horse Street, which is now William. This, perhaps, is the first example of one-way traffic that can be cited in American history.

At the opening night of this theatre John Henry made his New York début. In the second bill of the repertoire, in Garrick's "Clandestine Marriage," Ann Storer, the oldest of the three remaining Storer sisters, made her first New York appearance. Shortly after this we find her referred to as "Mrs. Henry." And thereupon we stumble on John Henry's supreme weakness. It appears that he did not possess what the Longer Westminster Catechism pleasantly calls "the gift of continence." The Storer sisters proved to be his passion. He simply could not resist them! Without benefit of parson or magistrate, Ann and John enjoyed their illicit state for many years. During this time she bore him a son who, later, failing to follow in their footsteps, became a sea captain.

Since we will have more to say of Mr. Henry's relations to the Storer sisters, we may leave him here with the reminder that, so far, he has now captivated two out of the four—and the dramatic history of America is still young!

However, we cannot leave this season of 1768 without recording a romance that marked another premier in American stage history. In that year the fascinating Miss Cheer, of the company, was wooed and won by the Rt. Hon. Lord Rosehill in Maryland. She had played no less than fifty leading rôles up to this time and was a competent and beautiful actress. She, then, was the first woman of the American stage to acquire a title through marriage, thus becoming godmother to a select little coterie of our theatrical peerage.

Also during this New York turn we come across an old name and an old custom. On April 24, 1769, in the intermission between the tragedy of "Alexander the Great" and the farce of "The Citizen," it was announced that Mr. Wall would "deliver a critical dissertation on 'Noses,' in which he will exhibit a Turning-up Nose, a Ruby Nose, Rose Nose, Gluttonous Blunt Nose and Hook'd Nose." This is the same Thomas Wall who had taught the guitar in

WILD OATS.

Mr. HENRY *in the character of Ephraim*
I say unto thee, a Play House is a school for the old
Dragon, and a Play Book the Primer of Belzebub.
N. York Publish'd by John Reid

JOHN HENRY, LEADING MAN OF HALLAM'S THEATRICAL COMPANY
AND LOVER OF THREE OUT OF THE FOUR STORER SISTERS
From the Collection of Harvard University

Charleston. Among his accomplishments he evidently was a lightning-change artist; indeed he was a man of many parts, for in his time he had played at the Theatre Royal, the Drury Lane, and the Haymarket in London. Following his act Maria Storer sang, thus filling up the interval until the curtain rose on the farce.

Two seasons were played at the John Street Theatre, closing in June 1770. Not until 1773 did this company perform again in New York. Meantime it appeared elsewhere along the lower Atlantic seaboard. Of these seasons on the road the most famous was the run in Charleston.

Douglass burst upon Charleston with the full panoply of his repertoire. In the five months between December 1773 and May 1774, his company played fifty-nine nights and produced seventy-three plays, of which twenty were operas, eleven Shakespeare, among them "Julius Caesar" for the first time in America, and eight comedies of Garrick's. An astounding record, that, a veritable cataract of industry! What stock company in America today would dare aspire to such a repertoire? Imagine the state of the nerves of the prompter after such a mixed season!

When the cast was not busy rehearsing and performing, some of its members found time to take part in concerts. Thus, in February 1774, Maria Storer, together with Miss Hallam, Miss Wainright, and Mr. Stephen Woolls, are assisting Peter Valton, organist

of St. Phillip's Church, in a concert given under the
auspices of the St. Cecilia Society. This organization
was among the first in America to foster the appreciation of music.

Charleston covered Maria with compliments that
would have flattered a duchess; it took her raptur-
ously to its bosom and she, on her part, accorded
Charleston the same. Years afterward, whenever
she could get away, we find her down there, singing,
acting, happy among old friends. As yet she was
young: only seven years before had she made her
début in Philadelphia, come on to sing her little song
at the end of the play and to do her little act. Now
she was a full-fledged ingenue, grown up and with an
enviable reputation. Little wonder that she became
a great pet! "Dowered with beauty and magnetism,"
she was considered the best public singer in America
up to 1792.

It was during this Charleston season that for the
first time she played *Ann Lovely* in "A Bold Strike for
a Wife." We shall be recalling this subsequently
when she plays it twenty years later with Mr. Henry,
under tearful circumstances.

From every point this Charleston season was a
great success. Had not the people supported the
building of a new theatre? Were they not glad and
willing to pay thirty-five shillings for box seats,
twenty-five for pit and twenty for the gallery? New
Yorkers paid no such prices at the John Street!

Having finished the run, the company goes its

several ways. Mr. Henry departs by the brigantine
Sea Nymph for Philadelphia. He seems to have
become attached to that city, for he built a house
there back of the theatre, a house that was to shelter
the dismal end of one of the Storer sisters. His
companion Ann went along with him, the sailing
records show. Likewise Maria, who was headed for
London and hoped to carry on further conquests.
These three eventually find their way back to
Jamaica, whence the rest of the company went when
it disbanded.

III

These advances and retreats of the stage may
seem puzzling at first, but, considering the temper
of the people scattered along the Atlantic seaboard
in those years before the Revolution, they are amply
justified. Certain sections looked upon the theatre
with a kindling and sympathetic eye; others considered it the Devil, intent on ruining men's souls.

North of New York, Puritan inhibitions were
virulent and active. Under the guise of preventing
unnecessary expense and encouraging industry and
frugality, Boston prohibited any manifestations of
play-acting by its regulation of 1750. Nor did the lid
come off for many years after. Following the Revolution, we find one owner of a Boston hall begging for
immortality by stating that he would sooner burn
down the place than to suffer it to be used for plays.
Even so late as 1824, Timothy Dwight, the worthy

President of Yale, offered as his expert opinion that a taste for theatre-going was a proof of the loss of one's immortal soul.

New York had its mingling of Dutch and Anglican English, both more liberal than the Calvinist New Englander, but even here the theatre fought an uphill fight against prejudice. Philadelphia, the palpitating centre of culture as well as the seat of governmental affairs and rebellious movements, protested that the theatre needed watching and curbing. Going farther south we come to Baltimore, where people have always enjoyed themselves and, please God, always will! From this point southward to the Florida line very few towns sympathetic to the theatre existed apart from Charleston. Nor, as we have seen, did that city fail in this respect when the opportunity was offered it. The sole protest against the stage made there was by a "foolish woman who signed herself 'Cleopatra'" and who proclaimed in the public press that the theatre was "the Devil's Synagogue."

Apart from these questionably hospitable points, there wasn't the slightest chance of the theatre being accepted previous to the Revolution and for many years afterward. (⁷)

In the face of such persecution Douglass and his associates were obliged to make concessions to popular prejudices. They gave "lectures," ending with a pantomime into which play-acting was slyly introduced. In Philadelphia, David Douglass even gave a lecture "for improving youth in the divine art of psalmody and church music." Constantly they gave benefits for the poor or for charitable institutions or for some actor or actress who came over as an indentured servant and wished to buy off his or her time.

During those years preceding the Revolution there was cause enough to dampen the ardor of even the most ambitious theatre manager. The people were engrossed with the political issues of the day, and where this did not involve them, they were completely occupied producing their daily bread. The theatre does not flourish in a purely rural community, and most of America at that time was rural.

The final blow to the theatre was dealt it in 1774, when the Continental Congress passed a resolution recommending the suspension of all public amusements. This rebellion was to be a grim war!

With their work thus taken away from them, the American Company of Comedians, having finished in that grand blaze of glory at Charleston, retired once more to Jamaica.

IV

After the Revolutionary War the American stage crept back on to the boards from its hibernation in Jamaica. Many of its actors were looked upon with suspicion, since they were obviously Loyalists. So the theatre became violently patriotic. Its posters flamed with the phrase, "Viva Republica!" But even this did not deceive many. Such plays as they dared to offer the public were described as "moral." The "lectures," previously described, were given at the slightest encouragement.

Among the actors of the old company at Charleston before the war was Thomas Wall—he who had taught the guitar and delivered the talk on "Noses." This gentleman, blessed with a turn for humorous and eccentric parts, may claim the honors for reviving the American stage. With a canny knowledge of our towns, he selected Baltimore for his initial venture. In January 1782 he opened the theatre there.

Meanwhile the handsome John Henry, still a member of Douglass's company in Jamaica, comes to Philadelphia and petitions the President of the Supreme Executive Committee of Pennsylvania for permission to open the Southwark Theatre with that lecture on "Heads." The subterfuge was too obvious, and he was promptly turned down. What did Philadelphians want with a lecture on "Heads"? Those who had been loyal to the Revolutionary cause were either too busy cleaning up the mess the British left when they evacuated the city, or were preparing political swaddling clothes for the new nation shortly to be born. Those who had held Tory sympathies could console themselves with recollections of the days when the British occupied the place—those hectic and brilliant years crowded with parties and the "Machianza" and the plays staged by that brilliant and lamented Major Andre. Obviously Philadelphia was no place for him, so Mr. Henry returned to the West Indies.

This "feeler" by Henry is an indication of the status he had acquired in the intervening years. Having wearied of theatrical labors, David Douglass exchanged the buskin for the ermine: he settled down to being a British judge in Jamaica. Considering his great contribution to the American stage, we can wish for him many years of mellow recollection. Henry assumes his place. He calls his troupe, "The Old American Company."

Meantime in London, Lewis Hallam, who was Douglass's stepson, had been playing, patiently awaiting the opportune time to return to New York and re-open the John Street Theatre. During the four years of the British occupancy the building was used, under the name of the Theatre Royal, by officers and their wives for amateur theatricals; otherwise it stood idle. Arriving from London in August, Hallam started with a skeleton company giving "lectures" that began with a dramatic prologue and ended with a pantomime.

In one of these pantomimes America's first native actor made his début—John Durang of Lancaster, Pennsylvania, who appeared as a dancer. A strange place for an actor to come from, Lancaster; he evidently broke out of the corral of Pennsylvania Dutch restraint!

Toward the end of 1785 John Henry comes up from Jamaica via Philadelphia and reinforces Hallam.

They soon form the partnership of Hallam & Henry and together control theatrical activities north of the Mason and Dixon Line for the next seven or eight years. During their 1787 season was produced the first public performance in a regular theatre of a play written by an American. Other dramas had been written and published, but this was the first to be accorded professional presentation. It was a five-act comedy called "The Contract"; its author, Royal Tyler of Massachusetts, who subsequently repented of his youthful folly and attained the ermine as Chief Justice of Vermont.

In May of this season, it may be noted, the Storers had their benefit. It was doubtless the most complete "sister act" New York had ever seen or was destined to see for some time. "Richard III" was played with Fanny as the *Prince of Wales*, Ann as *Lady Anne*, and Maria as the *Duke of York*. Between the third and fourth acts Maria enraptured the audience by singing "Sweet Echo." The benefit concluded with "Miss In Her Teens" in which Fanny played *Captain Flash*, Ann played *Tag*, and Maria filled the rôle of *Fribble*. Their appearance together is memorable, for shortly after that it would have been impossible.

During this busy era of reinstating the theatre, John Henry's private affairs had undergone a change. He broke with his paramour, Ann Storer, or, to be precise, she with him. His attentions to her younger sister had become too marked for her to overlook.

Though she realized that he naturally had a paternal and proprietary interest in Maria, since she had literally grown up under his hand, yet when his attentions went beyond that point, she revolted. Would Maria now be billed as "Mrs. Henry"?

To those who were aware of such things at the time, Henry's intimacy with Maria was obvious and pronounced, and equally obvious and pronounced was his neglect of the faithful Ann, who had certainly done her duty by him in bearing him a son. What other course was there open to Ann but to retire from the stage? Her time was probably engrossed in raising her boy. In addition to this failure of her companionate marriage, her decision to retire from acting was further prompted by another circumstance. Not only was her younger sister's rising popularity beginning to overshadow her, but there had come to the company a Mrs. Hodgkinson who was "very pleasing in high comedy" and won mighty applause in parts of "lively girls and singing romps." Opinions on Ann Storer's capability as an actress seem divided: some say she was good, some claim that, were it not for Henry's association she scarcely would have been tolerated. Mrs. Hodgkinson's appearance and Henry's infidelity finally crystallized her decision: she chose not to play.

How familiar all this reads! Doubtless in the history of the American stage there have been many such cases; this owes its value to history in being the first.

In the seasons that followed, Maria Storer, playing opposite to Henry, became the darling of the
American stage. "A perfect fairy in person," they
called her. As a singer she was in great demand. A
good actress in both tragedy and comedy, she met
with instant applause whenever she stepped on to the
stage.

We find her playing in New York, Philadelphia,
and her beloved Charleston. To old Charleston
records we are indebted for the clues to her movements. The *South Carolina Gazette* of March 11,
1785 under "West Indian Intelligence" states, "We
are assured that Miss Maria Storer, that celebrated
Disciple of Calliope, intends taking her departure for
Charleston the latter end of this month, and from
thence will sail for Great Britain in order to be in
time to get a winter engagement in one of the theatres in London." Imagine the flutter this caused
among the young blades of Charleston! Note how
precisely her plans are revealed to the public—her
intentions, her engagements! Even in those early
days the theatrical profession laid all its cards on
the public table. And how true to type does she
follow up this first announcment. In May of the
same year the *South Carolina Gazette and Public
Advertiser* says that "the celebrated Miss Maria
Storer, who has performed for several years past at
the theatre in Jamaica and one winter in this city
with great applause, arrived here a few days ago from

Kingston on her way to London." There, we know her every move!

But a bird in the Charleston hand was worth two in a London bush. After all this publicity, after all the excitement of anticipating her arrival and her glittering appearance on Charleston's streets, for only a few days before she sailed, Miss Storer decided that she simply could not refuse the demands of her "public." She stayed in Charleston. Those chimerical London engagements faded in the warm light of local popularity. On May 9 the whole élite turn out for a concert given to her benefit in the City Tavern, and they cheerfully pay the price of a guinea each for seats. After such a reception, how could she leave these adoring friends? It is supposed that she played for a while with Dennis Ryan's company, which was in the city at the time. Then in June we find her announced in another concert, and about this event no little scandal was circulated.

With the generosity characteristic of theatrical folk, Miss Storer lent her talents for a concert given in St. Michael's Church for charity. She sang anthems from Handel's "Messiah." As the audience passed out, a collection was taken at the door. Thus the church wardens veiled the affair in a semi-religious guise and at the same time sweet charity benefited. But some there were—envious and Puritanic women, easily shocked perhaps—who began circulating the story that Miss Storer had taken her share of the "benefit."

Noah Webster, our famous lexicographer, happened to be in Charleston at the time and he notes in his diary: "Go to St. Michael's Church. Hear Parson Smith. Miss Storer sings part of Handel's oratorio. Very odd indeed! A woman sings in public after church for her own benefit. I do not like the modern taste in singing." Just what this "modern taste" is, he fails to explain, but evidently Handel's arias did not sit comfortably on him. His New England frugality melted to the extent of a quarter which he dropped in the plate and reports in his diary, but he also reiterates his opinion—"She sang well in the modern taste but I cannot admire it." Somehow we feel that it wasn't half so much the "modern taste" that riled this Connecticut Yankee as the fact that he couldn't get out of the church gracefully without contributing.

Today such qualms never enter the heads of church-goers. Practically every Sunday in the year is pre-empted by some charity or organization asking preachers to expatiate on their worthy aims and, if possible, turn the collection their way. So insistently have these "Days" come—Mother's Day, Father's Day, etc.—that the modern pastor is hard pressed to find time for preaching the Gospel. Parson Smith of St. Michael's didn't know what he was starting! He probably flattered himself with the notion that his was a brilliant idea and he a veritable Balboa standing before the undiscovered sea of church benefits. Well, he was. But so many of his townspeople criticized him for lending the church edifice and service to this worldly affair that a few days later Miss Storer was obliged to insert in the local paper a card to the effect that she had not benefited one penny by her participation in this service. We hope Noah Webster read it!

Finally in January 1786 she tears herself away from Charleston and starts for New York in the sloop *Diana*, there to join the American Company of Comedians. Charleston papers refer to her as having "afforded so much amusement by her vocal abilities to the polite circles of this city." On May 29 her name begins to appear in the bills as "Mrs. Henry." She plays under this guise at the John Street Theatre in "Maid of the Mill" and "Daphne and Amintor." Alas, there is no record that Henry actually married her!

Thus the amours of three of the Storer sisters are accounted for—the first Mrs. Henry who lost her life in the fire at sea; Ann Storer, Henry's mistress for a number of years and mother of his child; now Maria, the youngest, his present companion in love.

John Henry evidently had a way with him. He is said to have stood six feet high and was one of the most accomplished actors of his time in America. True, his conception of rôles may have been somewhat unorthodox—or maybe the limitations of the wardrobe obliged him to adopt the disguise, but he was accustomed to play *Othello* as a very black negro

in a white woolly wig and dressed in a British officer's
cast-off uniform! (⁸)

The years and his manner of living began to take
their toll of John Henry. He developed the fashionable complaint of the era—gout. It distressed him
terribly and slowed up his activites. His old cronies
saw him less around the taverns and when he went
about town he rode in his crazy old coach. This
equipage made a place for itself in early American
stage history. It was not much of an affair as
coaches went in those days—a second-hand acquisition, gaudily tinted. On the door Henry had painted
crossed crutches with the device, "This or These." A
wag was Henry. You can hear him chuckling to
himself, "That'll fix the boys!"

When he and Maria went to the theatre they made
an occasion of their descent from this ramshackle
old coach. She usually came fully dressed and ready
to step on to the stage. Wearing the extravagant
hoops fashionable in this era, it was necessary for
Henry to lift her out sidewise. He always carried
her in his arms from the coach door to the stage entrance, and quite an adorable scene they must have
made of it—this six-foot, jolly Irishman with the
dainty little fairy that was Maria cradled in his em-
brace, her hoops wantoning about her fluttering feet.

In those days Maria Storer had no rivals in the
affection of the people. When she went South, a
local poet strummed his lyre and wrote this ode to
her in the *Maryland Gazette* of October 14, 1773:

Genius of Harmony, descend,
In all thy smiles appear,
And pleased, thy Storer's voice attend
For her thou lov'st to hear.
Bid every ruder sound remove,
Bid care, bid sorrow fly.

For now thy Storer wakes the lay
And, mistress of the heart,
Does with our yielding passions play
Submissive to her art.
'Tis hers to lead the mind along,
With love's own ardor warm;
Hers all the various powers of song,
And music's magic charm.

'Tis portion of the ethereal flame,
This high-wrought charm is given
To those alone of finer frame,
The favorite of Heaven.
For sure, it asks celestial art,
And all the Seraph's skill
To rule th' emotions of the heart
Or fix the wavering will.

As on the banks of Nile's famed stream
Old Mennon's lyre renown'd,
Touched by the sun's enliv'ning beam
Return'd a tuneful sound,
So warm'd by some diviner ray,
Some emanation bright
Of harmony, fair Storer's lay
Thus pains us with delight.

Now while she wakes the living lay,
And fills th' enraptured soul,
I feel my beating heart obey,
And own her soft control.
Sweet Harmonist, prolong the strain,
The melody of Heaven;
And soothe with songs the tender pain
Thy tender songs have given.

Although this ode might be improved on, one gathers from its ecstatic effusion that the unknown bard was smitten not only by Maria's singing but by her beauty as well. Such is the privilege of poets and artists. For not alone were these lines inscribed to her, but the artist Peale, so it is said, begged the honor of painting her, and she consented to sit for him in the costume of "Ariel."

With such adulation poured out at her feet Maria Storer needs must act the part of those who live upon applause. To her we are indebted for our first recorded exhibition of artistic temperament on the boards. Though a little person, she had the wilfulness of a huge and pampered prima donna. Time and again her capricious and jealous fits directed at some member of the company necessitated a last-minute change in the cast, "A slender box sheet or a stinted proportion of applause" would bring on terrible tantrums.

For years these two, John Henry and Maria Storer, enlivened the American stage, shuttling back and forth along the Atlantic seaboard with the Hallam & Henry troupe, playing now in New York, now in Philadelphia, Baltimore, Richmond. She was acclaimed wherever she went. On many occasions, too, Maria appeared in subscription concerts, the public patronizing her generously.

After many seasons they finally reached that time when all good stage folk take their benefits and begin making farewell performances. In 1794 Henry

winds up his affairs. His theatrical interests are sold
to Mr. Hodgkinson for the neat sum of $10,000 and
Hallam and Hodgkinson form a partnership to carry
on the enterprise. (⁹) On the seventh of May of
this year Mr. and Mrs. Henry gave a benefit performance of "Jane Shore" and two acts from a "A Bold
Strike for a Wife," entitled "The Guardians Out-
witted" that Henry adapted for the occasion. He
advertised that he had expurgated it so that it could
give "no offense to Morality or force a blush from
the cheek of Modesty." Maria played the same
part that she had ventured on twenty years before.
Thus these two reach their final curtain amid tears
and applause. And for the present we shall leave
them bowing there.

V

Her sisters meantime had not been altogether
idle. The rejected Ann, attaining age and her son
reaching manhood, found favor in the eyes of one
John Hogg, an actor twenty-four years her junior.
Hogg made his début in March 1796 but played so
wretchedly that he retired for the rest of the season.
However, in 1798 he married Ann Storer, and with
this union his luck changed. He became a lively
member of the company. She, too, after twenty-five
years' absence from the stage, appeared again, recit-
ing the "Masonic Epilogue" that followed a benefit
performance of "The Clandestine Marriage" given
especially for them. They became quite popular.

When she was playing the comic old woman at the Park Street Theatre toward the end of the century—*Mrs. Malaprop, Mrs. Hardcaſtle, Lucretia MacTabb,* and such—he was filling the rôle of eccentric old man, bluff, old, country-fellow parts. He also gained notoriety as the genial hoſt of a local tavern, which won him the name of "Honeſt John Hogg." In 1807 Sully painted his portrait, which indicates the position he had attained in New York: the notice in Sully's regiſter of portraits ſtates that he was "formerly of the theatre," from which we surmise that he had retired by this time. Mrs. Hogg doubtless retired with him, thus ending a diſtinguished career during which she had played forty-three rôles.

From this union, which turned out so happily in the end, sprang a theatrical family that graced the American ſtage for many years. Mrs. Hogg in her generation proved a worthy ſtage mother. She bore several sons and a daughter. The laſt was known to theatrical circles of the early nineteenth century as Mrs. Claude, famous for singing ballads of the day. Her laſt ſtage appearance was in 1816.

In this same year her mother died, having survived her husband by three years.

When the old people passed away, the children petitioned the New York Legislature to change their name. They evidently suffered from the gibes that muſt fall to anyone with such a porcine title. So they became the Biddles. George Edgar Biddle, known as George Edgar on the stage, was Mrs. Hogg's grandson.

Since we are accounting for them one by one we may note that two of the famous Storer sisters have been checked off the list of life. We now retrace our steps and contemplate the dismal end of pretty little Maria, whom we left bowing before her final curtain with her lover John Henry some time back.

After this performance she and Henry boarded a boat for Providence. Roads in those days were far from safe and traveling by them very uncomfortable; wise people took the boat. Henry had not been well. En route he had an attack of "galloping consumption," as they called it, and died. He was buried unceremoniously on an island in the Sound. At Providence Maria turned back and made the dreary, lonesome journey to Philadelphia, finding shelter in the house back of the South Street Theatre that Henry had built before the Revolution. She was miserably poor. The terrible experience of his death began to unhinge her reason. She ordered his body disinterred from its quiet grave in Long Island Sound and brought to Philadelphia. The mind, already weakened, broke completely under the strain of its reception. She died shortly afterward. The date was the 25th of April 1795—and she was a little over forty.

Of the four Storer sisters there remains only one to account for—Fanny. Unceremoniously we left her in New York playing at the John Street Theatre

with the old American company back in 1768. The
stage, somehow, did not seem to attract her. After
appearing in five rôles, she left it.

A wise virgin was Fanny. Let Ann yield to the
blandishments of Mr. Henry, let little Maria bask
in the sunlight of his smiles, for her this wild Irishman
and his blarney held no charms. A pert, turned-up
nose she must have had, and she probably told John
Henry just what she thought of him. Fanny can
boast the unique distinction of being the only one of
the four Storer sisters who did not succumb to his
amorous onslaught. Very definitely she proved her
determination to save "that first, fine, careless rap-
ture" for someone else.

In due time this fortunate fellow came along.
Melcher was his name, and she evidently was happy
with him. They went to England to live. We find
her back here again, however, since she had a voice
that was not to be despised.   In September, 1792, the
New York *Advertiser* announced a series of three
subscription concerts at Corre's Hotel ([10]) on Broadway: "Mrs. Van Hagen, lately from Amsterdam,
will perform concerto's, sonata's, and accompani-
ments on the piano-forte, and, to render the enter-
tainment as satisfactory as in their powers, they
have engaged Mrs. Melcher, lately from England,
whose vocal powers they hope will be a pleasing
acquisition to these concerts."

And so we leave the last of these Storer sisters
singing her way into the hearts of a New York
audience.

CHAPTER III
DAUGHTERS OF ZION

THREE SCHEMING LADIES SET THEIR CAPS AND TRAPS FOR THE WESLEY BROTHERS AND OUT OF THE ASHES OF THEIR INTRIGUES ARISES THE PHOENIX OF METHODISM

I

A GROUP of men were discussing, in measured and judicious terms, this new venture in religious practice called Methodism. Seated pontifically in one chair was John Wesley, a short, stocky, square-jowled man, vigorous and muscular, with ruddy complexion, aquiline nose and a penetrating eye. His clothes bore the evidence of simple, fastidious taste: a neatly-plaited narrow stock showed in the opening of his coat and above its upright collar. His gestures were formal, his speech dogmatic. Force and finality lay behind his words; when he spoke, he spoke *ex cathedra*. His brother Charles sat near by, and gathered about them were other men of like mind.

They were discussing, and would discuss for some time, rules and counsels designed for those who chose to follow their footsteps. As they asked their questions and John answered them, these were taken down in a notebook entitled "Longer Minutes." Eventually from the notes of these *conversazioni* was evolved the Discipline of the Methodist Church, that spiritual constitution which was to guide the work and lives of countless men and women for decades to come.

But as yet Methodism was still in a nebulous state. Some in that group still held Orders in the Church of England. Methodism was then merely an awakening within a well-established but badly-run organization. These men were hewing a path through the undergrowth of corruption and bad practice that sloth, simony, and worldly distractions had sown in the noble forest of English faith. They must consider and weigh each phase of the new work. Already they had arrived at a decision on many things. They now approached the subject of the ministry.

As John Wesley preached and practised it, the ministry of Methodism was a peripatetic calling with the whole world for its parish. He summoned young men to go out into the fields, into the byways of towns and cities and carry the Gospel to the ecclesiastically neglected. What Francis of Assisi had done, what Peter the Hermit, his young followers were to do. They were to have no encumbrances. In no manner was the world to hold these fiery preachers, and yet, in no manner would a lack of necessities hinder their work. They were to be provided for, but not too well.

"And should they be encouraged to marry?" someone asked. "Shall we make provision for them and their families if they marry shortly after they join the ministry?"

The question was a serious one. It encountered

a long silence. Charles Wesley glanced at John understandingly, and John's gaze traveled out the window, past the garden, far, far away. . . .

II

From its very beginning, Savannah was a pleasant place to live in. The men who conceived and managed its settlement, idealists of the highest order, dreamed great dreams for it; and the climate of the region and the fair place they chose to build their town conspired to make them come true. Here was to be a cosmopolitan city, unrestricted by race, or creed, or nationality. All save Papists were given freedom of religious opinion and observance. Here toil was to be relieved of slavery, then casting its dark shadow across other colonies by cutting into the labor of free workingmen. Here they were to live without the devastating temptations of strong drink (although they were allowed light wines and beer), and without extravagant habits of luxury. Such abundance as eventually surrounded them would come from their own honest toil and Nature.

Landing on Yamacraw Bluff, the first settlers laboriously hauled provisions from boats that lay in the river below by a crane up the forty-five-foot steep cliffs and began laying out their city. A beautiful spot, this plateau, covered with pine and heavy with the fragrance of jasmine and cooled by balmy airs. Around its rim, a circumference of about a mile and a quarter, they ran up a stockade against possible

attack from Indians and Spaniards. A lighthouse
was built to guide river traffic. The town was divided
into four wards, with plenty of breathing-space
between them. Houses, some two, some three storeys
high, were erected of clapboards, their lots fenced in
with palings. Streets were cut generously wide.
The central square they named for Robert Johnson,
Governor of Carolina, a civic compliment well deserved, since he rendered yeoman service in escorting
and provisioning the first Georgian settlers and aiding
Colonel Peter Purry to settle his Swiss émigrés in the
town named after him. A sun-dial, set up in this
square, told the time of day, there being no town
clock as yet.

To the east of the town was laid out a public garden, or nursery, of ten acres, designed to supply the
settlers with mulberry trees, oranges, olives, vines
and other necessary plants for the beginning of a
vast horticultural industry. From England came all
manner of seeds, slips, and plants to stock the garden.
The trustees in London set aside annual appropriations of £50 to £100 for its support. Robert Millar,
with an annual salary of £150, was appointed bot-
anist and agricultural director.

Provision was also made for the spiritual life of
the colony. A split-board tabernacle was projected,
and some pious soul in England sent a bell for it,
which, proving too heavy, rested in the soil of the
church yard for a long time. Other presents came
for the church—books and money and a silver chalice

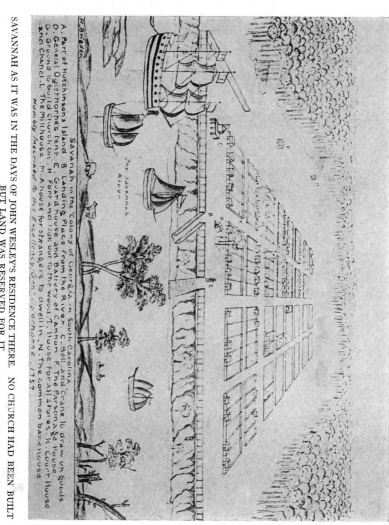

Savannah in the Colony of Georgia in South Carolina
A. Part of Hutchinson's Island B. Landing Place from the River C. Bell and Crane to draw up goods
D. General Oglethorpe's Tent. E. Guard house and Battery of Cannon F. The Parsonage House
G. Ground to build Church on. H. Font and House out to the wood I. House for all Strangers K. Court House
and Chapel L The Millhouse M. A house for strangers to dwell in N. The common bake house
Humbly Inscribed to his Excellency Gen. Oglethorpe, 1757

The Savannah River

K. Brigden

SAVANNAH AS IT WAS IN THE DAYS OF JOHN WESLEY'S RESIDENCE THERE. NO CHURCH HAD BEEN BUILT BUT LAND WAS RESERVED FOR IT

and paten from the Rev. Samuel Wesley, rector of Epworth. But long before the church, a house was built for the minister, and three hundred acres set aside to be cleared and cultivated as his glebe.

The idealism of the trustees and the pleasant situation soon attracted foreigners from all parts. The city grew and the colony began to spread out. On St. Simon Island, at the mouth of the Alatamaha River, Oglethorpe founded a town and called it Frederica and built a fort there. Here also three hundred acres were reserved for a pastor. Between this point and Savannah, on each side the river, little settlements began springing up, each with its group of national colonists. Germans settled at Hempstead, a mile east of Savannah: French at Highgate, five miles south: and in Savannah itself were Piedmontese, come to help in the silk worm industry, and Italians, Greeks and Spanish Jews. By 1738 one-third of the colony was estimated to be of birth other than English.

Over this cosmopolitan colony Oglethorpe ruled as master and final court of appeals, representative of the trustees in England. His second in command was Thomas Causton, one of the local trustees of the colony, who served as magistrate and keeper of the stores and, when Oglethorpe was absent, director of the colony. A man of the highest idealism, of unquestioned bravery, a great organizer and a wise counselor, Oglethorpe represented the best element in Georgia. As time went on, Causton proved to be his antithesis, in fact, a thoroughly unprincipled rogue. His reputation in England had been none too good, but he managed, by apparently aiding Oglethorpe's efforts at keeping the colony moral, to ingratiate himself into his favor and patronage. Having attained this position of trust, he set about feathering his own nest, and soon acquired ten farms and eight gardens, each garden being five acres, and each farm forty-four, a considerable holding. Scarcely had Oglethorpe turned his back when he began imposing tyrannical restrictions on the colony. Couston represented the element that was to give Georgia trouble for a long time to come.

Begun as a charitable and philanthropic venture to provide homes and a new opportunity for unfortunates in England, Georgia was soon to see advantage taken of its idealism. The prohibition of rum and strong spirits bred a race of bootleggers who supplied whatsoever was required, from boats that came up the river. A wave of silly luxury swept the colony following the importation of a shipment of gold and silver tinsel. Laws to suppress this extravagance had to be clamped on the populace. The people began bickering among themselves; they bandied scandal about from doorstep to doorstep. The Germans, Austrian Salzburgers, French, Italians, Spanish Jews, and Greeks brought with them their foreign ways. Among some classes was soon manifest a spirit of levity and a persistent laziness. They wanted to have a good time and nobody wanted to work. The Moravians, a pious and hard-working people, were an exception and among the English at Savannah there may have been a handful who had the colony's interest at heart, but it was not a universal sentiment, nor did a religious idealism direct their manner of toil and living, such as guided the destinies of the New England and Pennsylvania colonies.

Two ministers had served this flock—first the Rev. Henry Herbert and then the Rev. Samuel Quincy. The latter built his parsonage, which was also a guest house for the town, and worked to clear the land of his glebe. But neither of them seem to have made much of an impression on the life of the colony, Quincy especially lacking in this respect. The trustees in London were soon convinced that if its religious life were to survive, someone of deep spiritual convictions must be sent over.

At Lincoln College, Oxford had been a young man who made a vivid impression by founding the "Holy Club," "The Bible Bigots," or "The Methodists," as they were variously dubbed by the wits: a band of undergraduates who withdrew from the worldly distractions of the university, spent their available time in prayer and meditation and adopted a strict rule of life. So rigorous was the discipline they imposed upon themselves that one boy died as the result of excessive fasting. This young leader was now in Orders, and held a fellowship at Lincoln. His younger brother Charles also was a parson. They were sons of a well-known clergyman of the Church of England, the Rev. Samuel Wesley, of Epworth, the same one who had sent the silver chalice and paten to the Savannah Church. Casting about for the right leader to guide the religious life of Georgia, Oglethorpe chose this young man—John Wesley. His salary was to be £50 a year. He appointed the younger brother, Charles, his own secretary under the title of Secretary for Indian affairs.

The two brothers sailed for Georgia on the *Symond* in October 1735, accompanied by Benjamin Ingham of Queens College, Oxford, and Charles Delamotte, son of a London merchant. Oglethorpe was aboard, as were a number of pious Moravians headed by their saintly bishop, David Nitschman. Also included in the passenger list of the *Symond* were a Mrs. Hawkins and a Mrs. Welsh. The former lady appeared to John a very religious woman and to Charles decidedly questionable. Indeed, the two brothers quarreled over admitting her to Communion. Later events proved Charles Wesley to be the better judge of women.

From the first day out Wesley and his companions began strict religious exercises. They avowed that their purpose in going to Georgia was "to save our souls and to live wholly to the glory of God." On the long journey over—which lasted from October till February—they rose at four each morning; devoted an hour to private prayer; read the Bible together from five to seven; held public prayers at eight; studied from nine to twelve; at noon met to give account of what they had been doing; read to others from two till four; held evening prayers, expounded the Lesson for the day and catechized the children; passed from five till six in private prayer; from six to seven read to other passengers; at seven joined the German Moravian service; at eight met to exhort each other; and finally went to bed at ten. A very strenuous schedule, even for one on land, and not the sort calculated to be adopted by many passengers either at that time or since. During this regime John Wesley and Delamotte tried living on bread alone. Like athletes traveling to a foreign country for the Olympic games, these young zealots never broke training for the difficult work that lay ahead.

In some way John Wesley had gotten the mistaken notion that he was being sent over to Georgia primarily as missionary to the Indians, and his first act on landing on February 5, 1736, was to seek out the chieftain Tomochichi, whom he had previously seen in England ([11]) and with whom he now stayed for a month. Finally he came to Savannah, was met by Mr. Couston, and, to a congregation that packed the courthouse—for as yet there was no church—preached his first sermon. This idea of being missionary to the Indians became such an obsession that Oglethorpe had to do a good deal of persuading before Wesley was convinced that his work lay there in Savannah; if any time remained unoccupied, then he might work with the savages. And there was work enough:

his parish was two hundred miles long and the people, to his manner of thinking, were either ignorant or "disposed to licentiousness."

Meantime his brother Charles had been given the missionary outpost on St. Simon's Island, to serve the people of Frederica. Delamotte, one of their companions on shipboard, organized a school in Savannah, whilst John Wesley took over the work of catechizing the children.

Both the Wesley brothers kept detailed diaries and journals, a habit they had practised from youth. Some parts were written in legible English, others in the shorthand of Dr. Byrom, one of the early cypher writers. And in these very personal records we find one of the strangest stories of early America: strange in the light of John Wesley's career—he who at twenty-eight had declared it unlawful for a priest to marry, at forty published his sentiments in favor of clerical celibacy, and at sixty-two, under bitterly ironic circumstances, gave to the world his "Thoughts on a Single Life." But he was only thirty-three at the time of his Georgia experience. Consequently, as we read along this record of daily doings, we feel no sudden transition of thought nor do we suspect the pressure of the thumb of Destiny on his impressionable clay, when we encounter the fact, set down as happening on Saturday, March 13, 1736—a little more than a month after he landed in Georgia—that he meets a Miss Sophy Hopkey.

III

Sophia Christiana Hopkey was eighteen. A niece of Mrs. Couston, she lived in their house and enjoyed the position and benefits in the colony's life that naturally derived from being related to the magistrate and storekeeper-trustee and owner of eight farms and ten gardens. Of the young women in Savannah she was the most desirable "catch." The youth who won her hand would be fortunate indeed. And there were two who considered their chances promising.

One was Tom Mellicamp, a brilliant young scallawag, given to bothering the authorities and keeping tongues awag with his pranks and misdemeanors. Shortly after Wesley's arrival Tom was assigned to the lock-up for fraud. His dishonesty and incarceration didn't seem to worry Sophy at all. Some time before, in a burst of adolescent infatuation, she had promised her hand to him, and his brilliance still secretly fascinated her.

The other was William Williamson, who eventually steps into this comedy in the rôle of ponderous lover. His name betrays a Welsh extraction, and the Welshman at times can be almost as dour as the Scot. Wesley draws a jaundiced picture of him in his diary, says that he was "not remarkable for handsomeness, neither for greatness, neither for wit or knowledge or sense, and least of all for religion." Discounting Wesley's jealousy and natural dislike of the man, and considering him in the light of later events,

Williamson appears to have been the sort of man who takes himself too seriously, who resents outside interference in his private life, especially from the clergy, and who has acquired the habit of questioning the sincerity of people whose piety was pronouncedly ecclesiastical. He probably was a substantial citizen, was William Williamson and, were he living in Savannah today, would be a prosperous business man, highly respected.

Mellicamp, the scallawag, was still well in the saddle of Sophy's favor when John Wesley descended on Savannah with his fiery and insistent piety.

His spiritual muscles supple from the training aboard ship, he began to institute a rigorous campaign of services for the seven hundred inhabitants of Savannah that literally "drenched the people with the physic of intolerable discipline." His first Sunday morning service was at five; Holy Communion and sermon followed at eleven, and Evensong at three, with prodigious daily work in between, both in Savannah and at various towns thereabout. He read prayers for the Germans at Hempstead, for the French at Highgate and for the Italians in town, each in their own tongue. He made constant house-to-house visitations of his flock, catechized the children and counseled their elders. Now and then he journeyed down the river to Frederica and helped his brother Charles with services.

In the first few days of his pastorate in Savannah he scandalized people by refusing point blank to immerse a sick baby, whereupon the parents carried it off to a denominational parson who was not so strict an interpreter of rubrics. He added to the scandal by refusing communion to Bolzius, a saintly Salzburger minister, one of the holiest men in the community, on the ground that he was a dissenter and had not been "baptized by a minister who had been episcopally ordained." Bolzius later forgave him, but the impression was too vivid in the minds of the towns-people to forget. Some of them said they had "never heard of such a religion before" as John Wesley insisted on preaching; they objected to his sermons as being satires on particular members of the congregation. Some of the malcontents told him to his face, "You may preach long enough, but nobody will come to hear you!" Nevertheless, in that first year he believed he was making progress, and reported to the trustees that "many Ill Practices seem to lose ground daily and a General Face of Decency and Order prevails." Among most of his parishioners he was respected for his diligence and piety; indeed, from their viewpoint, he was a model shepherd of his sheep.

At times the humanity of this fiery young religionist broke through the shell of piety; he labored in his glebe, clearing land, growing vegetables and flowers; he used to stroll along the waterfront and swim in the Savannah River; he helped start Georgia's first lending library; and had a pleasant word for everyone. As Sophy Hopkey later testified, he was a man of "singularly attractive and susceptible personality."

After the manner of the religiously inclined from the beginning of time, he counseled the serious people of Savannah to form a society which could meet once or twice a week, "to reprove, instruct and exhort each other." This group eventually was assembled. Then from this band he selected a smaller group of the intensely pious designed "for a more intimate union with each other." These circles within circles are found wherever mysticism and introspection lead the religious thoughts of people; there are always those who huddle together in esoteric groups. So commonplace is the custom that this banding of people by John Wesley would not warrant recognition from history were it not for the fact that out of it grew both the conception of Methodism ([12]) and the scandal that clouded the last months of his stay in Georgia, causing him to flee the colony ignominiously. To this very select inner circle of the devout, John Wesley admitted Sophia Christiana Hopkey; and with that association he himself joined the equally select group of her admirers.

Their contact, purely religious at first, soon blossomed into mutual attraction. Sophy was eighteen and John Wesley thirty-three. Old enough to know better, to be sure, but wholly lacking the wisdom of the world, he was soon captivated by her charms. And she—well, what maiden of a colony would not be overwhelmed by a man who was graduate of

Oxford, well-born and well-known in England, master of many languages, a great student and a leader of the people? Mellicamp paled into insignificance beside the light of this brilliant new lover.

Between instructions in religion, he began by teaching her French each morning between eight and nine and set her an hour of French reading to do. When Wesley fell sick, she nursed him. The latter incident is amusing. One day General Oglethorpe called on Wesley and asked him to dinner. Wesley accepted and the General, seizing the opportunity, remarked, "Mr. Wesley, there are some here who have a wrong idea of your abstemiousness. They think that you hold the eating of animal food and the drinking of wine to be unlawful. I beg that you will convince them to the contrary." So at the dinner John partook of both, shortly after which he was seized with a fever which kept him to his bed for five days. Hearing of his illness, Sophy, the good vestal virgin that she was, insisted on fluttering over to the parsonage and nursing him day and night.

When he preached against extravagance in dress, she learned from General Oglethorpe what kind of clothes Wesley liked to see women in, and thereafter wore only white—neat, simple, and elegant.

The community was well aware that a romance had begun. Oglethorpe looked on this budding love affair with sympathetic eyes; he hoped it would tame the fiery religionist who had given him no little bother with his strict discipline and insistence on going off to the Indians. Married to a nice girl like Sophy Hopkey, John Wesley would settle down—and he wouldn't have to worry about church matters any more. He probably visualized him as being hobbled with the usual curate's brood of eight to ten snuffling children.

Those autumn months of 1736 must have been pleasant indeed with the last wild flowers flinging their blossom censers in the air and the walks of John's glebe garden aglow, where Sophy and he strolled, and the balmy breezes bringing blissfully cool nights. Under this kindly patronage of Nature the romance grew apace.

To some, however, this affair was very distressing. From the security of his cell Tom Mellicamp sent word that he would shoot the blighter who dared make love to his girl. Williamson buzzed in the background like an over-honied bee. To Delamotte the situation was very grave. But meantime even graver things were happening to Charles down in Frederica.

IV

Both the Wesleys had been confused as to their work in the colony. John believed that he had been sent as missionary to the Indians, whereas he was rector of the Savannah Church; Charles had come over as Oglethorpe's Secretary for Indian affairs, only to find that he was in charge of a nondescript parish in an isolated town. The people at Frederica were even more lazy and licentious than those at Savannah, and on several occasions John had to come down to aid his brother in the work.

Among the townspeople were two women, Mrs. Hawkins and Mrs. Welsh, who schemed to set enmity between Oglethorpe and the Wesleys and thus tilt the lid of the discipline they believed Oglethorpe was imposing at the instigation of the two Wesleys. Charles had known both of them of old. They had come across with them on the *Symond* and from the first he had suspected Mrs. Hawkins' sincerity, although his brother John, as we have seen, considered her a worthy and pious woman. Oglethorpe, too, had accorded them kindly consideration on the way over. One day these two women came to Charles Wesley and, in an apparent burst of pious contrition, confessed that they had both committed adultery with the General. Though he was shocked, Charles believed he now understood why Oglethorpe had been so attentive to them on shipboard. Then these two vixens went to Oglethorpe and told him that Charles Wesley was circulating around Frederica the story that he had had relations with them. And Oglethorpe too, believed them.

The plot succeeded. Oglethorpe's anger burst on Charles like a whirlwind. So utterly crushed by this evil report was Charles, that he fell dangerously sick. John and he discussed the matter "in lonely places beyond the overhearing of informers, and in Latin; if they afterwards had to write to one another about

it, they employed the veil of Greek or shorthand."
Thus acquainted with the facts, John began investigating. His first point of attack was Mrs. Welsh,
whom he flatly called an adulteress, to which she
answered, "with such a mixture of scurrility and pro-
faneness" as he had never heard before. The following Sunday Mrs. Hawkins sent for him and he obeyed
the summons. We will let John tell the story in his
own words:

> When I came in, she said, "Sir, sit down." I
> sat down on the bedside. She stood close to me,
> with her hands behind her, and said, "Sir, you
> have wronged me, and I will shoot you through
> the head this moment with a brace of balls." I
> caught hold of the hand with which she presented
> the pistol, and at the same time of her other
> hand, in which she had a pair of scissors. On
> which she threw herself upon me, and forced me
> down upon the bed, crying out all the while,
> "Villain, dog, let go my hands," and swearing
> bitterly, with many imprecations both on herself
> and me, that she would either have my hair or
> my heart's blood. I was very unwilling either
> to cry out, which must publish to all the world
> what, for her sake, I desired should be more
> private; or to attempt rising by force, which
> could not have been done without hurting her.
> Just then the maid came in, whom she ordered
> to reach a knife, swearing she would be the

death of her if she did not. The woman stood trembling, not knowing what to do. Her two boys (servants) came in next, whom she bid to hold my hands, and I desired to take hold of their mistress. But they did not dare to do either. Then came in Mr. Davison the constable, and Mr. Reed, who, on my desire, were going to take her by the arms, when Mr. Hawkins came in, asked what that scoundrel did in his house, and commanded them at their peril not to touch his wife. Upon this encouragement she struggled again to get her hands loose; but not being able, seized on my cassock with her teeth and tore both the sleeves of it to pieces, and then fixed upon my arm, four men (for Mr. Robinson and Ward were now come) standing by, and not daring to hinder her. I then spoke to Mr. Hawkins, who, seeing the company increase, took her round the waist and lifted her up. I went to Mr. Oglethorpe and gave him a simple narration of what had happened. He sent for them both and for Mr. Horton. She defended all, saying he had not done her justice for the wrong she had received, and therefore she had done herself justice. After a long hearing, her husband and she, promising better behaviour for the future, were dismissed."

This brawl was certainly not calculated to swell the prestige of the Wesleys in Frederica. Charles was convinced that his work in the colony had come to an abrupt end. He departed shortly afterward, never to return. In subsequent years, when he married the lovely and saintly Sarah Gwynne and lived blissfully with her, the while he penned such exquisite hymns as "Jesus, Lover of My Soul" and "Hark, the Herald Angels Sing," Charles Wesley could look back on this sordid episode at Frederica as a bitterly bought but salutary experience.

After he left, John undertook to convert Frederica from its evil ways, and on several occasions he journeyed there for that purpose. But Frederica remained adamant to his appeals. After twenty solid days of preaching, he shook the dust of the town off his feet. Frederica could stew in its own revolting juices. Moreover, his heart lay in Savannah.

V

Sophy's religious evolution grew apace, and with it many problems. This "seriously affected" young woman, as her lover calls her, is constant on attendance at services early and late. Dawn finds her at the altar rail, with another girl, comprising Wesley's entire congregation. They talk solemnly of holy things after church, walking side by side in the parsonage garden. The French lessons continue from eight to nine. Occasionally of evenings he reads her a sermon. This was fairly solemn courting; however, it had its lighter sides. John goes to the Couston's for breakfast, he dines there frequently, and is a welcome guest. They beam upon this intent lover, for does he not offer a solution to their problem? Married to Sophy, they would no longer have the girl on their hands.

Not content with seeing her constantly, John writes reams about her in his journal and pens fervid letters to her. Whenever anyone mentions her name—the General or his brother or Delamotte—he is "set up." Nor for a moment does either he or the General note any disparity between them. Though he was educated far beyond her, Sophy Hopkey seems to be just as good a woman as he a man. It was a worthy match.

> The simplicity of her behavior was a constant voucher for her sincerity. (He writes.) Her soul appeared to be wholly made up of mildness, gentleness, long suffering. She was the friend to humankind. To whomever was distressed she was all sympathy, tenderness, compassion. To a friend her behavior can only be conceived, not expressed, such was the spirit of gratitude that ran through it, such the softness, the sweetness.

One could ask for no more beautiful tribute. Yet he was afraid of her. In the back of his mind lurked that old idea, first expressed when he was twenty-eight, that priests should not marry. He writes her: "I find, Miss Sophy, I can't take fire into my bosom and not be burnt."

October 1736 saw her go to Frederica. She was really fleeing from the pressure that was being brought to bear on her at home. And her plight was growing desperate. The incarcerated Mellicamp and his lurid past stood on one hand; John Wesley, the holy man, on the other; and as background to these amorous contestants were the Coustons urging her to seize the main chance. The girl was not well, she was worried, and they knew she would continue being unsettled and ill until she picked her man and married him. There was good common sense on their side: many a parent before and since has faced just such a situation.

Hot-foot after her, Wesley speeds to Frederica. She comes to morning prayer and, just as he feared, he finds her distant—"scarcely a shadow of what she was. Most of her good resolutions were vanished away." She tells John she has about made up her mind to go back to England. He argues with her for several days: she should not go. Her uncle entrusted her to his care. Finally, they agree to lay the problem before Oglethorpe, who is planning shortly to leave for England and could take her with him. As the General listens to their pleadings he sees a way out of the situation: no, Sophy should not leave the colony; John should take her back to Savannah. And he probably hoped the boat would be a long time getting there! Were ever lovers given such a chance?

They start off from Frederica in a little boat with six days stiff sailing and rowing ahead of them. At

nights they drop anchor and the two lovers, a boy and
the boat's crew crawl under a tarpaulin till daylight
comes again.   The nights were cold and the sound
rough; this journey was not exactly a picnic.

At St. Catherine's Island a rough sea keeps them
ashore three days and nights.   The crew build a fire,
and far into the night John and Sophy sit beside it
talking about this and that.   The conversation drifts
around to Mellicamp.   John is anxious to know his
status.   Sophy vows she has promised to marry him,
or to marry no one at all.   But John is not discour-
aged by this silly resolution.   "Miss Sophy, I should
think myself happy," he said, "if I was to spend my
life with you."   The average girl then, and since,
would consider this a proposal.   But Sophy is reluctant.   She won't marry Mellicamp because he's a bad
boy, and since she's given her word to him, she can
have no one else.   "Sir," she answered John, "you
don't know what danger you are in."   They end this
enchanting tête-à-tête under the stars and whispering
pines by singing a psalm.

Later they land on another island, and alone once
more, John brings up again the subject of their relations.   She tells him how utterly unhappy she is at
the Coustons.   Like many men before his time and
since, John rose to this plea for sympathy as a trout
to the fly.   He offers her a room at his house (for the
parsonage was really the guest house of the colony)
and suggests an alternative—that she can go live with
the Moravians, who are thoroughly good people.

Thirty miles from Savannah they are forced to land on still another island. The provisions are gone save bread and water and there is no firewood. Sophy makes a tent of her apron and lies down under it safe from the chill October winds. And through the long night Wesley talks with her in soothing whispers and watches over her when, exhausted, she falls asleep.

Gentleness and beauty and great mutual trust there are in these hours together. Most men and maidens would have come home from such intimacy with their future well decided. Not John—he is a hesitant lover. Nevertheless they continue their daily associations both in church services and outside.

The following January when he goes to Frederica, word is brought to him that Mellicamp is out of jail and headed for Savannah. Terror, stark, cold terror, seizes him. He prays fervidly for Sophy's safety and, as if not certain of Providential watchfulness, flies back to her side. Mellicamp's presence, however, causes him to move carefully. Perhaps he had better begin looking around for a way out of the situation. Sophy and he talk it over. After all, he argues, should a parson marry? No, she assures him, "it is best for a clergyman not to be encumbered with worldly cares."

The little ninny! She could have forced his hand then and there without an effort. "Had she closed with me at that time," he wrote, "my judgment would have made but faint resistance." In reading these diaries and journals we are as angry at her

shilly-shallying as at his misgivings. She feared
Mellicamp, she feared the Coustons, she was in love
with John, and John lacked the courage of his
amours. We feel like banging their heads together!

Meantime, lumbering into the situation, comes
William Williamson. This is almost the last straw.
John is at his wits' ends. In sheer cowardice he
rushes off to the Moravian pastor and spreads the
whole story before him. What shall he do? Shall he
keep on with Sophy? The wise old pastor asks,
"What if you do keep on seeing her?" "I fear I
should marry her," John answers. And the parson
assures him that he can't see anything wrong in that.

But John's friends thought otherwise. Ingham
and Delamotte fly post-haste at midnight to see the
Moravian bishop, David Nitschman. This incredibly
foolish situation must cease! John is called in. He is
informed that his friends have decided his course for
him, and he solemnly promises to abide by their
decision. "We advise you to proceed no further in
the matter," the bishop says. John bows his head.
It is God's will.

Immediately he retires to a little settlement by
himself, and, to rid his mind of the problem, chops
wood and prays. But all the time his heart is with
Sophy and her image troubles every minute of his
waking hours.

On his return to Savannah, he falls into his old
habits again: he is as much at the Coustons' as ever.
Left alone with Sophy, he is holding her hand and

making cautious love to her. Day after day he sees her. The noble resolve given the bishop has gone on the winds.

Finally his friends can stand it no longer. John is as putty in the girl's hands. When absent from her side, he can think of naught else; when with her, he is teetering on the brink of proposal. The whole colony is talking and giggling. The Coustons are growing anxious. His friends blush for the fool he is making of himself. It will utterly ruin their friendship.

So they take him in hand. They ask him point blank if he intends marrying the girl. No, he flatly states, he has no intention of marrying her.

From the viewpoint of decency and honor, John Wesley's relations with Sophy Hopkey—granted that he meant what he just said to his friends—was beneath contempt. But this was no time to argue such ethical points. They must snatch him out of the crisis.

In early Christian times sortilege, or drawing lots, was resorted to in desperate and serious situations. It was believed that this style of decision indicated the directing finger of Providence. And it was this that Ingham and Delamotte proposed. They wrote three slips of paper: on one, "Marry;" on the second "Think not of it this year;" on the third, "Think of it no more." Then the three put these into a hat, shuffled them, knelt down to beseech Divine direction on their matrimonial lottery—and John drew. The paper he unfolded read, "Think of it no more."

Thus the one thing which, as he attested, he longed for, the one companion whose like he will never find again though he were to "live one thousand years twice fold," is taken from him, and with her, "all the color of remaining life for her; but perhaps all my happiness, too, in time and eternity."

To put the matter out of mind, he sits down and writes an extended yearly report for the trustees. And—and the next morning he is walking in the Coustons' garden again with Sophy!

Take the ingredients of religious fervor, asceticism and love, and mix them in a balmy climate, and you have about as complete and easily-running a case of eroticism as any student of such affairs could wish. That is what this episode in the life of John Wesley amounted to: it was eroticism. It had its clearly defined pathological and psychological aspects.

Sophy presents no such problem. Her violent religious exercises under Wesley provided her with a novel form of diversion at a time when she was receptive to religious impulse. Away from Wesley's influence, she began backsliding to the normalcy of a girl in her teens. Her diffidence and uncertainty can easily be attributed to Wesley's overwhelming and insistent ardor on the one hand and Mellicamp's threats on the other.

On his part, John blew hot and blew cold, wavered piteously, ran to the fire and dashed away from it, trembled at the thought of rivals and exulted when he triumphed over them, vowed not to see her and promptly broke the vow, the while he leaned heavily on Providence and castigated himself with long vigils of prayer and fasting. Though he apparently lacked the wisdom of the serpent, there were times in this courtship and afterward when he manifested finished guile.

In the course of a conversation one morning, he discovers that Sophy has finally decided to put Tom Mellicamp out of mind. Good! But what about Williamson, who is now staying at the Coustons'? The propinquity is dangerous. Sophy shrugs, and promises never to take a serious step without first consulting him. But scarcely had Wesley gone when her aunt and uncle begin coercing and urging: make a choice! make a choice! In sheer desperation, she turns to William Williamson.

The next morning Wesley drops in for his usual call at the Coustons' and is met by the aunt. She calmly asks him to publish the banns of marriage for Sophy and Williamson the following Sunday. For a moment he couldn't speak. Sophy appears. Yes, it is true, she is going to marry Williamson—but only on the condition that John has no objection. Object? How can he object? The situation is out of his hands now. With as cheerful a face as he can muster, he congratulates them both, and retires to the parsonage garden, like a hurt beast, to lick his wounds. Well, the only reason she is marrying Williamson, he assures himself, is not because she loves him but because she can no longer stand the intolerable life at the Couſtons'. The Couſton household was the ſtar that fought againſt him in its course. He bows to the inevitable. Sophy is loſt to him.

And Williamson sees to it that she ſtays loſt. At once he assumes the knightly rôle of the protecting lover. She is not to worry about the Couſton matter; he will handle that in due time. And as for the parson, he much prefers that she didn't see him again unless he is present. A direct man was Williamson, and Sophy bent before his will. She was not accuſtomed to so direct a lover.

Though John had promised to publish the banns the following Sunday, Williamson could not wait on the niceties of ritual. Scarcely had Wesley turned his back than he bundled the girl off to Purrysburg, a little settlement across the South Carolina line outside Wesley's jurisdiction, and there married her. Wesley sets down the event in his journal as of Saturday, March 12, 1737, "this being the day that completed the year from my firſt speaking to her."

VI

Oglethorpe had gone to England the previous autumn, and Couſton was in charge. While the populace had reasons for diſtruſting him, since he had more than once proven to be a grafter and an unbearable tyrant, they accepted the situation. Trouble was bound to ensue, and the trouble that involved John Wesley came shortly after Williamson and Sophy married.

The ceremony over, they returned to Savannah, and she apparently intended to continue the religious practices that Wesley had taught her, but as time passed, and as she became more and more engrossed with her married life, her attendance at church was not as regular as it had been. Indeed, it was scarcely conceivable that it could be. In his inner circle of worshippers, John Wesley had assumed the rôle of religious tyrant. Not satisfied with being their spiritual director, it is said that he had servants spying on masters and induced women to tell him "their inmost secret actions, nay, even their thoughts and the subject of their dreams." This was none other than making confession. Williamson was evidently aware of this practice, for when Wesley sent for Sophy to come to meetings, she sent word that her husband objected to her attending them.

The marriage was scarcely a success. Two months after the ceremony Mrs. Couston confesses to Wesley that she wished he'd married the girl, and even intimates that the marriage might be annulled and John then take her to his bosom. From her suggestion, it is easy to gather the kind of woman Mrs. Couston was.

With the marriage threatening them trouble, both the Coustons turn on Wesley; whereupon Wesley loses his temper and informs Couston in no uncertain terms what the people are saying about his grafting and manner of running the colony. The outburst was calculated to create bad blood.

Meantime Sophy was backsliding more and more. In his journal John notes that nine times in three months she had absented herself from Communion. "God has shown me yet more of my deliverance by opening to me a new and unexpected scene of Miss Sophy's dissimulation." The next time he meets her—it was a pleasant day in June—he begins upbraiding her—accuses her of hypocrisy, of not being repentant. And having emptied the vials of his religious wrath, he turns from these spiritual matters to upbraiding her for having married Williamson instead of him.

It was soon evident that he would have to watch his step. When he felt that the ill-feeling between him and Couston had died down, he consulted with the governor pro tem on a question of policy relative to church matters. It concerned denying Communion to persons whom Wesley believed not worthy to receive it. The magistrate rendered his opinion: no one should be reproved or condemned for doing what he believed to be his duty, nor should he condemn a minister for repelling from Communion even a member of his own family if circumstances warranted it.

A month passes. It is the beginning of August. With the infinite care with which he records every detail, John sets down the fact, as of August 7, "I repelled Mrs. Williamson from the Holy Communion." And he gives his reasons: that she had not appeared repentant. Moreover, like many a parson before him and since, he sought sanctuary in a rubric. He gave as his second reason the fact that she had failed to observe the rubric in the Book of Common Prayer which requires a person intending to partake of Holy Communion to give notice beforehand to the minister.

Consider the scandal this refusal caused. Here is a little colony of seven hundred people in which everyone knows everybody else's business. Here is the parson who has daily been seen in company with Miss Hopkey and who recently lost out in the matrimonial race for her. In the presence of the congregation he deliberately passes her by when she kneels at the altar rail. Though his apologists may strive to exonerate John Wesley, the plain fact is that he offered a direct insult to the girl, and we can find no other reason for it save revenge.

But revenge breeds revenge. Two days later Wesley is served with papers, issued by Recorder Christie on the complaint of "William Williamson and Sophia his wife," charging him with "defaming the said Sophia, refusing to administer the Sacrament of the Lord's Supper, in a public congregation, without cause." The bill called for damages of £1000.

On being taken before the Recorder and Bailiff Parker, Wesley denies having defamed the woman and states flatly that on ecclesiastical matters they have no jurisdiction. He is permitted to go on cognizance.

Immediately Couston begins rallying public sympathy to his side. His tyranny ceases. He opens the public stores and permits the people to have all the supplies they wish. He slaps them on the back and they slap him. Consequently, when the case comes to trial, he has no trouble in packing the grand jury. A bill of ten counts is returned against Wesley, ranging from purely ecclesiastical matters to alleged relations between him and Mrs. Williamson since her marriage.

But there was better stuff in Savannah than Couston had suspected. Among his jurors were twelve men who scented in these charges against Wesley an effort by Couston to head off charges against himself. Couston's hands, as later developed, were not clean from fraud. The jurors began investigating him on their own, and within the year his estate—the finest in the colony—was attached and he had to answer for misappropriation of funds.

Meantime Wesley's case dragged on. Time after time the court sat and the case was not brought to trial. He knew that accusations against him had gone forward to England, and if he was to clear himself, he must be there to answer them. So he posted in Johnson Square a notice to the effect that he was leaving shortly for England. Immediately the magistrates demanded that he furnish bail and when Wesley refused, they placed sentinels around his house and ordered all persons to prevent his leaving.

On the night of December 2, having said evening

prayers, he slipped into a rowboat with three companions and headed up the river toward Purrysburg. Here he was safe in South Carolina, out of Couston's reach. Eventually he made his way to Charleston where, after twenty days' rest, he set sail for England. The date was December 22, 1737. He had been in Georgia one year and nearly nine months.[13]

. . . John Wesley's gaze came back from far away. He straightened in his chair and cleared his throat. The others bent forward to listen.

"As for those who marry during the first four years of their ministry, no provision shall be made for them. The Society should not be encumbered with them." His words had the air of finality. "Moreover, to prevent young Clergymen from forming unfavorable alliances in communities where they are not acquainted, they should take no step toward marriage without first advising with their brethren."

Ever since that day countless young Methodist parsons have lived in single loneliness through the beginnings of their church careers, little suspecting that a woman was at the bottom of it!

CHAPTER IV
THE CHASTE AMAZON

DEBORAH SAMPSON IN TROUSERS BLEEDS FOR HER COUNTRY AND SHOWS US CONDITIONS THE REVOLUTIONARY VETERAN FOUND WHEN HE RETURNED HOME FROM THE WAR

I

A HOST of figures march across the tapestry of the American Revolution. Some loom titanic in the estimation Time has placed on their services. Others are obscure to the point of oblivion. Yet these less spectacular figures often have an appealing human interest beyond the ordinary compass. As the ranks go tramping by, let us call two women out of the line.

The one is Mary Draper of Dedham, Massachusetts, forerunner of those Salvation Army lassies who lately served doughnuts and coffee to men going up to the front. The other is Deborah Sampson who fought, dressed as a man, in the Continental Army, "during which time," so the title of her biography states, "she performed the duties of every department into which she was called, with punctual exactness, fidelity and honor, and preserved her chastity inviolate, by the most artful concealment of her sex."

Mary Draper assumed a rôle that was short, sane and motherly. When the fighting opened around Boston and the "embattled farmers" began drifting

93

past her house, she set up a booth on the roadside where she dispensed brown bread and cider. This hospitality was offered without price and with no pious strings attached. She simply doled out food to hungry men, God bless her! And we picture her staying up nights to knead the dough and tend the wood-stoked oven, and shovel out the loaves, weary but indefatigable, that no soldier should want. At her roadside counter we leave this gastronomic heroine, busily ladling out cider, sawing off man-sized hunks of bread and telling her visitors what she would do to those damned redcoats, if she were a man.

Deborah Sampson evidently thought the same, only she determined not to let sex stand in her way. The ardent searcher after Americana might dub her a collector's piece, so choice and amusing an example is she. For although there were belligerent females before her time—valiant Indian fighters and a multitude of Revolutionary heroines—she is the first veritable enlisted American Amazon of which we have record. (14)

In their efforts to cast a robe of glory about her, early biographers exhausted their saccharine vocabularies. She was made to strike the posture of a plaster saint. Yet single women in barracks differ little from single men, and Kipling's dictum regarding the sort of saints they turn into was as true of Revolutionary times as it is today. In many districts through which they passed, soldiers of the Revolution (as did soldiers under Xenophon, Caesar, Genghis Khan, Napoleon,

Grant, Lee, Foch, Hindenburg) appear to have
applied a liberal interpretation of both the amount
of ardent spirits a man should consume and of the
Seventh Commandment. While we have her assurances that respecting such matters she was unap-
proachable, yet, after chipping the plaster off this
chaste Amazon, she stands forth a human being.

II

She was born December 17, 1760.

Her ancestry was the sort to give her immediate
and unchallenged membership in the Colonial Dames.
On her father's side one ancestor came to Plymouth
in 1629, having been a member of the English colony
at Leyden. Another was a Mayflower émigré. One
of her great-uncles married a granddaughter of Miles
Standish, and her father married a descendant of the
famous William Bradford. This stock was the excellent Puritan farmer type that gave New England its
best men and women and from which sprang leaders
in great affairs. In addition, Deborah's blood was
salted by a dash of Gallic, a grandfather having
espoused a French wife.

Of her father we read that he had little or no
property and that he was fickle and "perhaps too
loose in his morals." Well, that's not uncommon
with sailors. This particular salt went down to the
sea on his lawful occasions, leaving his wife to scrape
along as best she could. Deborah's mother had a
difficult time making ends meet. Finally news came

that he had perished at sea. Deborah had just turned
five. Although his death lifted the burden of uncertainty from the mother, she found it beyond her
skill to keep the family together. She farmed the
children out among friends and relatives. Up to the
time she was ten, Deborah had a peripatetic childhood, being shunted about from house to house, poor
little waif! Finally she came to a standstill in the
home of one Jeremiah Thomas in Middleborough.

"We now view Miss Sampson," says her biographer, "advancing into the bloom and vigor of
youth." In other words, she was old enough to make
herself useful around the Thomas place—she milked
the cows, fed the pigs, tended the chickens, raked hay,
spun and wove and did countless other chores until
she was eighteen. A farmhouse drudge with little or
no chance for schooling. "During Spring, Summer
and Autumn," continues the same devoted chronicler,
"she was peculiarly attached to rural speculation."
What she did in winter he does not say. But regard
the pathetic picture she makes in these rural speculations—gazing at the monotonous fields, in a dumb
wonder if ever she'll break away from this treadmill
of dreary work. She is said to have "despised
revelry, gossiping, distraction and orgies," which
leads us to surmise that such things went on in
Middleborough, but, since she was merely a slavey,
she wasn't invited to them. Most of us dislike the
kind of parties we aren't invited to. For a time,
when she neared twenty, she taught school, a rather

courageous undertaking, seeing that she had had no schooling herself.

Meantime the war had broken out and history was being made swiftly all around her—battles and raids, advances and retreats. Urged by this excitement a brilliant idea came to her in one of her rural speculations. Some would call it a temptation. For it appears that one night she borrowed a man's suit of clothes, went to the local "ordinary," as the tavern was called, and enjoyed its bibulous hospitality with the rest of the yokels. The Thomases were doubtless shocked, and berated her mightily. Besides she had just been received into the Baptist Church. Her masquerading "and other very loose and un-Christian-like behavior" amazed the elders. They labored with her "without obtaining satisfaction" and concluded it was the church's duty to withdraw fellowship.

With a sentence of excommunication dangling over her head Deborah began day-dreaming about distant places, about getting away from that dreary *milieu*, the sort of thing a spirited young woman would be apt to do under the circumstances. She decided to take the chance—she obtained men's clothes and set out to see the world. Womanlike, she consulted a prognosticator to have read for her what fortune would attend the venture. For a while she wandered about aimlessly (some say she enlisted and deserted) but lack of funds prevented her attaining her vagrant dream. As in these days, so

then; if you couldn't afford to travel and see the
world as a gentleman, you joined the army. At
Worcester, in May 1782, she signed up for the dura-
tion of the war. Her "enlistment as a soldier was
not the original plan, nor patriotism the original
impulse." To the recruiting officer she gave the
name of Robert Surtlieff.

Determined to get her into the campaign that
wrecked Cornwallis, one biographer pictures her
enlisting long before she did and battling in patriotic
frenzy up and down the Atlantic seaboard. The
amount of action this Amazon saw was really negligible, however. From Worcester she was sent with
others to West Point, and from there went on several
raiding parties. One, during June, headed across the
Hudson to Stony Point, went as far south as Harlem
and then turned back to White Plains. At Tappan
Bay—between Sing Sing and Tarrytown—her company contacted with Tories and in the mêlée she
received a sabre slash. She appears to have made a
good accounting of herself despite the fact that her
"buddies" referred to her as the "blooming boy" and
"Molly," because she had no beard.

Her sudden and unexplained departure from the
bosom of the Thomas family had caused concern.
Her brother, we are told, went on a wild-goose chase
to Maine to find her, and a friend came to West Point
on another clue. Through his gossip she heard news
of her mother, although he did not recognize her. To
comfort her anxious parent she wrote a letter saying

that she had found agreeable work in "a large but well-regulated family," which was certainly paying an unwarranted compliment to the Continental Army. While this was a terrible fib to have told, we must remember that the mother was distracted and that the girl was fighting for freedom, or as a certain wag put it, referring to New England, fighting to make the world safe for the Congregational Church.

Some weeks later another Tory-raiding party included Deborah, this time going down the west shore of the Hudson. At East Chester, shortly after midnight, they ambushed a band of Loyalists. A stiff fight ensued, during which Deborah was shot in the thigh. Lest she reveal herself, she told her buddies she had received a mortal wound and begged them to leave her by the roadside to die. This subterfuge didn't work; they carried her back to a dressing station conducted by the French (the French did some of the best medical work in the Revolution) and only by the greatest fortitude and nimbleness of wit was she able to convince the surgeon that she was perfectly all right. She crawled off by herself and for days suffered untold tortures until the wound began to heal. For this perversity she later paid a heavy price.

In November the army retired into winter quarters, but it was no vacation for Deborah. With a detachment she was sent to the headwaters of the Hudson up to Ticonderoga, thence west—to quiet the Indians who had gone on the warpath. This proved an adventure. We read of Deborah, in one of the fights, about to despatch an Indian only to find he was white. Of course she did the only decent thing one could do under the circumstance, she rescued the unfortunate captive.

Next we see this Amazon appointed orderly to General Patterson. This easy berth took her to Philadelphia where the General was sent to help quell a riot of unpaid drunken troops that threatened Congress, and had driven it to sitting in Trenton. Malignant fever was running through Philadelphia at the time and Deborah fell victim to it. She was carried unconscious to a hospital, and during the examination, her sex was disclosed. She recovered almost as quickly as she had fallen ill. To the doctor she confessed her rôle and won from him a promise not to reveal her secret. And good reason she had for it— she was enjoying her life in the army and also, at the time, as the story goes, she was intrigued by a little "affair."

A girl had fallen in love with her. An anonymous letter is delivered to Deborah, a letter breathing warm admiration. Later Deborah meets the girl. "Timorous as a young roe, yet pliant as the bending osier, with the queen of love resident in her eyes, she rehearsed her plaint of love with that unreservedness, which evinced the sincerity of her passion and exaltedness of soul." We marvel that Deborah kept a straight face through this meeting. Yet it seems she did. The biographer in his grandest manner

IN DEBORAH SAMPSON'S CASE, THE LASS WHO LOVED A
SOLDIER HAD A RUDE AWAKENING

further tells us that "had this unfortunate lover uttered herself in an uncouth, illiterate, unpolished manner, every word would have lost its energy and all her charms become vapid on the senses. Or had she assumed the attire, the cunning of a harlot, the desperate simplicity of the young wanton; had she begun her subtle eloquence with a kiss; and with the poison of asps under her tongue, had represented her bed of embroidery filled with perfume and finally had urged that the absence of the good man gave them an opportunity to riot in the ecstatic delights of love—while our young fugitive would have needed supernatural means to have answered the demands of venerous appetition, the simple might have found satiety in her seraglio." But this was not the case. Deborah listened to her plaint without cracking a smile and promised that the next time she came that way she'd look her up.

One probably wonders how Deborah managed to preserve her masquerade. Her stature, we are told, was erect, and a little taller than the average height of females. Her countenance and voice were feminine. In her memoir Deborah says that she found men's clothes more convenient than those worn by women. "Her waist might displease a coquette" but her limbs were regularly proportioned. "Ladies of taste considered them handsome when in masculine garb. Several instances are recorded where they were deeply smitten by her good looks." For her voluminous waist, her biographer accounts as follows: "She wore a bandage about her breasts, during her disguise. . . . It is not improbable that the severe pressure of this bandage served to compress the bosom while the waist had every natural convenience for augmentation." He further states that "she was never found in liquor" and that she "never wrestled nor suffered anyone to twine his arms about her shoulders." . . . That she managed to preserve her chastity moves him to state, "such a case, perhaps, was never before known. It certainly stood alone in the Revolutionary War."

In her rôle as orderly to General Patterson she is said to have crossed the Alleghanies, had thrilling encounters with Indians in what is now Ohio, and finally returned to Philadelphia, via Baltimore. While in the latter city she once again met the girl who was smitten with her charms. During this rendezvous the maiden gave her, as a token of her admiration, six shirts, a watch and twenty-five Spanish dollars. Deborah apparently accepted them in the spirit in which they were offered. Later we find her writing the girl a letter which, in modern parlance, would be to the effect that this affair simply mustn't go on any further. She signed it "Your Own Sex."

Finally the doctor who discovered Deborah proved to be a sieve. He wrote about her to General Patterson. When that lusty warrior found that his orderly was a woman, he is said to have exclaimed, "This is truly theatrical!" But he was not devoid of wit. Returning to West Point he allowed Deborah to assume women's garb and in this mufti she walked up and down the ranks of her erstwhile comrades. Never a one recognized her! Finally she was mustered out, receiving her discharge from General Knox with recommendations from General Patterson and others. She returned to New England in November 1783, having been away one year and a half.

Instead of going to Middleborough, where she had spent her dreary childhood, she went to Stoughton, and retired into tedious rusticity. She still wore her uniform and in this male costume found a job on a farm. She adopted the name of Ephraim Sampson. During that winter the usual farm chores engrossed her and for diversion, she flirted with the country girls! On the approach of Spring she assumed women's clothes and thereafter, except for veterans' parades and meetings of the contemporary equivalent of the American Legion, she never wore her uniform again. Once to gratify the curiosity of the multitude she visited Boston, and in the theatre, "clad in military attire, she went through at the word of a military officer, the manual exercise." Those who witnessed the performance said that "she would almost make the gun talk" every time it came to the ground from her hand, the sound was so significant. This happened about 1801, when she was past forty.

In April, 1784, she yielded to the manly attractions of one Benjamin Gannet, a young farmer, and shortly thereafterward married him.

At this point old-time books display their modesty

by saying, "We will now draw the veil." Let us do the same. For the present let us leave Deborah and her Benjamin to their connubial bliss.

What concerns us at this point is the condition of life and affairs the Revolutionary soldier found on his return home. How had his family fared while he was off fighting? What prospects were there of his getting a job? What sort of things that would affect him had been going on while he was away? How did people behave themselves after the Revolutionary War?

III

In unthinking moments we are apt to gild the lily of ancient patriotism, apt to believe that all decent men and women in America of 1776 rose with one accord to combat the Mother Country for life, liberty and the pursuit of happiness, apt to feel that everyone made Titanic sacrifices for the cause, that all were inspired by holy zeal and unimpeachable purposes, that even business men were ice to the guilty desire of profiting by dissension. Nevertheless human nature pursues its course unhindered in all such conflicts. The scandals, the economic and moral upheavals attendant on the Civil War, the Spanish-American War, the Great War, and all other wars, were as pronounced in the Revolution. The gilded lily of blind patriotism soon withers in the penetrating sunlight of facts.

There were those who went forth with a fierce

desire to fight—spirited young men especially. There were those who violently opposed the fighting, either through loyalty to the Mother Country or because they believed it the wrong method to take. And there were those who weren't interested in the controversy and who preferred to pursue their lives and business undisturbed. In modern parlance, the ardent patriot, the enemy alien, the slacker.

Instead of every available man taking up arms, we find that in 1776, when the Continental Army was at its peak, it mustered only 90,000, one-eighth of the men of fighting age at the time. Because of the slowness in enlisting, it was soon found necessary to offer inducements—money, suits of clothes, land grants. Bounty-jumping was common. Men joined up and then departed when their paid time expired, irrespective of what battle was imminent. After Washington's capture of the British at Trenton, he was obliged to pay his men a fresh bounty of $10 each to keep them in the ranks for another month.

In 1776 each state promised to supply its quota of troops together with their arms and ammunition, yet in 1781 Washington recorded in his diary that scarcely a state had one-eighth of its quota in the field. Conditions grew desperate. Congress and the states offered fabulous bounties—in paper money—Congress $200 to each man and $250 additional by New Jersey, $300 by Georgia, $750 by Virginia. By 1779 the Continental Army numbered only 45,000. It numbered even less when Deborah Sampson joined it, although by that time the men were better fed, clothed and sheltered. Looking over these meagre figures one cannot help marveling at the successes attained by Washington, at the man's superb generalship, his enduring fortitude and unflagging courage.

When those who had fought in the war returned they found these countless men who had never lifted a finger for the cause comfortably ensconced at home. The situation did not help to promote good feeling.

From the first, the Loyalists or Tories presented a problem. Here was a potential enemy, and often an actively treacherous one within the Continental lines. That they would remain neutral was too much to expect of human nature. There were about fifty distinct corps of Loyalist troops in the Colonies during the Revolution—men born and living here who were willing to fight for the Mother Country. Their number totaled about 15,000 men and officers.

More than a third of the men of influence in America were opposed to using force. John Adams estimated that in 1775 fully half of the educated, wealthy and respected citizens of New England were Loyalists. However, Massachusetts passed an act of banishment in 1778, and three hundred of her best people were sent to segregation points in the remote wilderness; others departed when the British Army left Boston. In New York, the majority of the property owners and many of the middle class held Tory sympathies. In Pennsylvania, the same. On the other hand, in Virginia and the other Southern

Colonies, sentiment for the Revolution was predominant. Without a waver Virginia and Connecticut threw their Tories into jail. The Anglican preachers among the Tories fared especially ill; one staunch, old Maryland parson for months mounted his pulpit carrying two loaded pistols to defend himself while he preached for the King, and even Bishop Asbury, John Wesley's representative here, was obliged to curb his ecclesiastical activities and pass many a "dumb and silent Sabbath."

During the war hysteria, people demanded the extermination of all Loyalists "by halter and gibbet." They were called "this stinking race." Washington ordered them seized; they were "preying on the vitals of the country." Even so worthy a citizen as John Adams was for fining, imprisoning and even hanging those who refused to take the oath of allegiance.

As a logical corollary, the states pursued the usual predatory policy of confiscation. This was suggested by Tom Paine in his famous pamphlet, "Common Sense." Lands belonging to Tories were forthwith seized. New Hampshire confiscated twenty-eight estates, including the property of the Governor. New York seized all lands and rents of the Crown, and the estates of fifty-nine persons. In Pennsylvania, the holdings of the Penn family, estimated to be worth a million pounds sterling, were swept in by the state. The same policy was pursued in Maryland and Georgia. The enemy alien property custodians showed no favor. Loyalists estimated their losses to amount to eight million pounds; Parliament paid claims to the tune of two million.

These seizures proved profitable to the states. The forfeited real estate in New York, for example, was valued at 3,150,000 Spanish dollars. After the war the sale of the property—usually in small parcels— not only recouped the depleted finances of the several commonwealths, but also effected an economic trans- formation in that it did away, by these small parcels sales, with many of the huge estates. This chance to buy property was one of the opportunities that awaited the home-coming Revolutionary soldier.

Even after the peace, Loyalists continued to be a problem. Many of them were in evidence on all sides, and they endeavored to ingratiate themselves into the good will of the community. Some crept back to make public recantation of their past errors, pay the costs and receive back the whole or part of their forfeited property, but in many places popular sentiment was not volatile; the "independence fever" ran too high to make life comfortable for Loyalists or to warrant them immediate success. They were objects of derision and scorn. Some fled and some were shipped to Nova Scotia, where the British Government awarded each 200 acres of land and two years' provisions. Those who stayed were often forbidden residence. Stamford, Connecticut, and Worcester, Massachusetts, conducted them uncere- moniously to the township limits. In Virginia, Maryland, and the Carolinas the feeling against them persisted for years. Watchmen on their rounds announcing the time of night and the state of the weather, shouted bawdy remarks concerning local Tories and people sympathetic to them. The memory of their activities was too fresh in the minds of the returning veterans to guarantee them an unmolested existence.

As in the late war, so in the Revolution, popular support had been aroused and sustained by propaganda. And what a familiar ring this propaganda has! It makes one wonder if the standards for war propaganda weren't definitely set thousands of years ago, and, so soon as activities commence, we merely bring out the old moulds, dust them off, and cast the same old stories over again. There was the customary yarn about helpless girls and women being ravished by the British, and the recurrent scandal of the enemy—Hessians especially—exhuming the dead and stripping the bodies, and of murdering the helplessly wounded. Such tales the returning veterans were not soon to forget or forgive.

As in all wars, profiteering rose to the proportions of a scandal. The merchant class in towns and cities, the jobber who supplied the army and the farmer as well took advantage of the occasion to feather their nests. Prices for commodities shot sky-high. Speculators, known as "engrossers," bought up the available supplies of foodstuffs and clothing in a neighborhood, thus controlling the market prices for them. Other speculators, known as "forestallers," tried to corner goods before they reached the market stalls. Things got to such a pass that some of the states clamped on price-regulating acts. A flood of paper money was let loose, which lost value almost as soon as printed. Speculators dealt in this, and since each state had its own paper currency of varying values, there was great monetary confusion. Through these two circumstances—the profiteer and the worthless money—the families of the soldiers paid the price that the proletariat usually does in times of war.

Between 1779 and 1782 taxes continued to rise as levies were imposed on the states. Since many of the men were away, the burden of paying this fell on the women. State and local officials tried to render them aid. In many sections the farmer faced dire poverty. On the frontier, farm areas were also harried by Indian and Royalist attacks that made life uncertain and work difficult.

Nevertheless the common people became avaricious. There was lively profiteering among the rural population. New England was mostly a place of small farms from which the crop was sufficient to support the family and perhaps leave a little over. During the war the surplus was held at a high figure. In Pennsylvania, many farmers preferred to carry their goods to Philadelphia, where the British paid higher prices than those offered by the Continental Army quartermasters. On the other hand, due to the absence of the men, many farms suffered a diminution of their crops and the loss of the utensils

that men used to make, so that it took some time
after the war for these farms and farmers to get back
to productive tillage.

Thanks to profiteering, old families that had held
places of prominence in the community were pushed
into the background, and others, that had acquired
sudden wealth, usurped their places. Even before
peace came, profiteers—vulgar and ostentatious—
swanked through the streets. The homespun class
assumed the broadcloth. Peddlers rose to affluence.

The Marquis de Chastellux observed of these times
that "the rage for dress among the women in America,
in the very height of the miseries of war, was beyond
all bounds." And this he found not only in seacoast
towns and cities, but the rural areas as well. Such
was the topsy-turvy social condition that the soldier found on returning home.

Nor did it add to his peace of mind. For while
these conditions were being evolved the men were
fighting, some of them pitiably under-armed, under-
clad and underfed, and certainly underpaid.

Toward the end of the war the shortage of pay
for both men and officers became the most serious
problem the Revolutionary Fathers faced. As we
have seen, Deborah Sampson's chief was summoned
post-haste to Philadelphia to suppress a riot of soldiers
demanding their money. As soon as the war was
over officers lost no time sending in their resignations.
They simply had to recoup, and the army was no

place for that. This loss of officers weakened the discipline of those who remained.

During the war the men had been promised half pay for seven years if they fought to the end. In 1780, this was increased to half pay for life, although Congress had no funds at the time to guarantee the payment. In 1783, the life pay was commuted to five years pay in a lump sum for which 6 per cent interest-bearing certificates were issued. In many neighborhoods, men who had been beggared by services to their country were bitterly criticized for accepting this or insisting that pay be given them. We saw the same controversy after the Great War in regard to the bonus.

Many men in the ranks took a different course from their officers. The war over, people demanded that the army be disbanded. Thereby taxes could be reduced. For people had gotten terribly behind in their taxes and no one wanted the unpleasant task of trying to collect them. So, cut down the army. But the army refused to be cut down. Some troops refused to be mustered out until they were paid. When Congress proposed its certificates, many citizens violently opposed the action. Irate patriots rose up in town meetings and argued ardently against any such augmentation of their taxes. In Massachusetts and Connecticut, both bulwarks of patriotism, the feeling against this veteran relief was particularly strong. Thus the returned soldier, whose needs were pressing, found himself caught between the devil of a

Congress that lacked the funds to pay, and the deep sea of a citizenry that would refuse the payment. The discontent among New England troops combined with the brutal debtors' law, later found an outlet in Shay's Rebellion. However, the army was reduced immediately. By 1785 it numbered less than six hundred men and two companies of antiquated artillery, and a few handfuls of useless soldiers at frontier forts.

The situation that many merchants found themselves in after the Revolution was likewise difficult. Scarcely had the peace treaty been signed than to Boston, New York, Philadelphia, and even to Charleston, factors and agents of British manufacturers swarmed with their price lists. And their prices deliberately undersold the goods American merchants could import from French and Dutch sources. England also required the goods to be carried in British bottoms. So America lost her overseas trade. Britain controlled it on her own terms. She continued to furnish nine-tenths of the imports into the United States. Even English clerks and merchants flocked over and took the jobs young Americans sorely needed.

In New England the cod-fishery, the backbone of the coastal business, had been obliterated by the enemy's ships. Likewise merchant ship owners could scarcely get together crews to man their vessels. Many of them were forced into privateering, each man aboard getting his share of the spoils. Thus alone were they able to man their boats. Newspapers and posters printed tempting pictures of the spoils these men would win. This drain on the available man power not only lessened the fighting ranks but it augmented the numbers of the *nouveau riche*, for these privateering merchants waxed fat on the spoils. Indeed, were it not for robbery on the high seas, many a New England family prominent today would have remained in obscurity.

As soon as hostilities ceased there arose the problem of rehabilitating the territory held by the enemy. In Rhode Island some of the best farm lands had been occupied, and for months after peace, refugees were returning to their homes. New York and Charleston, long held by the British, remained hot-beds of Tories, and patriots found difficulty settling their claims.

Nor did British troops leave the cities they had occupied in any presentable condition. Philadelphia was a filthy mess when they marched out in 1778—streets dirty and piled with obstructions, gutters choked with filth, trees and fences cut down, country houses on the edge of town rifled or destroyed—they put seventeen of them to the torch in one day. Nor were the morals of the evacuated Philadelphia anything to boast of. Chastellux describes it as being "a great sink wherein all the speculations of America terminate and are confounded together."

New York was accorded the same sort of neglect and destruction as Philadelphia. The week Howe entered New York a fire on the west side destroyed five hundred houses, and three years later a second fire leveled three hundred on the east side. Since the British did little or no building during their occupancy and made no effort to clean up the town, returning patriots found large areas covered with the usual chaos and heaped debris of a fire, when they came into it toward the end of November, 1783. For seven years New York had been a prison and a military depot, its population reduced to twenty-three thousand. Due to the poverty of the people and their lack of enterprise, no improvements were made in the city for fifteen years after the evacuation.

In rural sections, and in cities as well, schools had been sorely neglected during the long years of the conflict. The structure of education had to be fashioned all over again. Not until 1789 was there any legislation affecting the common school. Communities felt too poor after the Revolution to undertake educational activities. For years the common schools of New York and Pennsylvania were in desperate straits. However, in two such widely separated districts as Vermont in 1782, and in Georgia a year later, constructive action was taken to rewind the machinery of popular education.

To us who can remember the reaction to the Great War it is amusing to read the social changes that came to pass during the conflict. We find one New England parson complaining that children in church had gotten so out of hand that they shouted across the pews and otherwise acted boisterously. The flapper of the day, too, seemed determined to shock her elders. Young ladies who were previously accustomed to chat decorously over teacups, used obscene language heard only from the lips of sailors! Little or no respect was shown magistrates and others in authority. Rowdies soon presented a problem to the local constabulary. New England experienced a crime wave—burglaries and hold-ups disturbed the peace and decorum of well-regulated communities. Likewise did a wave of drinking hit the country after the war. John Adams complained, "dissipation has no bounds at present." Massachusetts had sixty distilleries going full blast and such inroads were made on the grains needed for food that both Massachusetts and Rhode Island had to restrict the amount of liquor distilled.

But after this usual post-war chaos and unrest had spent its force, hope slowly dawned for the veteran of the Revolution. Congress actually began paying them money. There was work aplenty to be done for those who were not too proud to work—in digging the canals that were projected over the Atlantic seaboard and in making the turnpikes that were to establish national communication. And roads were sorely needed. The year after the Revolution only two stages were running between Boston and New York and so bad was the condition of the roads that the journey required six days and was considered perilous.

America was expanding both in its settled areas
and along its frontiers. And it was on the frontiers
that courageous men of this time found their opportunity.

For some years Congress labored with the states
to surrender the undefined territory that lay to the
west of them or to contribute to opening it up. This
did not appeal to the commonwealths. Abortive
states were planned and little came of them. Consequently when in 1790 the Ohio Company proposed to
purchase a million and a half acres in the Ohio Valley
—the Western Reserve—it was welcomed as the
happiest solution of the problem. One million dollars was paid for this area. The land was made easily
available to men who had fought in the Revolution;
and from New England, led by General Rufus Putnam,
and later by the Rev. Manasseh Cutler, hordes of
veterans with their families and household goods
began the long overland trek that brought them to
Pittsburgh and the headwaters of the Ohio. The
Western Reserve became a Promised Land—a rich,
abundant soil, in contrast to the boulder-strewn
fields they had struggled with for generations; a
freer life where, in time, the Democracy as set forth
by Thomas Jefferson and preached by the local
"coonskin apostles of liberty and equality," made
every man the other fellow's equal, and eventually
developed the expansive, breezy type we know as
"Middle Western."

This migration drained New England of some of

its best agricultural stock. They abandoned their fields, shut up the old barns and forgot the desolation behind them for the advantages that lay ahead. Boldly they advertised their departure; everywhere along the roads and trails those days one encountered the wagons of the Ohio company, huge, lumbering, ox-drawn affairs covered with black canvas on which was painted in large letters "To Marietta on the Ohio." ([15])

IV

If Deborah Sampson and her spouse Benjamin were indeed the sort of people the quaint old records picture them, they doubtless had many an argument over this opportunity. Here was a veteran of the war, and here was the big chance of their lives to leap out of the narrow rut of New England farm life. To be sure, theirs was a nice enough place—a two-storey house embowered with willows, covered with woodbine and with roses growing up to the chimney-tops, a hundred acres or so of mowing and cultivatable land with brooks through it and raspberries in the hedges and along the stone walls. Having literally worn the pants, Deborah had a lot to say about its management. She had known adventure, she had crossed the Alleghanies. "Well, Benjamin, what about it? Shall we go?"

Then arose an embarrassing fact, one that gave Deborah the whip-hand over her husband all their married life: while she was out fighting, what was

The Hoosier Wagon.

THE HOOSIER WAGON BORE ITS ADVERTISING
BOAST PAINTED ON ITS CANVAS COVER

he doing? Did he put on the Continental uniform for Freedom? Did he slog-slog through mud and cross-country 'mile on end to take pot-shots at Tories? Did he help subdue wild Indians? Did he get a sabre slash and a bullet in his hip? Not Benjamin. He stayed at home, did the chores around the farm, and let the militant Georges of the time do the fighting. Although it is definitely established that he was not a Tory, he certainly was of fighting age, being only three years her senior. He had been a slacker!

We feel that Deborah really married beneath her. A high-spirited, adventuresome young woman with her war record deserved a man of better stuff than Gannett. Perhaps though, he wearied of her telling about the war, and she wearied of his cloddish ways. Little wonder that when she was forty-one she accepted the offer to do the manual of arms on a Boston stage. Whether or not she was paid for this act we don't know, but if she did receive money, she might lay claim to being the first American heroine to capitalize her prowess in vaudeville.

Time dragged on. Benjamin panned out hard-working but ambitionless. A son came and two daughters. Meantime the wound she received at East Chester kept bothering Deborah. The bullet had never been extracted. She was unable to perform any great labor. Benjamin was under heavy expenses for her care. In 1783 the Commonwealth of Massachusetts granted her an invalid bonus of thirty-four pounds, about one hundred dollars. In

1805 Congress granted her a pension of four dollars a month as an invalid soldier. Because she lacked sufficient credentials—due to her enlisting as a man —she had difficulty in establishing her claim. In 1818 the four-dollar pension was doubled and this was paid her until her death in 1827.

Then came Benjamin's little hour of reflected glory. He was alone. He could spin all the war yarns he wanted without fear of contradiction. He could boast about his patriotic wife and her contribution to the cause. But, poor old fellow, he had little else to enjoy. After her death, hard luck trailed his footsteps. In 1837, ten years after her passing, we find him eighty-three, infirm, in indigent circumstances, without property. His only son, who could have lent support, was dead, and the two daughters were dependent on charity. He remembered that six hundred dollars he had paid out for doctors to care for his wife's wounded thigh. So he sent a petition to Congress asking for aid. A bill was reported, granting him eighty dollars a month dated back to the 4th of March, 1831 and to be paid "for and during his natural life."

But even with this assistance, he evidently concluded that life wasn't worth the living if it had to be bought at the price of ignoble solicitude. He survived only a short time to enjoy the government's munificence.

CHAPTER V

THE DAMOSEL OF THE SLATE PENCIL

*MARIA MONK TELLS A PRODIGIOUS LIE THAT STARTS RIOTS AND INCEN-
DIARY FIRES AND WINDS UP IN THE ANTI-CATHOLIC PREJUDICE OF THE
KNOW-NOTHING DAYS*

I

AT THE moment she rammed a slate pencil into her head, Fame (or Infamy if you will) leaped on the shoulders of a tot of seven. What prompted her to do this, the drab and dusty annals do not disclose, but, thereafter this young lady was given to telling "whoppers."

To her mother we are indebted for the story of the offending pencil. Under stress mothers can recall even such minor accidents, and the occasion when Mrs. Monk recalled this affair was painful indeed. Her daughter Maria had just told a prodigious lie. She was destined to tell many more. Eventually, so finished became her prevaricating technique that she kept the ecclesiastical dove-cotes a-flutter and a-twitter for some time.

Before she accomplished this, and for many years afterward, there being evolved circumstances favorable to the reception of her type of imposture.

The intelligentsia and the genteel of America bathed in the tepid waters of Romanticism. At points here and there the stream was tinctured with the blood-red infusion of reform. Now and again came a buffeting backwash from exploitation, expansion, and adventure as the industrial life of the country attained potentiality and as its frontiers bit deeper into the hinterlands. From many diverse and far-flung springs trickled the forces that gave this eddying stream its volume.

One rivulet rose in Europe, when starvation followed the blight of the potato crop. Other traceable tributaries were in the decline of political probity under the nefarious Spoils System; the outcropping and pestilent flowering of Nativism, of the American Party, of Know-Nothingism, with numerous secret societies and bitter religious prejudice in their wake; the frantic pulsations of crusades against war, liquor, and tobacco; the Abolition Movement; and the early championing of the rights of women. Still another stream begins with a New York portrait painter penning fervent letters to the press about the designs of the Roman Church on the liberties of America.

A further source was a young woman hastily departing over the back fence of a convent in Charlestown, Massachusetts, the which she did in February, 1832, and a cold day it was. This incident might not seem important in the cosmic scheme of things were it not for the fact that convent-jumping became a habit. Quite a number of young ladies of this epoch, to misquote the "Ingoldsby Legends,"

"Bring me before a court."

Maria Monk

MARIA MONK'S "AWFUL DISCLOSURES" WAS A VOLUME
THAT CONTRIBUTED TO THE ANTI-FOREIGN AND ANTI-
CATHOLIC MOVEMENT OF THE 40'S CALLED "KNOW-
NOTHINGISM"

Stamped their feet and hired a hack
And fled from their convents and never came back.

From such various sources sprang the eddy that washed around Maria Monk's impostures and their consequences. In beginning her story, let us start at the stream of a persistent Colonial prejudice.

II

Americans have always distrusted the foreigner and the entangling alliances that the foreigner connoted. Whatever evils befell the country from time to time, the man in the street and the leader as well have eventually laid them at the door of newcomers to these shores. The manner of the first populating of America and the manner in which the population increased bred this distrust.

The Southern colonies, settled mainly by middle class English stock, attained a rural aristocracy under the importation of slaves and the redemptioners and criminals dumped on their shores. New England, also settled by the same class of British stock, developed an ecclesiastical and intellectual aristocracy and held itself aloof from foreigners. From 1640 until after the turn of the nineteenth century the population of New England increased solely from its own people. In both the Southern and the New England colonies the controlling stock was Nordic and Protestant. In the middle Atlantic colonies—New York, New Jersey, Delaware, Pennsylvania—although the colonists were of mixed nationalities, their religious prejudices tended mainly toward Protestantism. Excepting Maryland, the Atlantic seaboard was settled by people whose religious convictions were as far removed as possible from the influence of Rome.

And their convictions found voice! With one or two exceptions, the Colonies were established for the express purpose of affording freedom of religious belief, a purpose that in a short while came to mean freedom only for such as held the belief of those in power. Among the religions that fell under this ban was the Roman Catholic. From the beginning and for many years the enactments against it were pronounced.

The New Haven and Connecticut settlements forbade Catholics entrance. Despite this, many did come to New England. Because he considered the red crossed bars of the English flag to be a Papal symbol, in 1634 John Endicott ordered it cut out. Thirteen years later Massachusetts put up the bars on Jesuits, and so strict was their ruling that a second offense carried the death penalty. The passage of the Quebec Bill, giving freedom of religious observance to Canadian Roman Catholics, struck terror to the hearts of most New Englanders.

The variations of Catholic favor and disfavor as expressed in the laws of Cromwell's régime and the reigns of Charles II, James II, and William and Mary, were reflected in enactments here. In 1642 Virginia passed its law banishing priests and in 1756

The Mitre Mented.

THE QUEBEC ACT, GIVING RELIGIOUS FREEDOM TO CATHOLICS IN CANADA, STIRRED UP NO END OF PALPITATIONS IN NEW ENGLAND. PAUL REVERE CARTOONED HIS SENTIMENTS IN THIS DRAWING

forbade Roman Catholics to have arms or—a quaint touch!—to own a horse worth more than five pounds. The Carolinas and Georgia considered it safest for their welfare if they excluded Papists. In the colony of New York any priest found there after November 1, 1700 was subject to life imprisonment and Catholics were excluded from office and the exercise of the franchise. Maryland, Rhode Island, and Pennsylvania were the only colonies where freedom of religious belief was extended to Catholics.

In several sections of Colonial America, New England and the Carolinas especially, a popular expression of the anti-Catholic feeling was Pope Day, an annual festival on the fifth of November—the local interpretation of Guy Fawkes Day. Effigies of the Pope and the Devil were carried in rowdy procession to the Common and burned amid the explosion of fire crackers and the huzzas of the citizens. During the Revolution Washington forbade the army celebrating Pope Day. After the Revolution, the custom fell into desuetude.

From anti-Catholic prejudice the same distrust spread to all classes of foreigners.

No sooner had the United States become a reality than there arose the controversy with France and England regarding the activities of Irish and French rebels. Some thirty thousand French and fifty thousand Irish refugees had found sanctuary here. Out of this controversy sprang the Alien and Sedition Acts whereby the President was given power to eject foreigners distasteful and dangerous to the government. Americans shuddered when they contemplated the contamination that might come from contact with foreigners. These acts, however, caused the downfall of the old Federal Party. We still nursed our early reputation as a safe harbor for the oppressed of all lands.

In slow trickles immigrants began to arrive. By 1820 the foreign stream was flowing in at the rate of 10,000 a year. Between 1820 and 1830 it totaled over 140,000. From 1830 to 1840 it grew to nearly 600,000. The following ten years saw a veritable tidal wave breaking, to the extent of 1,700,000. By 1850, immigrants comprised one-seventh of the population of this country.

Of those that came from 1830 to 1840 fully a third were from Ireland, and of those from 1840 to 1850, fully one-half. Of all the immigrants landing up to 1850 two-thirds were Roman Catholics. The No-Popery agitation in England and the Irish Rebellion were responsible for the early migration, but starvation was the whip that drove great hordes here in later years. In Ireland and Germany, following a cold, wet, sunless summer, farmers found their potato crops failing and horticultural solons proclaimed these countries to be in for a siege of the dread potato rot, with starvation in its wake. Over 600,000 did perish of starvation due to this scourge in various parts of Europe. Immigration westward assumed the proportions of a stampede. America became the poorhouse of Europe.

Since the political and economic organization of America could not easily absorb these newcomers, our towns and cities found themselves in the embarrassed position of a housewife with more guests than beds. Moreover, these foreigners worked hard, and were snapping up the jobs. To the man in the street they were decidedly a menace.

New York City, at which port the majority of the immigrants landed, witnessed a premature flutter in 1806 when the police were called to quell an anti-Catholic riot. Though by 1830 high-visioned Americans were rejoicing over the new freedom that appeared in England when the Reform Bill gave Catholics seats in Parliament, nevertheless, the next year, a Roman Catholic chapel in New York was burned in a suspicious fire, and two years later, a seminary at Nyack in similar circumstances.

This era prior to 1830 saw the rise of a religious phenomenon—the beginning of country revivals and camp meetings and the increase in itinerant preaching. Starting from the rural areas of Kentucky and Tennessee, the camp meeting increased in popularity. Noted preachers joined its forces. In 1831 the nation was swept by a great religious revival. Over city and town and countryside spread the Gospel net. Since this was directed by Methodists, Baptists, Presbyterians, and their various offshoots, it was patently a Protestant effort. The revival became the

contemporary expression of 100 per cent American-
ism.   While ecstatic religious fervor characterized
most of the preaching, from many a meadow pulpit
ricocheted attacks on foreigners and Roman Catholics.

This epoch also found Americans acquiring new
humanitarian interests.   On the heels of a pacifist
movement, fathered by William Lloyd Garrison in
the late thirties, came the opening shots of a war on
drink.   Under Garrison's crusading the *National
Philanthropist* appeared in Boston, and soon attracted
a large body of readers.   The Massachusetts Society
for the Suppression of Intemperance called people to
the attack.   The Maine Law, prohibiting liquor in
that state, was being agitated.

Stimulated by these assaults on war and drink,
the humanitarian consciousness of New England
spread its urge to include anti-slavery, prison and
debtors' law reforms (which certainly needed reforming), women's rights, and many other public benefactions.   After the manner of the "bitter neat"
Yankee housewife, New England reformers determined to scrub out every smudge on the body
politic.   Here were topics that politicians and
preachers alike grasped at avidly—some to support,
some to attack.

In this mêlée of reform newcomers were caught
helpless.   After New York, Boston was the great port
of entry for the immigrant, and Boston was the cita-
del of reform.   Not immediately fitting into the current scheme of things, these foreigners were soon

The Spirit of our Elections; or, the Organs, (Barrel), of all Political Parties

NOT ALONE THE IRISH, BUT THE GERMANS AS WELL, WERE ASSAILED FOR THEIR ALLEGED INTERFERENCE IN ELECTIONS AND THEIR STOUT OPPOSITION TO TEMPERANCE

accused of being arraigned against them. In the North, in New England especially, the Irish and Germans were assailed for being opposed to temperance and Abolition. Much of the anti-slavery feeling in New England among certain classes was actually anti-Catholic feeling. From the beginning, the Methodists, especially the northern Methodists, had busied themselves with abolishing slavery and restricting liquor sales. Down South the accusation was just the other way around—foreigners were openly suspected of pro-temperance and pro-Abolition activities.

Nor were local politics in the average American town attaining a state of grace. Corruption became rampant. The excesses of the Spoils System under Jackson set a notorious example and helped to create a public mood for graft. City elections were rife with vote-buying. Into this net the poorer immigrants fell as children before the temptation of candy. Under the lead of corrupt ward heelers they swayed from one camp to another. Serious-minded citizens took alarm. These foreigners were even being elected to offices! America should be run by Americans!

Meantime, up in Montreal, Maria Monk was coming along as best she could; still suffering from the effects of having rammed that slate pencil into her head, still telling fibs, much to the vexation of her parents, pastors and masters, and gradually developing other naughty traits that were destined to bring a sordid finale to her rôle.

The prologue to her comedy, however, was spoken by three different characters—two women and a man, with a growing chorus of the easily excited.

III

On a hill in Charlestown, outside of Boston, was founded in 1820 the convent of Mount Benedict, a house of Ursuline nuns devoted to the care and teaching of children. For eleven years they went about their work without stirring any too violent ripples in the community. Then, in the autumn of 1831, there came to the convent a Rebecca Theresa Reed, a convert to Catholicism of two years' standing, who was hired to teach music. For six months (some say only four) she lived within the convent pursuing this vocation, rather unsuccessfully, it seems, until one cold February afternoon, without apprising the Mother Superior of her intentions, she left the convent by way of the back fence and went to the house of the nearest neighbor. She was in a highly nervous state. The tales she related of convent life were shocking indeed, and they ran through the community like wildfire. Miss Reed was given assistance by Protestant ministers and friends and, at their suggestion, set to writing the book of her experiences. The following March it appeared—"Six Months in a Convent." Though a committee of Protestant citizens had investigated her stories and reported them unfounded, 10,000 copies of this book sold in Boston (the Watch and Ward Society having not yet laid its censoring hand on literature) in the first week. Anti-Catholic feeling rose to fever pitch. People looked aghast at convents, calling them "domiciles of inordinate wickedness," or "dungeons of unmitigated despair."

Meanwhile another book was being composed. In New York, Samuel F. B. Morse, of telegraph fame, then a portrait painter, was contributing letters to the *Observer* under the pseudonym of Brutus. He was recently home from Europe where he had been alarmed by the political activities of the Roman Church. On seeing Irish Catholics about the streets of New York, he started expressing his opinion of what these things meant. His letters set the fire crackling under the pot. Their appearance between the covers of a book stirred leading ministers, such as the Rev. W. C. Brownlee, pastor of the Dutch Reformed Church, and business men, such as the Harper brothers, founders of the publishing house, to violent expression. What citizen would not be alarmed by a volume called, "A Conspiracy Against the United States"? Were not these conspirators within our very gates? Were we to stand idle whilst the dearly bought independence of this country disappeared before the machinations of Rome?

Not alone did New York devour these letters, but Boston as well. The New England citizenry was on edge. Its reforming dander was up. The slightest spark of conspiracy against reform must be stamped out. People had not forgotten the tales Rebecca Reed told when she escaped from the Ursuline Convent two years before. Mount Benedict was being closely watched. From the pulpit thundered the voice of Lyman Beecher in a sermon called "The Devil and the Pope of Rome." Then in August, 1834, Boston was plunged into a nasty mess.

Miss Elizabeth Harrison, for ten years a professed member of the Ursuline congregation, suffered a breakdown. During her delirium she fled the convent. The next day, accompanied by her brother and Bishop Fenwick of the Boston diocese, she returned. Her aberration was temporary. However, her return gave rise to the legend that she had been forced back into the convent. Ten days later the Boston *Mercantile Journal* published an editorial captioned "Mysterious" which hinted that a girl was being held against her will at Mount Benedict. Irate citizens called at the convent to see about it. Though the Mother Superior received them and they saw Miss Harrison, they turned away unconvinced. The Board of Selectmen appointed an investigation committee. Their findings gave the institution a clean bill of health.

But hotheads seized the reins. A mob began murmuring through the Charlestown streets. It approached Mount Benedict. Someone lighted a bonfire. Fire bells rang. The mob streamed into the convent. From garret to cellar it swept, destroying whatever it laid its hand on. Ten nuns and fifty children under their charge fled to safety. The torch was applied. By one o'clock in the morning the convent was ablaze. The bishop's lodge and farm building adjoining were also fired. Boston awoke next morning to the realization of a profound disgrace.

In New York, fanned by Morse's book and by the preaching and writings of such Pope-hunters as the Rev. W. C. Brownlee, the anti-Catholic embers burst into flame. While the Charlestown fire had shocked cool-headed citizens, many there were who thought their own thoughts. In July, 1835, they gave their support to a Rev. W. K. Hoyt, and his Canadian Benevolent Association which was "designed to arrest the progress of Popery and to enlighten and convert their ignorant, vicious and degraded subjects." Mr. Hoyt had been employed in mission work in Lower Canada, and he spoke from experience. He selected Dr. Brownlee for vice-president. Not content with this, Dr. Brownlee formed his own association—the Society for the Diffusion of Christian Knowledge, established to conduct public meetings at which the man in the street would be apprised of the menace of Catholicism. Meantime Lyman Beecher, moved to the Ohio Valley, published his "Plea for the West," in which he demonstrated the alarming influences of Romanism. The book found immediate reception.

It was after this varied prologue that there

stepped onto the stage the young lady who had rammed a slate pencil into her head.

IV

In casting his net for the lost souls of Popery in Canada, the Rev. Mr. Hoyt gathered in a girl whose name was Maria Monk. A sturdy girl was Maria, with alluring rosy cheeks and attractive brown hair. She had an interesting way with her, and she also told an amazing story.

For five years, she said, she had been a novice and two years a professed nun in the Hotel Dieu in Montreal. She had been born in St. John, a small town on the Richelieu River near Montreal, of Scotch parentage. Her father was an officer in the Government. After a time the family moved to Montreal. Both parents were dead at the time she related this experience. At six she had been sent to a Protestant school and at ten to a school conducted by Sisters of Charity, which was next door to the Hotel Dieu. When she had scarcely passed thirteen, she was seized with a desire to become a nun and so presented herself to the Mother Superior of the Hotel as a novice. The usual novitiate was two and a half years, but because of her extreme youth, hers was almost five, or until she was eighteen. Having attained this age, she left the convent without notice, and went to St. Denis, a town near by, where she found work teaching. There she fell in with an evil man, not named, and was lured by him into marriage. Immediately she repented of this error and started to retrace her steps. She returned to the convent so that she might continue her novitiate. With her went a woman, so she averred, who agreed to corroborate an innocent story she was to tell of her departure, "which would satisfy and stop further inquiry." She also borrowed money from her mother's pension and from friends so that she could have sufficient funds to see her through the novitiate. Without questioning this story, the Mother Superior welcomed back the wayward lamb, and a year later she took her final vows in the order.

Scarcely had she been admitted to the intimate companionship of the sisters than she was induced to commit and see unspeakable immoralities. For the slightest offense sisters were gagged and horribly abused. Local clergy had the freedom of the nuns. Infanticide was common. In the few years she was there "eighteen or twenty infants were smothered or secretly buried in the cellar." She claimed even to have witnessed the murder of a nun who was crushed and smothered under a mattress when she refused the advances of a priest. This crime, so Maria said, was committed with the knowledge and sanction of the Bishop of Montreal, the Mother Superior and five priests, of which she named three. Twice after she took the veil was she obliged to flee the place and, finally, finding herself about to become a mother, she went to New York and having been discovered in great distress by a humane citizen was given sanctuary in Bellevue Hospital.

The Rev. Mr. Hoyt had her repeat the story to the assembled and amazed Pope-hunters. Aghast that such things could happen in a civilized community, these worthy pastors decided that the world should be apprised of them. In the *Protestant Vindicator* for October 14, 1835, Maria Monk's disclosures first appeared, and again on November 4.

Newspapers in Canada made an instant and furious denial. The Hotel Dieu was the best organized hospital on the continent at the time. The Black Nuns who conducted it had served the poor and sick of Montreal since the earlier days of Montreal (1642). Never before had aught but good been spoken of them or their ministrations for nearly two centuries.

In spite of the warning given by the leading Presbyterian ministers of Montreal, the following January these tales appeared in book form under the title of "Maria Monk's Awful Disclosures as Exhibited in a Narrative of Her Sufferings During a Residence of Five Years as a Novice and Two Years as a Black Nun in the Hotel Dieu at Montreal." A Committee of Publication, which vouched for the book, stated that they knew every word of these stories to be true. Harper & Brothers were the publishers.

As the book caused a widespread uproar, the Committee in New York were with Miss Monk clamoring for an investigation. This they funked when, on his own initiative, Col. W. L. Stone, editor of the *New York Commercial Advertiser*, himself a Protestant, had secured all the necessary permissions and offered to chaperon Maria to Montreal and investigate her charges. She declined the invitation. So did the committee. Col. Stone went alone. As he reported in his paper on Oct. 8, 1836, he found no evidence to substantiate her story. Before this, five Montreal investigators, formally appointed, confounded her regarding the layout of the convent. Then a general committee of New York citizens was assembled, and they, too, found Maria's story faulty in many respects.

The first inquiries into Maria's tales had centered around the interior of the convent—secret cellar passages and various changes she alleged had been made since her residence there. They left the public straddling the fence. Her supporters vowed that they had entire confidence in her narrative. She "behaved in the most correct manner, modestly and virtuously." But the cat eventually got out of the bag through a suit at law.

V

Patched together, the disclosures of Maria Monk's "Awful Disclosures" make an astounding story. The true story of her career is more prosaic.

One night in November 1834 there was brought to the house of a Dr. Robertson in Montreal a girl who had been attempting to drown herself and who

said that she was his daughter. As this was obviously
untrue, he began questioning her and she finally acknowledged that her name was Maria Monk. She
told a wandering tale to the effect that her mother
had kept her chained in a cellar for four years. When
he examined her, Dr. Robertson found no marks of
ill-treatment or confinement. He then turned her
over to the police as a vagrant. The following August
he was visited by three excited citizens who related
tales of horrible things going on inside the walls of the
Hotel Dieu. He found the source of these tales to be
the same girl who had been brought to him the previous November. This is the doctor's contribution to
the story.

Further checking up on Maria's eventful life
revealed that at the time she claimed to be in the
nunnery and (to the doctor) chained in a cellar, she
really had been a servant at William Henry, St.
Ours and St. Denis, towns not far from Montreal.
Moreover she was never a novice or a nun for she was
never a Catholic. Her father had been no officer,
but a non-commissioned soldier, a barrack yard
orderly. Her mother had no pension. She was the
nimble house cleaner of the officers' quarters attached
to the Chateau de Ravezay, the Government Headquarters at Montreal.

Meantime her mother, a widow, was asked what
she knew about her daughter. She forthwith related
the incident of the slate pencil in extenuation of
Maria's queer behavior and said that the girl had

been unmanageable ever since. She was sent to a day school (for a short time until she was sent away) conducted by the Sisters but had never been in the convent. She had a police record and at one time she had been confined in a Magdalene Asylum for reclaiming prostitutes. This was close by the Hotel Dieu. It was after leaving this asylum, from which she was dismissed, that the Rev. Mr. Hoyt re-encountered Maria and at his suggestion she straightway journeyed to New York with him to become his mistress and partner in conspiracy. It was he who arranged for her, on her arrival in New York, to go to the Bellevue Lying-in Hospital, where she bore a child.

Continuing her story, Mrs. Monk stated that in August, 1835, Hoyt called on her and said that he had journeyed to Montreal with Maria and her five weeks' old baby, and that she had abandoned him, leaving the child. Poor girl, said he, she was unaccountable for her actions because of her terrible experiences in the nunnery. Mrs. Monk denied the nunnery yarn, but offered to give the child a home. This apparently was contrary to Hoyt's scheme. He departed, shortly afterward returning with two others, and this trio attempted to convince Mrs. Monk that she was wrong. Surely her daughter had been a novice and a nun in the Hotel Dieu. Mrs. Monk replied the contemporary equivalent of "nonsense." But Hoyt was a persistent beggar, and a third time he called. His tactics on this visit were to offer Mrs.

Monk £100 if she would ſtate that Maria had been
in the nunnery. The inducement made no difference.
That was her ſtory and she clung to it with maternal
tenacity. Maria had rammed that slate pencil into
her head when she was seven, and she'd been queer
ever since, and now designing men were taking advantage of her. Balked in this final attempt, Hoyt
departed for New York with Maria, and there were
made her "awful disclosures" to Dr. Brownlee and
his friends among "the anti-Papal bulldogs."

Though he had invited the shame and ridicule of
exposure, it muſt be said to his credit that Dr.
Brownlee (a ſtern-looking person was Dr. Brownlee,
with imposing side-burns) eventually acknowledged
having been taken in. It was as though the Bishop
of New York and the paſtor of the Collegiate Church
were today to give recognition to the wandering gossip of a mentally defeÂªctive proſtitute. Dr. Brownlee's
firſt indignation turned on Maria's paramour, Hoyt.
In a ſtatement in the *New York Herald* he said that
he had loſt all confidence in him because "he had
been laboring to get her (Maria) under his influence
so as to induce her to make him her heir in case of her
death, that he might have the whole proceeds of her
writings if she died, while he affeÂªcted to secure her a
living as long as she was alive." While Dr. Brownlee
claimed not to have had a finger in writing the "Awful Disclosures," he ſtated that it had been done by
"able and moſt respeÂªctable gentlemen and publishers." In none of his later writings on the Papacy,

and the priesthood—and pretty torrid writings they were—do you find any reference to the Maria Monk affair.

When Hoyt first brought her to New York Maria lived near the Dry Dock, a swampy area, which was where the foot of Rivington Street is today. Dr. Brownlee and others immediately endeavored to get her out of Hoyt's hands and to have themselves appointed her guardians. She was a minor at the time, not reaching her twenty-first year until June 1, 1837. The plan was about to be consummated in favor of these "able and most respectable gentlemen" when Maria met the Rev. John J. L. Slocum, "fell in love with him and was carried off by him in triumph." Thereupon the conspirators began to disagree. Having become her "next friend," as the law puts it, Mr. Slocum sued the publishers of Maria's book, Harper & Brothers, in the Vice-Chancellor's Court, for Maria's share of the proceeds of the book. During the trial it was revealed that the Committee of Publication had profited by its sales. It also later appeared that not only was Maria's part in the writing of the book negligible, but that it came from the pen of Theodore Dwight, nephew of "Old Pope Dwight," the worthy president of Yale who was responsible for a renewed religious revivalism in New England and especially among its colleges. Young Theodore was of the firm of Van Nostrand and Dwight, publishers. Mr. Dwight was called in by Dr. Bourne, editor of the *Protestant Vindicator* to act as "scribe," and his

firm would naturally have printed the book, but
Howe & Bates (Harper & Brothers) by Maria's con-
nivance made a scoop. Maria's original title had
been innocuous enough but the publishers, being
good journalists, saw better sales in a book called
"Awful Disclosures."

Although Dr. Brownlee recanted, Mr. Slocum
apparently remained unabashed by the revelations.
The first book having made good money, he urged
Maria to compose "Further Disclosures" and, to give
this the right publicity send-off, she alleged that she
was abducted to a Catholic asylum in Philadelphia
by six priests, one of whom was anxious to marry her.
This escapade was soon exploded. However the book
appeared and sold well. Shortly thereafter Mr.
Slocum departed for London where he brought out
an English edition of Maria's works and evidently
profited by the venture. Of him we hear no more.

Present-day psychiatrists might say that Maria
Monk suffered from *Pseudologica fantastica*. She may
have been induced to believe the ingenious and palpable myths she related. Into what category they
would place the reverend and most respectable gentlemen who swallowed her story, hook, line, and sinker,
it would be uncharitable to repeat. Or of the people
who read the "Awful Disclosures" and believed them.
Two editions of 40,000 each were sold in a very short
time and Maria is said to have made $30,000 in royal-
ties. It is estimated that over 300,000 copies of her
works have been sold, and it is a commentary on the

credulity of some people that the book is still circulated, still read, still held to be gospel truth. It is the
sort of book that careful parents keep hidden away
from childish eyes—in lower bureau drawers beneath
the winter underwear!

Many people in those years may have bought and
read, the "Awful Disclosures" in the same spirit of
fun that our own generation reveled in "The Young
Visiters" and "The Diary of a Young Lady of Fashion." Nevertheless, thousands enjoyed the episode.
That, however, is the way with New York.

Montreal, on the other hand, dealt with the
scandal seriously, and the report of those dealings
ought to end the controversy forever. Prof. William
Henry Atherton, historian of Montreal, an expert
on Maria Monk literature, has recently found in
the files of a bilingual paper flourishing at the time,
a lengthy account of a representative meeting of
prominent Protestants of Montreal, assembled to
discuss Maria Monk's impostures. The paper is
L'Ami du Peuple, of April 5, 1836.

At this meeting the Hon. Peter McGill, then
Mayor, occupied the chair and leading Protestant
citizens made addresses. The resolutions adopted
by this meeting reveal "astonishment at the circulation and credence which these impostures have
received in Great Britain and the United States."
The writings of Maria Monk were stigmatized as
"gross and absurd fabrications, unworthy of attention or refutations." The credence given these vile

stories outside Montreal "is the only reason which leads us to honor, even with a denial, the lies of an abandoned prostitute." A committee of leading Protestant citizens was appointed to make all arrangements and accompany an investigating committee from the States. Neither Maria nor the delegation from the States accepted the invitation. By that time the game was up.

VI

Of Maria Monk's appearance we know little. An editorial writer for the *Herald* said that "she was no better than she should be and not nearly as pretty as a couple of other young ladies we saw there on the same evening."

Her daughter, Mrs. L. St. John Eckel, writing of her thirty years later, gives a pen picture of what she was at twenty-six. She "might once have been handsome, but a life of misery and sin had already robbed her cheeks of their roses and her form of the graces of youth. She was short in stature, thick set, with oval features, dark gray eyes and long brown hair." This description represents Maria when she was last seen to be remembered, a drunkard in a dram shop.

For after she had been cast off by her promoters, her descent in the social scale was precipitate. She devoted her energies to a licentious and obscure life in the dingy purlieus of the city. Having had her crowded hour of notoriety, she returned to the course she naturally would have followed had not Hoyt lured her from it to suit his own designs. For twelve years she haunted the gin shops and baudy houses of the tenderloin. Then, on October 11, 1849, caught in the act of picking the pocket of her paramour of the hour in a dive near the notorious Five Points, she was arrested, tried, and sentenced to prison. There she died shortly afterward.

The slate pencil had scrawled its last for Maria Monk.

From beginning to end Maria's tales were fabricated. Whether she herself evolved them entirely out of her disordered brain or whether Hoyt evolved them out of his venomous stupidity and elected to fasten them on this poor little prostitute, we cannot say. He evidently took his cue from the success Rebecca Theresa Reed had made with the sales of her "Six Months in a Convent." As one of her erstwhile supporters acknowledged, "Maria was dragged about by various parties and her mind kept in a perpetual state of excitement for several years so that she could be made to say or consent to anything. This was the source of her disclosures rather than any peculiar or natural depravity of mind."

Her promoters, it must be remembered, took her in hand when she was eighteen, and for four years they profited by her exploitation, profited either financially or profited in the causes they were championing.

The whole affair was an unparalleled case of

ecclesiastical white-slavery. There was no romance
to it. It lacked the picaresque spirit of robust
robbery or the fine flourish of piracy on the high
seas. It was just a sordid little hoax. And a plebeian
and grotesque episode it would have remained, had
not Maria Monk gathered energetic imitators in
her train.

Having profited by her first book, Miss Reed produced "A Supplement to Six Months in a Convent,"
prepared and presented by the same Boston Committee of Publication, which as in Maria's case, was
composed of quick-witted promoters. It is incon-
ceivable that either she or Maria ever wrote their
books, since neither was literate enough. Then came
Frances Partridge, an alleged runaway nun; Rosamund Culbertson, who made "disclosures" that professed to reveal the iniquities of the confessional.
Like Maria, Rosamund was obliged to sue her backers
for her share in the profits. Then followed a stream
of books with such lurid titles as "Open Convents,"
"Secrets of Female Convents Disclosed," "Thrilling
Mysteries of a Convent Revealed," "The School Girl
in France, or the Snares of Popery," "The Female
Jesuit," etc.

Nor indeed would Maria Monk and her imitators
be remembered had not their martyrdom (in books)
become the seed of a church wrangle that was later
to disrupt many sections of the country. The little
prostitute who died obscurely in the prison shambles
was destined to be the harbinger of Know-Nothing-

ism, the glittering Jeanne d'Arc of the American
Party. Her soul went marching on.

Having finished writing her sorry tale, the slate
pencil made still uglier scrawls.

VII

It was an age of riots. At the slightest provocation, city streets became Donnybrook Fairs. In
June of 1835, New York had its Five Points Riots, an
anti-Catholic brawl caused by the forming of an Irish
Regiment. In June of '37, a mob of 15,000 rioted
in the streets of Boston, the result of a clash between
a fire engine company and an Irish funeral. This
battle, known locally as the Broad Street Riots,
necessitated calling out the militia and ended in
sacking the Irish quarter. [16]

In the same year a Boston wag, Laughton Osborne,
composed "The Vision of Roberta," a poem in three
cantos, pillorying the whole Maria Monk investigation, much to the delight of the intelligentsia. Newspapers, too, were poking fun at it. But Romanism
was still no laughing matter with the lower and
middle classes. In 1839 a mob of riff-raff got out of
hand in Baltimore—a city where mobs had a habit
of getting out of hand—and attacked a convent.
The following year the Whig Party, casting around
for a plank in its platform, hit on Native American-
ism. It waved the flag, but people failed to rally to
the cause. The only result was the establishing in
New York of a Native American Democratic Associa-

tion. Thus far Anti-Catholic feeling had been centered in New York and Boston. Still the people
were on edge. The tinder of religious prejudice still
lay around. Any spark could stir it into flame.
And that spark eventually was struck.

In Philadelphia and New York arose a sharp controversy over the reading of the Bible in the public
schools. The Roman Catholic hierarchy opposed it.
The peace of December 1843 was disturbed by a din
of ecclesiastical back-chat all over the country. The
following May, rioters began rushing through the
Kensington district of Philadelphia, the textile section
where the Irish lived. The fight lasted three days.
Two Catholic churches and a convent were destroyed
and several lives were lost. In a foolish moment
Bishop Hughes advised his people to arm themselves
to protect Catholic property. The following July
guns were found in two Kensington churches. They
were claimed to be antiquated weapons stored there
and designed to be used for drilling a local military
company. The rioting broke out anew. This time
seventeen died in the gutters and bloody barricades
of Kensington.

Making political capital out of this disturbance,
a pronounced Nativism movement cropped out in
such widely separated districts as New Orleans,
Philadelphia, New York, Boston, and St. Louis under
the guise of the American Republican Party. America was to be for Americans. There was talk of imposing a long period of initiation before foreigners

THE INTERFERENCE OF THE IRISH CATHOLIC IMMIGRANT
INTO THE PUBLIC SCHOOLS WAS A TOPIC FOR MANY CAUSTIC
CARTOONS. THIS IS FROM AN ISSUE OF *VANITY FAIR* OF 1860

could be naturalized and hold office. In a year, however, the excitement had died down. The people were too much absorbed by the "54-40 or Fight" controversy with England over the Oregon boundary, that put Polk in the White House. But though the party had gone, anti-foreign and anti-Catholic sentiment cocooned itself in secret societies—The Order of the Star-Spangled Banner, or the Sons of the Sires of '76, Native Sons of America, The Order of the United American Mechanics, the American Protestant Association, the Protestant Irish Order of United Americans. Leading and humble citizens alike joined them. It is not recorded that any members of these societies attended the funeral of Maria Monk in '49. They were too busy making America secure against foreign conspiracy. They had completely forgotten their Jeanne d'Arc!

Such successive high and low pulsations of anti-foreign and anti-Catholic feeling cannot be laid wholly at the door of religious prejudice. One must look for a cause that touched people's pocketbooks. This era saw a mania for road, canal, and railroad building. It also saw the rise of industrialism. All these gave employment to the foreigners. New England was gradually changing from an agricultural to a manufacturing section; its first cotton mill was opened at Lawrence in 1822 and the next year the Merrimac Mills at Lowell, from which start the factory system grew by leaps and bounds. Philadelphia, too, was growing in the number of its factories, into which the foreign proletarians poured to the saturation point. An oversupply of labor threatened. Wall Street had its sudden ups and downs, with disastrous reactions in other parts of the country. There were panics in 1837-39, followed by great distress and accompanied by labor riots, other panics in '49, followed by wild speculation, and another in 1857, when paper money far exceeded the gold deposits. Moreover our cities were passing through a social transformation; the leadership of the old and established families was being displaced by newer blood.

Meantime the causes of increased immigrations were piling up fast in Europe. Emigration agents scoured the byways of Europe for more and more men to pack their ships. The Irish famine came in '46. France, Germany, and Italy had their governmental disturbances followed by the departure of uncomfortable citizens. The cry of "Gold!" set the faces of thousands in all parts of the world toward America and California. Then it was, due to these stimulations, that the rising stream of immigration became a terrifying flood. When the census of 1850 showed one-seventh of the population to be immigrants, native-born Americans awoke to the reality of the menace that faced them. Foreigners were issued a solemn warning: "You may come to live but not to rule."

The old Nativism movement that had lain hidden away in lodge halls of secret societies, crept out into the air. In 1852 the American Party became a reality. With a program worked out secretly three years before, it gathered into its ranks old Whigs, dissatisfied Democrats, and political malcontents of every kidney. And there was reason for the alarm this party voiced.

The Irish among the immigrants were blatantly antagonistic to the government at first, and then proceeded to elect their own kind into office with gusto. Revolutionists from Germany, Italy, Ireland, and other countries failed to leave their ardor behind them at Castle Garden. They continued plotting in their new homes. With amazement, Americans watched alien military organizations drilling—German Jaegers, Irish Greens, Swiss Guards. Of the six thousand uniformed militia in New York in 1853, four thousand were of foreign birth. They wore foreign types of uniforms and in many companies orders were given in foreign tongues. So alarmed became native-born citizens that they refused to join the militia and they organized "shooting societies," which soon outnumbered the militia.

Other contributing factors to the discontent were the rise of foreign-language newspapers and the multiplication of congested cities and industries. At the polls the foreign vote was openly bought and sold. To add to the confusion appeared in June, 1853, Monsignor Bedini, a Papal nuncio, come to America to pay a visit of courtesy to President Pierce and to tour the country. Unfortunately he came at a time when the spirit of the mob overrode efforts at hospitality and good manners.

Many among the foreigners were liberals, and their broad views collided rudely with reform movements then under way and with the conservatism of the older classes. The Germans clustered in their beer gardens and saw only women's folly in the war on drink. The Irish, congregated in their gin shops, spat symbolically when temperance was mentioned. Consequently, irate Carrie Nations broke into grog shops and beer gardens and smashed bottles with frenzy. Equally opposed to all other reforms seemed these foreigners—to Abolition and to women's rights.

These years heard pulpits and hustings echo the noisy discharge of patriotic emotion. All patterns of ranters arose and the public read all manner of anti-alien and anti-Catholic propaganda. One of the picturesque figures was Gavazzi, an ex-monk, sworn foe of the legate Bedini, who lectured in many cities. Wherever Gavazzi appeared trouble ensued. In Montreal he escaped from the city at the risk of his life, however. Another ranter was the "Angel Gabriel," Saunders McSwich, ([17]) an eccentric and disreputable Scot, who called his audiences together by tooting a brass trumpet. The anti-Catholic pamphlets and novels that people of those times devoured make pretty dull reading today. We turn their pages and marvel at the minds that composed and enjoyed them. Yet enjoy them they apparently did.

THE IRISH IMMIGRANT AS VIEWED BY A CONTEMPORARY
CARTOONIST IN *YANKEE NOTIONS*

Patriotic Americans thought of the Pope and shuddered.

Such shudders were speedily induced by the secretive methods of the Know-Nothings, as the American Party was popularly called. For this party was, in reality, a vast secret society. Like the Indian *kivas*, it assembled underground in many places. Its three secret degrees, its solemn initiation, its ritual and its terrific oaths were enough to keep even the most strong-hearted on edge. No man of Catholic parentage was admitted. Members were sworn to vote only for Protestants and for men whose families had been in America three generations. In each political area the members formed a council, or cell, in the Soviet manner—New York City boasted one to each ward. To call a meeting, triangular pieces of paper were passed around, and the bearer would ask, "Have you seen Sam?" A red paper meant that members must come at once, prepared for trouble. To all questions members replied, "I don't know." This became the password of the sons of "Sam" and gave its name to the movement.

Under these auspices cities and towns were kept in a constant turmoil. Disorder was always just around the corner. Time and again Broadway echoed the shout of "To Hell with the Pope and burn his churches!" Street riots disturbed the peace of Chelsea, Philadelphia, New York, Brooklyn, Rochester, St. Louis, Providence, and many other places. In Boston a Protestant mob assaulted a Catholic church, whereupon a Catholic mob returned the compliment on a Unitarian edifice. Ostensibly to protect street speakers, rowdy gangs were formed, although they really were out only for trouble. And picturesque names they took—Wide Awakes, Rip Raps, Plug Uglies, Tigers, Black Snakes, Blood Tubs, Rough Skins, Rattlers, Rosebuds, White Oaks, Washingtons, Thunderbolts, Little Fellows, Babes. There also appeared in Pennsylvania the Mollie Maguires, who later were to make bloody history.

By 1854 the Know-Nothings had gained such political following and power as to elect governors in nine states and claim a majority in the House of Representatives. The pinnacle of the movement was attained in 1856 when at a convention in Philadelphia Millard Fillmore was nominated for the Presidency. Shall the Pope or the President guide the destinies of these United States? Such was the campaign slogan. It was a noisy, valiant demonstration of religious bitterness—and the last one.

Fillmore made a very poor showing at the polls. The balloon deflated as though pricked. The Papal scarecrow was abandoned in the fields. The party had split over sectional and national differences. Popular imagination was being fired by more serious affairs.

The Kansas-Nebraska strife of 1854 had filtered down from the political leaders to the people. It became the topic of general man-in-the-street conversation. States' Rights and the Abolitionist Move-

The Anti Know Nothing Meeting at Washington.

INDEPENDENCE OF MR. RATCLIFFE.

MR. RATCLIFFE.—*Fellow citizens—(Take your hat off)—Who is it that asks me to take my hat off? If it is a gentleman, I will; but if it's a blackguard Know Nothing, I'll be damned if I do. (Explosive laughter.)* (Mr. Ratcliff strikes an attitude, and looks defiance at the crowd.)

AN ANTI-KNOW-NOTHING MEETING AS DEPICTED BY THE CARTOONIST FOR *YANKEE NOTIONS*
A HUMOROUS PAPER OF THE MIDDLE OF THE LAST CENTURY

ment gained the ascendancy in the thoughts of common citizens. Before the weight and seriousness of these problems, religious prejudice paled into insignificance. The generation that thrilled at Maria Monk's "Awful Disclosures" had been succeeded by one that wept over "Uncle Tom's Cabin."

The slate pencil had made its last scrawl for many years to come. Occasionally it still scrawls. ([18])

CHAPTER VI
THE WIDOW
WITH THE SERPENT'S TONGUE

*ANNE ROYALL'S REPORTORIAL WANDERINGS AFFORD US A VIEW OF THE
ANTI-MASONIC TIMES IN THE 40'S AND THE CONTEMPORARY STATE OF
JOURNALISM IN AMERICA*

I

BETWEEN Tarsus and Virginia is a great gulf
fixed. St. Paul's experience with widows was
limited to two kinds—the old and the young. The
old prayed night and day and were to be honored because they were "widows indeed." The young any
wise man would avoid. They went from house to
house, "tattlers and busybodies, speaking things
which they ought not." It wasn't within his ken that
an aged widow would be found doing that—tattling
and busybodying from house to house. But then,
St. Paul had never heard of Mrs. Anne Newport
Royall, journalist, traveler, and widow *extraordinaire*.

For the story of Anne Royall is primarily the story
of a widowhood, a bustling, pitiful, valiant, productive
and vagrant widowhood such as is given few women
to live, such as few of them would have the courage
to try. Mistress of spirited invective, Mrs. Royall
was a sort of female William Cobbett, and, in another
sense, she anticipated Janet Anne Ross, Margot As-
quith, and the others who write "uncensored recollections" and books about things they admit they

156

shouldn't tell. She fits snugly into an adaptation of William Watson's discerning title: she was "The *Widow* with the Serpent's Tongue."

Her life spanned the eventful years of America's adolescence. Born June 11, 1769, as a chit of a child she heard the reverberations of the Revolutionary firing and looked upon the faces of Washington and Lafayette. It ended in 1854, by which time the long shadow of Lincoln was creeping across the destinies of the nation. Her widowhood covered the last twenty-six years, but the years that preceded them had not lacked a vivid color of their own.

II

Being a child of a Loyalist was no sinecure. ([19]) Indications justify the assumption that her father's sympathies lay with the British and his activities were directed toward their benefit. When the Revolution opened, Maryland was a hotbed of virulent patriotism. William Newport found it more comfortable to pull up stakes and move his family out upon the frontier. They made a home in Westmoreland County, Pennsylvania, near where Pittsburgh is today. Anne was then three. There he left them, while he disappeared on mysterious journeys. Living was hard on this frontier and Indians a menace. Finally he died, the mother married again, and the new head of the house led the family to the more civilized atmosphere of a town—Hannastown, Pennsylvania. At least it was civilized to the young Anne, for there she first saw the American flag, an event she recorded years later in a stirring passage.

She grew into a wiry, quick-witted child of the border, unlettered, unschooled save in the ways of the woods. When Indians ran amuck through Hannastown her mother moved the family back to the safety of Virginia, where they became attached to the household of William Royall, and with this attachment the sun of romance burst upon her life.

Royall had served as general with both Washington and Lafayette. He was squire of a large Virginia plantation, a strangely run plantation where the stock went native but the mind did not—it was known for its lack of steers and geldings, and for the size of its library. Into this atmosphere he took his bride, this frontier hoyden many years his junior. The date was 1797.

A quaintly contrasted picture they made—the backwoods bride and the roustabout eccentric squire of many slaves, many acres and many books. Under his tutelage she learned to read and write. Thus grounded, he turned her loose in his library, set her to reading the English classics and Voltaire and other French rationalist philosophers and the democratic writings of Jefferson. Being an ardent Mason (he was a member of the same lodge to which Washington and Lafayette belonged) he schooled her to look upon this order as a Heaven-sent boon to mankind, a belief that later played an important rôle in her career. Likewise his talk was of the war and the battles he had fought and the great men he knew. She became saturated in patriotism and love of country. And a good wife she made him too—ran his house and his slaves and graced his table when leaders of the time were his guests. Then, having lived sixteen years of this idyllic existence, he died.

The blow stunned her beyond recovery. Throughout a long life his memory was never absent from her. To bring surcease to her misery, she took three of her slaves, hitched up the best coach and started on a tour of the far South—to Alabama. The going wasn't easy then by any means, but the servants looked after her wants and she had enough money to satisfy her needs. She found her worrying ceased when she scribbled down impressions of the country through which she passed, and of the people thereabouts, and she got into the habit of doing this. Nevertheless the worries were very real. Other heirs were laying claim to the estate. A suit had been started to break Royall's will. With this cloud menacing her horizon, she stayed in Alabama for ten years, scribbling industriously, waiting for news.

When the news came, it dealt her another wicked blow. She had lost the suit. The plantation, the slaves, the house, the books, the money all were assigned to the other heirs. The spectre of poverty fell across her path. She was alone and practically penniless. Her age was then fifty-four.

Under similar circumstances and at such an age most women would have capitulated to the overwhelming evil destiny. Not Anne Royall. She found in it the beginning of a brilliant career.

III

Taking what little money she could scrape together, she saddled her horse and headed alone through the wilderness for the nearest coach route. Her destination was Washington. There she would lay before Congress her claim for a pension as the widow of a prominent Revolutionary general. To keep her mind off her troubles she continued writing. This time they were letters addressed to her lawyer —vivid reports of the country she passed through, the people she met at inns and on the coaches, local legends and dialects, the state of crops, reports of tavern brawls, adventures and anecdotes. "I am fertile in anecdotes," she writes, and she missed none of them—from the tale of the young girl who took religion violently at a camp meeting and shortly afterward was encountered in the woods acting in anything but a religious manner, to the description of Lord Selkirk whom she meets en route and whose consumption of eggs each meal was a good, round baker's dozen. Later these letters and other things she had written over a period of years were preserved in "Letters from Alabama," and in others of her eleven volumes.

She reached Alexandria penniless, and sick from exposure, worry and lack of food. On the verge of collapsing, she recalled how William Royall used to talk about the kindness of the Masons back there in those ideal days of married life. She took a chance on it, and threw herself on the charity of a prominent Mason. As if in a fairy tale the legend came true. He gave her a home and care until she was sufficiently recovered to launch forth on Washington. This she did in 1824. A crusader, bristling with purpose, she landed in the Capital. Surely a grateful country would not dream of refusing her a pension for the services of her valiant husband! But getting a pension in those days was even more difficult than it is today. She encountered the delays, procrastinations and vain promises of Congressmen. Meantime her pen itched for use. She worked valiantly at her diary.

With almost unbelievable energy this widow of fifty-four started out to set her case before everyone of influence in Washington. She began at the top, at the White House, but was rebuffed by the President's domestics. Then down the line from one cabinet member to another. Thence to the heads of departments. Each night toddling home and faithfully setting down in her diary what she actually thought of these people. Some were sympathetic, some were cold. There was John Quincy Adams, then Secretary of State, who, during the interview, "neither frowned nor smiled," and regarded her with "a calmness peculiar to him." Adams promised his support, and never did he fail his word. Year after year he championed her cause. "A virago errant in enchanted armor," he called her. Mrs. Adams, taking pity on her, gave her a shawl, which was later to figure in Anne's travels. Lafayette, here on his final tour, presented her with a letter breathing warm appreciation of her husband's services.

After six weeks of vain endeavor it was evident that her pension would be delayed. She must do something to make ends meet, so she conceived the idea of traveling around America writing intimate impressions of people and places. Books of this kind were popular then. Adolescent America was preening itself. It enjoyed reading what visitors and observers had to say of it. Scarcely a season but one or more such books appeared. Nor was the exploring and reporting limited to men alone—Miss Martineau, Margaret Fuller, Mrs. Trollope, and Fanny Wright D'Arusmont were all sharpening their quills for the writing. To some good-hearted Masons Mrs. Royall proposed that they underwrite this sort of trip, during which she could take subscriptions for the book, as was the custom of the day. It seemed a reasonable idea, and the money was raised. Decked in the shawl Mrs. Adams had given her and with unquestioned confidence in her ability to see the job through, this doughty little widow—she was small and stout and had sparkling blue eyes, very white teeth, and a quick laugh—set forth on her journalistic wanderings.

The itinerary for this first journey wound through Baltimore to Philadelphia, to New York, thence up the Hudson to Albany, east to Springfield, Hartford, Worcester, and Boston, and then back to New Haven. In each city she called on booksellers and prominent citizens soliciting subscriptions and seeking information for her forthcoming book. This first volume, which appeared in 1826, was called "Sketches of History, Life and Manners in the United States." It is a book with a tang, a snappy foretaste of what Anne Royall could do were she given the chance.

Of Philadelphia she observed that were Market Street to be taken away anarchy would immediately ensue, which was true at the time. She visited all public institutions, and sat in a synagogue and a Friends' meeting with equally eager interest. New York men astonished her by "the untaught nobility" of their faces and their bold fashion of smoking in the presence of women. Here also she saw her first play—"The Saw Mill, or Yankee Tricks" at the Chatham Square Theatre. At that same theatre the Masons gave a profitable benefit for her. Among her observations in Albany was that the librarian there was "the greatest boor except two," but notes that Albany children are to be seen in the streets carrying Euclid. The ladies of Hartford "have a slight tinge of melancholy in their countenance; it is softened by a shade of placid tranquillity." Hartford of those days didn't countenance the theatre, but did tolerate the circus. There seemed to be a lot of drinking in the town, too,—and Mrs. Royall was strictly for temperance. In Boston she finds that "a chambermaid will read as correct as the most finished scholars" (Anne herself occasionally manages to manhandle the King's English) "yet their dialect is wretchedly defective." Money spent on common education in Boston, she concluded, was spent in vain. However, Boston was hospitable to her, for whereas in Philadelphia she lacked even the creature comfort of a chair, the Bostonians were veritable Chesterfields and swamped her with chairs. Observations such as these she scatters in with serious descriptions, statistics, and vitriolic and genial personalities.

When this very personal book clattered from the press, it caused no end of palpitations. America broke into a rash of resentment. Mrs. Royall called people by name and as to those she didn't name in full, there was no mistaking them. Her book was read far and wide. Immediately she established a reading public—of those who chuckled over her personalities and those who hated her for making them. Quantities of her books were bought and destroyed by those she descanted upon unfavorably.

Between 1824 and 1831 she continued her nomadic journalism, covering the entire established and civilized areas of the United States, visiting every village, town and city of importance and interviewing all the great and the near-great. In all she wrote ten books of travel and a novel.

Of the novel, "The Tennessean," the less said the better. Romance was not her forte. It is a dreary tale in which the author attempted to describe cities—Boston in particular—which she had never visited, with disastrous results. Later she apologized for her "injudicious" color. So her fame as an author must rest on the travel books—the "Black Books," in three volumes; "Sketches of History, Life and Manners in the United States," in two volumes; "The Southern Tour," in two volumes; "Letters From Alabama," and "Pennsylvania." Of these the best known are the "Black Books," published in Washington in 1828 and 1829.

On this grand tour she covered some of her old ground and readjusted her observations. The women of Baltimore, she decided, were the worst dressed in America, although a previous volume set this sartorial stigma on Washington. In New York the women have so many amusements and distractions that they rarely buy books, and then only when they are bound in red. Ignorance is prevalent in Richmond (she had once said the same of Baltimore!), and the town lacked civic pride in that it did not mark its streets. Wherever she goes she calls on the local editors. "An editor, of all classes of men, lies nearest my heart. I have a paramount predilection for them."

Although she made friends with editors, they were not always so friendly with her. They penned caustic words about her activities. As witness the *New York Mirror and Ladies' Literary Gazette* for October 13, 1827. "This fair dame, it is said, is now paying her addresses to Governor Lincoln of Maine.

Should he refuse to make her Madame Governor, she will probably give him the most prominent place in her 'Black Book.'"

But she had no predilection for another class of unskilled laborers that she constantly encounters. Avoid them though she did, she was always running afoul of missionaries, colporteurs, distributors of tracts and solicitors for religious funds. Her names for them are colorful—"Holy Willies," "Muckle-wraths," "Hallelujah Holdforths." "Their visage is long, their complexion a dirty wan; they are generally tall, gaunt and supple, distant and vulgar in their manners, the gloom in their countenance is never interrupted with a smile. They usually have a trail of women after them with the same lowering look." These females she calls, "Miss Dismals." This description comes pretty close to being the standard caricature of the Prohibitionist of our own day.

Ninety pages of the "Black Books" are devoted to a brilliant and unrelenting attack on them. "From Maine to Georgia, from the Atlantic to Missouri, they swarm like locusts; and under the name of foreign missions, home missions, Bible societies, tract societies, societies for educating pious young men to spread the Gospel, pin cushion societies, cent societies, mite societies, widows' societies, children's societies, rag-bag societies, and Sunday School societies, they have laid the whole country under contribution." These pestilential tracteers leave their pamphlets in tavern parlors, and Mrs. Royall delights in casting them from the window. If a missionary enters the room where she is, she shouts, "Treason! Black Coats about!"

By the time she reached Vermont her reputation had gained considerable momentum and rolled up an active bitterness. Pious merchants, fearful lest they lose the custom of the genteel, bustled her out of their shops. Innkeepers refused her their hospitality. So bitter became the feeling against her that in Burlington it brought serious consequences. A Mr. Hecock (may his name go down the ages in infamy!) "a fanatical Presbyterian" and anti-Mason, deliberately pushed this harmless old woman down a flight of icy steps. She dislocated her ankle, broke a bone in her leg and bruised her entire body. This was in December of 1827. For six months she never walked and not until 1829 was she fully recovered. The story of her painful progress over the rutted roads and in dismal coaches from Burlington to Washington is one of the most ghastly migrations in American literature, and one of the most amazing examples of fortitude. But not for a moment was her spirit broken. When finally she arrived in Washington and cast her eye about her she wrote, "All the difference I perceive in Washington since I wrote the Sketches is that the people eat more, drink more, dress more, cheat more, lie more, steal more, pray more and preach more, and are more ignorant and indigent."

This old widow's journalistic prowess was beyond belief. Her resourcefulness and versatility would be the envy of even a modern reporter. She would worm her way into a convent and bombard the nuns with personal questions. Where she found a university, she investigated the faculty and let the undergraduates make a rowdy fuss over her. She interviewed the Cherokee Indians and smoked the pipe of peace with them. She ransacked the garret of Thomas Jefferson's house, Monticello. She took down the drunken conversation of tavern brawlers and eavesdropped on a parson and his female companion in an adjoining room. She went into bookstores and berated the clerks for not selling more of her books and for "pushing" books written by British authors to the detriment of American writers.

There was nothing of splendor about her vagrant journalism. She was merely a fussy and persistent old woman barging about the country. Her writing has the chatty intimacy of a personal column in a country newspaper with all its localism, solecisms, and crudity. Nor did her books constitute literature or aspire to that plane.

How she ever managed to live while on these travels is a constant source of wonder. As fast as she made money she gave it away. In Philadelphia, not being able to afford a hack, she tramped about with blistered feet and her footprints were marked with blood. All day she would walk the streets seeking information on the slim breakfast of a single cup of coffee, and then come home to dine upon a dish of tea. On her Pennsylvania tour—this was after she

had written several books and was well known—she
existed for thirty-two hours on four cents. Most of
her books were composed in the drab bedrooms of
cheap inns. Often she would enter a tavern and in
sheer desperation for food and rest throw herself on
the mercy of the keeper. While in Washington, she
managed to live by the aid of friends, by private
donations bestowed on her for food, clothing and fuel
—"I live in a house upon humiliating charity, without furniture, and the coldest nights this winter was
without a bed." Nevertheless, she would proudly
claim, "I do not write for profit or for fame. I write
for the benefit of my country, and to please my
friends." She made no money from her books: "Of
all the works I have published," she writes, "I have
not been able from sales to pay for the paper, much
less the printing." Booksellers cheated her out of
the profits.

The purpose of her travels, as we have said, was
not alone to gather information for these books, but
also to take subscriptions for them, and many a time
she received a rough reception. Picture this incident,
and remember she was nearing sixty at the time—
"I approached Mr. F. in his office with my best
curtsey and told him I had come to pay my respects to
him, hoped he was well, etc. To which he replied,
in a voice that suggested the hoarse croak of a
raven, 'I want none of your respects nor your books.
Get out of here, you old hag!'"

Her clothes were pitiably inadequate. One mid-

November she had only a thin dress and the shawl
Mrs. Adams had given her.   Once later, when she
was publishing her newspaper, she stopped its issues
for a week.   "We really must take one week once in
ten years," she explained editorially, "to fix up our
wardrobe which is getting shabby."   In her more
prosperous days the costume she considered suitable
for the well-dressed Washington female correspondent
consisted of a clean calico gown with mutton-leg
sleeves, and a big poke-bonnet.

In her books of travel Mrs. Royall described, in
all, 274 people whom she named and 237 places, no
little accomplishment.   Her pen portraits of personalities comprise as valuable a gallery of the times as
did the silhouettes of Auguste Edouart.   One wonders
why some enterprising publisher doesn't rescue these
writings from the oblivion into which prejudice and
hatred forced them.   They are invaluable documents.
People who had not been flatteringly pictured would
ask her, "Why don't you wait till we are dead?"   To
which she invariably retorted, "I might die myself
in the meantime, and many a good and bad man
would be consigned to oblivion.   Besides, I wish to
write books that people will read, and I find that there
is nothing like throwing in plenty of spice."[20]

Her spice was scattered with a lavish hand.
Picture the explosive indignation from Senator Chambers of Maryland when he read, "He has a slim
person, a slim face, a slim nose and, if I were to
spend my opinion on him, I would pronounce him

ACCORDING TO ANNE ROYALL, THE ELITE OF RALEIGH RELISHED THE INDOOR SPORT OF
"SNUFF DIPPING"
From *Frank Leslie's Weekly*

to have a slim soul." The New York delegation
must have buried their chins in their stocks when
they found themselves described as a rough-hewn and
simple lot—"what can the people mean by sending
such boobies to Congress only to be laughed and
pointed at!" She had a way of following people to
get a good look at them. When men saw her
coming, they'd exclaim, "My God! I'll not stay
here!" Women wrapped their veils around their
faces and the men held up their hats to theirs and
off they scampered. "They always commit themselves by taking flight," she observed. Perhaps they
were justified. Did Senator Bibb relish being called,
"A low blue skin not worth naming?" Or Counselor Ogden of New York enjoy being described as,
"An oxen standing on his hind legs"? Or Hon.
Speaker Taylor, "A thick-headed, broad-faced man,
with a blue eye, bald head and vacant countenance"?
Imagine the civic wrath of staid old Charleston on
being dubbed, "the receptacle for the refuse of all
nations on earth—the only reputable people there
Jews." (Mrs. Royall had a penchant for Jews,
Germans and Roman Catholics and made no effort to
mask her sympathies.) Philadelphians resented hotly
her description of their city as "a den of British
Tories, domestic traitors, missionaries and Sunday
Schoolism." The University of Pennsylvania she
called "a den of ignorance." How the élite of
Raleigh must have squirmed at her description of
their disgusting snuff-dipping parties; and the proud

mothers of Baltimore when she pictured their offspring as dirty-faced brats who trailed her about,
sucking their thumbs and staring her out of countenance! And the stiff-backs of Virginia must have
become even stiffer when she repeated the catch—

> Hail Virginia, old and crazy!
> The people poor and proud and lazy!

Well, Virginia of those days deserved the berating.
It suffered "the imbecilities of premature age."
Its roads were as bad as its schools, "impassable
roads" that William Alexander Caruthers, one of its
famous native sons, acknowledged protected it "alike
from the pity and contempt of foreign travelers."

In our generation the spirited invective that
sparkled through Anne Royall's pages would be considered bad taste and libellous, yet such was the
custom of the times. Journalism was a very personal
affair in those days and editors were no shrinking
violets when it came to describing a foe. Consequently, it required more than such rapier thrusts as
she made to arouse the ire of politicians and citizens.
They could forgive Mrs. Royall's insults but they
could not forgive her political sympathies. Anne was
a fighter—only she fought on unpopular sides. She
championed the Masons when they were very much
disturbed. She battled against those who were
threatening to establish a state religion, and in later
times, she fought the United States Bank. Of these,
the Masons wrangle and the Church and State con-

troversy were the most vivid. They formed the background for the great comedy of Mrs. Royall's life, and in fact, for the great comedy of American justice—her trial as a common scold.

IV

During Revolutionary days and the Federal Era most men of affairs were Masons. The craft, having inherited its reputation for dignity and noble character from lodges in the Mother Country, stood high in the estimation of the people. Its members were the leaders and instigators of patriotic movements and were patrons of the cultural arts, even extending their interest to the development of the theatre in America. Masonry flourished and its lodges increased. And thus it was until 1826.

In that year there came to Batavia, N. Y., with his family, a William Morgan. He claimed to be a Mason in good standing, although members of the local lodge soon had reason for disputing this assertion. It was whispered about that he was compiling a book which would expose the secret degree work, pass words, etc., of the Masons. On investigation his past proved him to be an undesirable character; he had been a stonemason by trade and a wanderer by choice or compulsion and his trail was marked by shady transactions, heavy drinking, and a complete disregard for debts he incurred. His associate in the present venture was David C. Miller, local printer and editor of the Batavia *Republican Advocate*, who was to edit and publish the work.

The report struck terror at the hearts of several local Masons, and they completely lost their heads. As was later found, on discovering some of the manuscript, this was merely a reprint of an alleged "exposure" of Masonry written by Richard Carlisle, a London atheist, and as yet not circulated in America. However, a local movement against the two conspirators was begun. Having been found guilty of petty theft, Morgan was sent to jail, since he lacked money to pay his fine. The same night, September 12, 1826, six men called at the jail, paid the fine and conducted him away. He was taken to Fort Niagara, thence to Canada and back again. The intention had been to hand him over to Canadian Masons, but in some way the plan miscarried.

From that night on no sign of Morgan alive was seen. He was believed to have been drowned or smothered by violence. People opposed to the Masons raised a hue and cry that spread over the nation. Governor DeWitt Clinton, himself a Mason, issued a proclamation on the case, following it with another offering $200 for information and $300 for discovery of the offenders. A third proclamation raised these sums to $1000 and $2000 respectively. The offers were never claimed.

Meantime anti-Masonic distrust was speedily piling up. Morgan was held up as an innocent victim of Masonic machinations. Certainly the men who

took him from Batavia jail were of that order. Then
in October 1827 there was found at Oak Orchard
Park, Lake Ontario, forty miles east of Fort Niagara,
to which Morgan had been abducted, the body of a
drowned man. It could be none other than Morgan's.
Anti-Masonic sympathizers prepared an elaborate
funeral. A few days later the body was disinterred
and positively identified by his wife as being that of
Timothy Monroe, a Canadian drowned the previous
month. So the poor cadaver, over which so much
conflict had raged, was taken back to Canada and
finally given a peaceful grave. Of Morgan's end no
one knows. Three Masons were indicted for complic-
ity in the crime, pleaded guilty and were sentenced
to varying terms.

These sordid affairs would never have assumed
the proportions of a national scandal were it not for
the fact that they happened in the closing days of a
bitter political campaign. Politicians, quick to grasp
at straws of popular favor, exaggerated the story and
stimulated the attack with hectic ardor. Masons, or
"Mingoes," as they were called, found themselves
read out of parties, their private lives made miserable
and the order held to be an enemy of the people.
Legislatures threatened to abolish it.

The Baptists condemned Masonry with a wholesale sweep as "accommodated to the prejudices of the
Jews" and "receiving and adopting Orders of Knight-
hood from the Pope." Other denominations followed
their lead. An Anti-Masonic Party arose. It

gathered to its fold an increasing number of patriots, and its power spread over the entire country until it invaded the elections in New England, Pennsylvania, New Jersey, and many Southern States. In New York 1827 saw nineteen anti-Masonic conventions held and three years later that party came within 8000 votes of electing an anti-Masonic governor. At one time the state also had no less than thirty-two anti-Masonic papers. In fact, outside of New York the feeling against Masonry was by no means so vitriolic. Vermont did elect its candidate. In 1832 the party nominated William Wirt of Virginia, late Attorney-General, for the Presidency. Wirt polled 340,800 votes, but was snowed under by the popularity of Jackson.

The years of this anti-Masonic movement are 1826 to 1836, with the embers of it smoking for still another decade. As a result, hundreds of lodges stopped work. Before the outbreak there were five hundred lodges in New York state alone, with a membership of over twenty thousand; by 1830 there were only eighty-two lodges with three thousand members. Not until after the Civil War did Masonry recover from this blow.

It was Mrs. Royall's misfortune to be traveling and writing during this period—an ardent believer in Masonry, who insisted on proclaiming the fact in the face of suspicion and hatred. Little wonder that the alarmed citizenry read her diatribes with indignation!

These same years also saw the rise to power of the

Evangelical churches of America. The hordes of Roman Catholic immigrants who swarmed here, together with the growth of Universalism and Unitarianism, brought about a new ecclesiastical alignment. The Roman Catholics were set down as foreigners conspiring against the free institutions of America; the Unitarians were held by Fundamentalists of the time to be a peculiarly offensive and dangerous type of pagans, whose heterodoxy was as a stink in the nostrils of the pious, because they would substitute a God of Love for a God of Wrath, because they preferred a humanitarian religion to the ascetic and unyielding tenets of Puritan righteousness.

These elements, colored by the countryside rantings of itinerant preachers and camp-meeting exhorters, as well as established preachers in towns and cities, finally crystallized into a definite and determined movement to form a union of the Church and the State, designed to tear out "the noxious weed of infidelity" that William Wirt, the Virginian lawyer and biographer of Patrick Henry, said "had struck a deep, a fatal root, and spread its pestilential branches far around." At no time in American history have our religious liberties been so near to annihilation as in this era.

Among the methods adopted by those who would make America safe for the Evangelical Church was flooding the country with tracts and lobbying in Washington. Tracts were franked through the Post Office and lobbied into the Congressional Library.

For more than 30 years these "missionaries" kept
up their endeavors. In her time they found no more
bitter foe than Anne Royall. Persistently and fear-
lessly she opposed them. Her enemies soon made
capital of her sympathies.

In 1829, on returning from one of her trips, her
house became the target for gangs of rowdy boys
who stoned it. On the heels of this annoyance she
was arrested and charged with being a common scold.
Two clergymen of an obscure Presbyterian congregation were her immediate accusers, although it was
soon evident that they represented a larger and
nationally extended cabal. It is among Mrs. Royall's claims to fame that she is the only woman in
America ever convicted on this charge. The trial
proved one of the most laughable travesties in American legal history. The famous Anti-Evolution Scopes
case that brought fame to Dayton, Tennessee, in
1925, pales beside Mrs. Royall's trial in Washington.

No sooner was she arrested than the court ruled
that it had no jurisdiction in such matters, that the
District of Columbia had no law under which she
could be tried. She was released. Undismayed, her
persecutors led mass meetings and congregations all
over the country, vociferously shivering the gates of
Heaven with their imprecations against her. Meanwhile their subsidized investigators kept digging into
dusty law books. Their patience was finally re-
warded. They unearthed the fact that the code of
the District, being derived from the British, inherited

a law covering the case, although English jurists had long since discarded the law as obsolete. Under this ancient and forgotten relic, she was hailed before a jury of her peers—twelve Bladensburg men, with Chief Justice Cranch presiding on the bench. According to this hoary document the penalty for using intemperate language was the ducking stool. A model of such a stool was built at the Navy Yard and solemnly brought into court. Anne Newport Royall, sixty years old, poverty-stricken and unpensioned widow of a Revolutionary hero, stood before the bar and heard herself charged with being a public nuisance, a common brawler, a common scold.

The court was packed. The Postmaster-General and the Secretary of War testified in her behalf. The Librarian of Congress, Mr. Waterston, testified that she had called all Presbyterians, "cut-throats." Capt. John Coyle, under oath, averred that not only once but three times did she call him, "a damned old bald-headed son of a bitch." The examination kept the court in a roar of laughter. Its echoes resounded throughout the country. Nevertheless, when the jury returned, it brought in a verdict of guilty. Since the court could not stomach the idea of strapping this old woman in a ducking stool, it set her fine at $10 and obliged her to give a bond of $50 to keep the peace for a year.

Although the trial was a travesty and she made a great joke of it (she spent most of her time in court penning portraits of the jurymen, justices and witnesses) Mrs. Royall was sorely hurt by the ignominy and ordeal. She was sixty then and in the midst of her travels.

Shortly afterward she left for her Southern Tour. News of the trial caused her embarrassment and discomfiture wherever she went. People fled at the sight of her. Although she managed to get as far south as New Orleans, it was evident that her importance as a wandering observer was ended. Moreover, she was determined to win that pension from Congress. For twenty-five years, session after session, the bill was reported and voted down. It became the standing Congressional joke. Although in the end Congress did vote her a small sum, Mrs. Royall eventually received very little of it.

But her experience in and around the houses of Congress and with the great and near-great in all parts of the country did bring Mrs. Royall some benefit. It was on the basis of these experiences that she ventured on the last and great work of her busy career. In 1831 she settled permanently in the Capital, and in December of that year brought out the first issue of the Washington *Paul Pry*.

V

Her equipment for plunging into the deep waters of newspaper publishing consisted of a second-hand Ramage press which she set up in her kitchen and a couple of fonts of battered type; her staff, a porter and two boys. Mrs. Royall served as editor, re-

porter, and subscription agent. She not only collected
the news, wrote it and the editorials, but herself
solicited subscriptions among Congressmen and others
in Washington.

The name of her paper, *Paul Pry*, was rather an
unfortunate choice, for it connoted undesirable
methods of collecting news, but the contents of this
four-page weekly sheet (Saturday was its publishing
day) soon set the reader at ease. It contained no
personal gossip. Political editorials and political and
local news filled the sheet. "Public men are fair
game," she stated, and she continued penning
portraits of them as she had done in her books. In
her twenty-three years of newspaper publishing she
wrote over eleven hundred of these portraits. The
paper, considered first as a local curiosity—for it
was execrably printed and proof-read—soon gained
a reputation. It attained national fame and circulation. By January 1832 Mrs. Royall had agents in
every large city and town in the United States. With
a fine disregard for local reputations, she published
the names of those who failed to pay their subscription. If in one issue she erred in damning a person,
in the next she blithely apologized. And for all her
vitriolic and explosive writing in *Paul Pry*, Mrs.
Royall gained a following of loyal readers. The
same quick laughter that characterized her personality went into her editorials. She fought, but she
fought clean. Washington was the first centre of
her solicitude. It ought to be cleaned up. "Our

Congressmen are too valuable to be killed off as rapidly as they are by the unsanitary conditions here at the Capital."

President Jackson, whom she held in unwavering adoration, found in her a constant supporter. When the famous Eaton case divided the social ranks of Washington, Mrs. Royall was on the side of the President and the Eatons.

She had a nose for graft, and wherever it existed she hunted it down. Her first great assault—and she was the first to make this assault—was on the United States Bank. Holding a monopoly of all the national funds, it became one of the most influential financial powers in the world. Nicholas Biddle and his board of twenty-five ran the institution with an iron hand. Fortunes were made in it and fortunes lost. The common people had little to say about its management. Mrs. Royall continued her attacks. Other papers took up the cry. The country was aroused. When Jackson vetoed the bank's charter there was rejoicing such as had never been seen before.

One after another she sought out sources of public scandal and fought the devils with pen and ink. The causes for which she battled during the twenty-three years of her publishing are high points in American political and economic history. Besides the exposure and punishment of corrupt officials and the complete dissociation of Church and State, she battled for sound money, Free Masonry, for free, non-denominational public schools, a just management of the

Indians, especially the Cherokees, liberal immigration and tariff laws, transportation of Sunday mail, ([21]) appropriations for scientific investigation, the betterment of conditions of wage-earners, the abolition of flogging in the Navy, States' Rights in regard to slavery, appropriations for internal improvements and territorial expansion, and for free thought, free speech, and a free press.

Out-of-town newspapers, seeing that she was seriously in the fight for national advancement, gave her their support, excepting those that championed the anti-Mason and the Evangelical causes. And these could scarcely find bitter enough words to fling at her. When she ran short of newsprint paper, local editors would send her a supply and tell her to forget the bill. Mrs. Royall very soon commanded a position of respect. A number of the Presidents had her to dinner at the White House.

Some Congressmen, however, looked on her as a terrible old nuisance, for her reportorial persistence could be annoying. There is, for example, the famous instance of her interviewing John Quincy Adams when that President was as Nature made him. One early morning he left the White House and slipped into the Potomac for a nice, quiet, little swim. In the manner of small boys he left his clothes on the bank. Stroking around, he chanced to look up, and there comfortably seated on his clothes was Mrs. Royall. Several times, she shouted, she had been at the White House to get his opinion of the United

States Bank and had been refused an audience. Pencil in hand, she was now ready for the interview. When he gave it to her he could have his clothes, not before. Keeping his head above water as best he could, the President of the United States capitulated to the exigencies of the occasion. Mrs. Royall got her interview and John Quincy Adams his underwear, shirt, socks, shoes, pants, and coat.

For five years Mrs. Royall continued publishing *Paul Pry*. Many a time she had hard sledding, and once she was offered the insult of a bribe of $2,000 to hold her peace. She promptly printed an account of the affair.

Having ended *Paul Pry* in November 1836, she started another newspaper the following month. It was called *The Huntress* and assumed a different character. The style of rancorous journalism was gradually going out. So this paper boasted a literary flavor. It contained stories, poems, anecdotes, editorial comment and a "column" written by Mrs. Royall. But though the paper was changed, Mrs. Royall's journalistic ardor was not, nor was the keenness of her pen dulled. This sheet she continued for many years. When she reached eighty-five she started a new *Huntress!* There was simply no stopping this indefatigable woman!

Running through both *Paul Pry* and *The Huntress* was the colorful thread of an intimate friendship that gave these papers an unusual savor. In 1831 Mrs. Royall had found a companion and secretary in Mrs.

THE FIRST ISSUE OF ANNE ROYALL'S "THE HUNTRESS," A NEWSPAPER SHE FOUNDED AT THE AGE OF SIXTY-SEVEN

THE HUNTRESS.

EDUCATION.—"The sacred pillar which sustains the Temple of Liberty."—JOHNSON.

VOL. I.   WASHINGTON CITY, D. C., DECEMBER 2, 1836.   NO. 1.

THE HUNTRESS,

WILL BE PUBLISHED EVERY SATURDAY,

BY

MRS. ANNE ROYALL.

TERMS:

Two dollars and fifty cents, or three numbers for five dollars per annum, paid in advance. One dollar and fifty cents for six months, including the Session, if paid in advance. Where it is convenient for subscribers to pay the money down, they are hereby ...

All letters sent by mail, must be post-paid.

☞ The Office of the HUNTRESS is on Capitol Hill, within a short distance of the Capitol, at the corner of East Capitol and 2d streets, near the Hill Market.

Advertisements received at this Office, as usual.

SONG—THE BLOOM IS ON THE RYE.

My dearest Jane, my pretty Jane,
Ah, never look so shy,
But meet me in the evening,
When the bloom is on the rye.
The spring is waning fast, my love,
The corn is in the ear;
The summer nights are coming, love,
The moon shines bright and clear.

Then pretty Jane, &c.

But name the day, the wedding-day,
And I will buy the ring;
The lads and maids in favors gay,
...

Sarah Stack, who shared her labors, her poverty, her struggles, and, in the end, finally closed the eyes of this tired old journalist.   Sarah was Anne's *alter ego.* She became the second person of the editorial "we." Side by side with attacks on national evils were chatty reports of what Sarah did and said.   Readers got into the habit of looking for Sarah just as the followers of comic strips today look for the doings and sayings of their pet buffoons, or as readers of "columns" follow the domesticalities of their writers. And just as Anne Royall was the first of the tribe of muckraking editors, so her companion, Sarah, was the first of the column figures.

In the annals of journalism these two accomplishments would be sufficient to give Mrs. Royall a permanent and honored place.   Yet, strangely enough, her enemies dug a grave deep enough to keep her in obscurity.   A great patriot, a valiant soul, a strong bridge spanning many eventful years, Mrs. Royall occupies a unique place in American history. In her trembling old handwriting the last words of her final editorial spelled out the great hope of her heart —"I pray that the Union of these States may be eternal!"

On the first of October 1854 she passed away.   A place in the Congressional Cemetery was found for her body but there was no money forthcoming to mark the grave.   Today no one knows where she is buried.   No portrait of her has been found.   Copies of her newspapers and books are rarities that collectors hunt for and envy. The obscurity that closed in on Anne Newport Royall was final and overwhelming. Perhaps her enemies quieted their consciences by quoting "Julius Caesar"—

"When beggars die there are no comets seen."

CHAPTER VII

THE MADONNA IN BUSTLES

I

A T ABOUT the middle of the last century, female costume reached a sex *impasse*. This dizzy height was attained only through a long and arduous succession of fashions.

In 1800 a smart woman's clothes were counted by ounces. Her entire costume, including shoes and ornaments, did not tip the scales at more than half a pound. Society amused itself (pretty picture!) by weighing a lady's garments. So light became her covering that the illness it caused was known as "Muslin Disease." The underclothed woman of that day probably kept herself from chills with the same method used by the underclothed woman of today; with what the Germans call *Eitelkeit waermt*—vanity warmth. The style also appears to have affected their conduct: "the absence of hoops brings the ladies into such close contact that some of them quarreled and were near pulling one another's feathers." Thus did John Wilson Crocker, the Irish statesman, observe in his diary of a "Drawing Room" in 1822.

Toward the Forties the graceful and languishing

silhouette that characterized the dress of smart women began to spout flounces. With unabated vigor the spate of flounces increased both in size and number. Women were forced to don heavily ſtarched petticoats to hold them in place. By 1850 this flounce cataract had swollen to terrifying proportions. Under its pressure the levees of mere ſtarch proved inadequate. Wire hoops were rushed to the rescue— moderate hoops at firſt, then larger ones. The hoop-skirt spread like a mighty fountain around its wearer. It pre-empted every available inch of space. At social functions three women were about all a room of normal size would hold. Man was literally backed againſt the wall.

Whereas the entire coſtume of 1800 weighed only eight ounces, by 1860 a lady of fashion could not hold up her head in society unless it was weighed by pounds. She was a poorly dressed woman indeed unless she wore "a flannel petticoat, an under-petticoat three and a half yards wide, a petticoat wadded to the knees . . . a white ſtarched petticoat . . . two muslin petticoats and finally the dress." There is even recorded of this era a tulle dress that required eleven hundred yards of material. Thus did woman swathe herself in the Age of Stuffiness.

Meantime men were reacting in their own ſtuffy way, for a man with his back againſt the wall will take desperate measures. If woman asserted her dominance, so would he assert himself. Hitherto his

Monstrosities of 1827.

IN THE EARLY PART OF THE PAST CENTURY THE WELL-DRESSED MAN REFLECTED IN HIS CLOTHES THE CURRENT MODES OF THE LADIES. CRUIKSHANK HAD LITTLE TO EXAGGERATE IN HIS DRAWING

Courtesy of The Rosenbach Co.

costume had trailed the ladies' with ready complaisance: when their skirts swept the floor, the tails of his coats did the same; hitherto he repeated in clothes, in vests especially, the gaudy colors affected by women. Being crowded against the wall, he declared his independence by adopting a more standardized garb, and letting the colors of his clothes pale to the innocuous or assume the unsullied puritanism of black.

It is an amusing coincidence that this parting of the costume ways, this dominance of hoop-skirts, this male flight into Stygian black, all happened about the time that the feminist movement in America attained its first apex. Perhaps the one was symbolic of the other. And it is also an enlightening coincidence that the same woman who for many years was believed to be an arbiter of fashions was also a leader in the feminist cause—Sarah Josepha Hale—for forty-nine years editor of women's periodicals.

Her fashion dictatorship extended from the Romantic revival of the 30's, when Scott's novels roused renewed interest in mediaeval costuming for women, through the successive pulsations of flounces, hoop-skirts, crinoline, and bustles, to the period of the jersey and the kilted skirt. She lived to see the dawn of the tailor-made suit. Under her aegis women changed from the delicate, weeping, sighing, and fainting types who spent their days in suffering,

self-sacrifice, and self-devotion, through the harden-
ing of the female fibre in the fires of the Civil War, up
to the saucy and extravagant feminists of the Cen-
tennial. She lived long enough to see her sisters
venture on "high bikes."

She lived also to see the modes of women assume
a spiritual—if we might use that word—independence. In the days when first she took up her pen
to champion the hour-glass silhouette, the bertha cape
and bonnets of Milan straw heavily decked with
flowers, fruit, lace, and feathers—in those days
respectable fashion wore also the garb of righteousness and innocence. Vanity, which is ever woman's
most charming weakness, hid itself in the folds of
virtuous endeavor. Ladies of fashion were leaders
in public good. Respectability was smart. Through
successive years vanity gradually emerged as a spiritual entity. It became bold. It assumed a personality of its own. It no longer borrowed the
habiliments of its respectable |sister. The smart
woman was no longer of necessity a goddess of public
righteousness. As women attained sophistication and
power in the land, so did their clothes attain the right
to be a vain parade. Though Mrs. Hale did not live
to see it, and perhaps was unconscious of its evolution, the day came—and we are living in it—when,
due greatly to her endeavors, the erstwhile vice of
vanity attained the full stature of a feminine virtue.

The story of this transcendence is the story of
her life.

SARAH JOSEPHA HALE, FOR FORTY-SEVEN YEARS EDITOR OF *GODEY'S LADY'S BOOK*, AND ONE OF THE FEMALE GENIUSES OF THE PAST CENTURY

II

The same year that witnessed the agitation of
Washington for the first president, the states busily
adopting the constitution, and Marietta, in Ohio,
the haven of discontented and frontier-hungry Yankee
farmers, come into existence, saw also the birth of
Sarah Josepha Buell. The spot was Newport, New
Hampshire, to which her parents had moved from
Connecticut after the Revolution—for those who
didn't flee to the Western Reserve at this time of
heavy taxation moved to the upper tier of New
England States. The date was the thirtieth of
April, 1788. Under the guidance of her mother she
saturated herself in the Bible and the English poets—
Addison, Milton, Cowper, Burns, Shakespeare—the
sort of mental pabulum fed to minors in that time.

When she was twenty-five she married David
Hale, a young lawyer of Newport, and a good catch
he was. The Hales were identified with New Hampshire from the beginning. David's brother, Salma,
had already acquired a reputation as a local historian,
had written an English grammar, was a lawyer, an
editor and well on his way to Congressional fame.
The two were eminently compatible. Though many
years her senior, David found her a companionable
person. Each night from eight to ten, they undertook a systematic course of study and reading together. In the next nine years four children blessed
the union.

But there the romance snaps. David died. A fifth child was born shortly afterward. With these five bairns Mrs. Hale was left to face the long years to come. Her equipment for this uncertain future were the domestic gifts of a good housekeeper, and that broad acquaintance with the Scriptures and the English poets given her by her mother. Had she been a different type of woman she might have taken consolation from "A Winter's Tale"—

> I, an old turtle,
> Will wing me to some withered bough, and there
> My mate, that's never to be found again,
> Lament till I am lost.

But she was made of sterner stuff. The problem of providing for those five children and herself drove her to seek support from the pen. "The Genius of Oblivion and Other Poems" appeared the first year of her widowhood, thanks to the munificence of local Masons who took pride in the poet-widow of a loyal member. This fledgling effort could scarcely have been remunerative. It was a tale of the savage aborigines of America in three pompous cantos, followed by "occasional poems" of inconsequence.

Her next flight into the realms of literature proved more successful. "Northwood, or Life North and South, Showing the True Character of Both," appeared in 1827. It was written literally with her babe in her arms—the child born after the father died. From the first the book was a best seller. England published it as "A New England Tale."

THE CELEBRATED MRS. M. E. SOUTHWORTH BRADDON COBB, ENGAGED IN WRITING HER LAST NEW SENSATION NOVEL, TO CONTAIN 25 ELOPEMENTS, 43 SEPARATIONS FROM "BED AND BOARD," AND 742 DIVORCES FOR NEGLECT, ABANDONMENT, ETC., ETC., ETC.

THE FEMALE GENIUS, ESPECIALLY THE LITERARY KIND SUCH AS MRS. HALE REPRESENTED, CAME IN FOR HER MEASURE OF CRUEL CARTOONING

From *Yankee Notions*

Though not so speedy in action as modern readers might demand, and though spotted with dreary moralizing, "Northwood" is still a fascinatingly readable book. Written when first Abolition was beginning to arouse sectional feeling, its locale sways from a Yankee farm to a Charleston plantation. The story itself is negligible compared with the vivid and authentic descriptions of contemporary life in both places—the houses, the furniture, the manners, the day-to-day life of average people. In the style of novels of that time, the author's propaganda crops out boldly at the last: she suggests as a solution of the slavery problem that the forty thousand churches of America contribute each five dollars for the purpose of "educating and colonizing free people of color and emancipated slaves"—the Liberia idea. The final words of "Northwood" are, "The mission of American slavery is to Christianize Africa."

With "Northwood" Mrs. Hale leaped into literary fame. The success that was to enable her to educate her children liberally, was thereby assured. To make her position doubly safe, she casually won the prize in a poetry contest conducted by a Boston publisher. Thereupon this same enterprising publisher,—it happened to be the Rev. John L. Hale, an Episcopal clergyman—offered her the editorship of the *Ladies' Magazine*, and in 1828, being then forty, she moved to Boston and embarked on the editorial career that was to engross her until she was eighty-nine.

The *Ladies' Magazine* was to be a new kind of publication—the first in America devoted exclusively to women's interests and edited exclusively by a woman, the fore-runner of that great army of women's magazines that crowds our newsstands today. (²²)

Being a rank amateur, Mrs. Hale walked in where other editors feared to tread. Her editorial candor is engaging. In the first issue of the *Ladies' Magazine*, which she edited up in the rural innocence of her New Hampshire home, she appears purposeful but without guile. She shows her complete hand. She is not writing for fame. She is animated by the hope of thereby being able to support and educate her children. She asks the patronage of her readers because she intends to deserve it. And, at the end of the volume, having evidently received adequate patronage, she thanks her readers in the name of her children for their support. One could hardly resist such frankness.

Editors of today might try that—and with equal interest from readers. Were the editor of the *Atlantic Monthly*, for example, to tell his subscribers that all this pother over manuscripts and printers was undertaken merely to afford him the money to finish his collection of Georgian furniture, he would doubtless meet with amazing success. Were the author of this book to state boldly in his magazine that his only reason for editing it was to get enough money for him to keep his garden well-stocked and meticulously maintained, he might be able to retire

shortly to that rural Nirvana—and to the delight of
numberless subscribers.

Equally frank was the statement of Mrs. Hale's
editorial policy.

Her earliest female emotion, she says somewhere,
was "to promote the reputation of her sex." [23]   And
in the *Ladies' Magazine* she launches on this crusade
without hesitating.   Her one motive is "to make
females better acquainted with their duties and
privileges as women."   She recommends that, since
women are the real tutors of the race, they become
teachers in schools, and she urges parents so to educate their daughters that they can undertake this
work.   Through issue after issue she keeps hammer-
ing away at this theme.   Women as teachers!
Women as leaders in temperance!   Women as eman-
cipators of the slave!   All this is sandwiched in
between poems, articles, stories and Mrs. Hale's
own series of "Sketches of American Character,"
which were slightly fictionized portraits of American
domestic types.   Whatever she wrote, the accent was
on the word *woman.*   Any other title given her sex
filled her with destructive wrath.   Her aversion to
female was positively withering.

This early propaganda for women teachers,
fostered by Mrs. Hale, found an example in her own
daughter.   This young lady, named after her mother,
for several years conducted a boarding and day
school for young women in the fashionable Ritten-
house Square in Philadelphia.   It also found great

encouragement when Mary Lyon founded her Mount
Holyoke Seminary for young women in 1837.

Mrs. Hale's strenuous efforts to induce the
education of females by females may have struck
her readers as a quixotic notion, and yet the cause
warranted her championing it. The education of
girls had never been given the serious attention
that the education of boys had received. In seven-
teenth-century New England they were either taught
by their mothers or went to a "Dame's School"—
kept by a dried-up spinster. To read and write and
do a little figuring afforded them sufficient education
to read their Bible, learn the catechism and cast up
household accounts. In a later era they learned cultural arts—to sing and dance; but on the whole,
the ideal of the education of women was to make
them good housewives. So we find from a government survey of the women signing legal papers in
Massachusetts between 1653 and 1656, that half of
them were obliged to make their mark instead of
signing their names; up to 1697, thirty-eight per cent
were illiterate; New York showed a sixty per cent
illiteracy among women, and Virginia seventy-five.
However, both Massachusetts and Virginia had their
schools for boys and girls early in the seventeenth
century and Pennsylvania led them all in educational
advantages.

The latter part of the eighteenth century saw
the boarding school for girls come into favor. The
Moravians conducted their seminary at Bethlehem,

Pennsylvania, and there were like institutions in North Carolina and Massachusetts, where girls of genteel parents received schooling in the three R's, the classics, dancing, music, French, and polite manners. Girls of poorer homes, however, did not fare so well. As we have seen, Mrs. Hale's education was received primarily at her mother's knee. The very year she was born, the town fathers of Northampton, now the seat of the flourishing and prominent Smith College, voted down an appropriation for a girls' school on the grounds that it was a needless waste of public funds.

Always Mrs. Hale is the champion of righteousness and orthodoxy. When Fanny Wright began shocking conservatives with her lectures on rationalism and sex emancipation, Mrs. Hale attacked with thundering fury her "open and impudent attempt to advocate the cause of infidelity and disorder." "A shameless and impious woman," she calls her. Nor is it surprising that she should use such intemperate language, for was not that radical hussy aiming to destroy the very foundations of the American home? Abolition of the marriage rite and an equal footing for legitimate and illegitimate children were doctrines too advanced for women of those times.

The charge of advocating free love was to trail the feminist movement from its beginning up to those colorful days of the 70's when that amazing spiritualist-broker, Victoria Woodhull, led the insurgents and split the feminist party by announcing herself as candidate for the Presidency of the United States. Her followers in those days boldly paraded under a banner labeled "Free Love," and when the howls of the righteous came whipping around their ears, they hastened to assure the world that their interpretation of this unshackled state was purely academic and quite innocuous.

For thirteen years Mrs. Hale stuck to her desk at the *Ladies' Magazine*, never wasting a stroke of her busy pen. And when she wasn't conning manuscripts, she was busy at her own writing. Six books were turned out in this period—"Sketches of American Character"; "Traits of American Life"; "Flora's Interpreter"—a quaint little volume on the sentimental symbols of flowers; "The Lady's Wreath" —an anthology of English and American female poets; "The Way To Live Well"; "Grosvenor, A Tragedy"; and "Poems For Our Children."

Today no one dreams of reading these books, but it does bring a thrill to encounter the slim paperbound volume of "Poems For Our Children—written to inculcate moral truths and virtuous sentiments," —and find there "Mary's Lamb." Out of all her many volumes and forty-nine years of editing, this one poem remains and will remain to be lisped by the young. The female emancipation that Mrs. Hale battled for has been accomplished. Few remember her part in it. But we all will remember

Mary had a little lamb,
Its fleece was white as snow.

And a moſt accommodating person was Mrs. Hale
withal. If there were any little odd bits of editing to
be done around Boſton, she was always willing to
undertake them. The Bunker Hill Monument cause,
for example.

The movement to cap this battlefield with a suitable monument began in 1794 and by slow degrees it
proceeded until 1828 when, the work reaching forty
feet, funds were exhauſted. For years the pile ſtood
there, a mockery to Boſton. Visitors twitted the
Boſtonians about it, the way we twit Philadelphians
about their recent Sesquicentennial. Mrs. Hale
began agitating its cause the second year of her editorship of the *Ladies' Magazine* and pursued it relent-
lessly for ten years. Finally, the public dander
being aroused, citizens determined to rid themselves
of the disgrace. Two patriots offered $10,000 each,
leaving $30,000 to be raised by popular subscription.
Into this breech rushed the women with Mrs. Hale,
pen in hand, at their head. For months, New England housewives negleƈted their family chores to do
embroidery and crochet hug-me-tights. In September 1840 they opened a grand bazaar in Boſton. For
seven days the crowds poured into Quincy Hall and
prodigally diveſted themselves of their money. Mrs.
Hale conduƈted a daily paper, "The Monument,"
that kept the female spirits on tiptoe. On the laſt
night when the final embroidered bertha had been

sold and the one remaining hug-me-tight knocked down to the highest bidder, the treasurer announced that the bazaar had rolled up $30,000 profit. The monument was assured! Boston's honor was saved! Two years later the final capstone was set in place. Mrs. Hale could witness the ceremony with gratified and kindling eyes.

But even while all these exciting events were taking place, others were laying the steps to her future career. In 1837, the *Ladies' Magazine* was amalgamated with another female publication started in Philadelphia in 1830 by Louis A. Godey and known as *Godey's Lady's Book*. Mrs. Hale was made editor. She stayed on in Boston and, thanks to the patronage of her readers, saw her sons through Harvard. Then in 1841 she moved to Philadelphia, which thenceforward became the centre of her activities. This date marked a definite transition in her career: from a local celebrity, with this move to Philadelphia, she leaped to national fame.

Her coming there also marks a new era in Philadelphia's history—its rise in importance as a magazine publishing centre.

Prior to 1800 Philadelphia had been the cultural and political hub of America. Boston, New York, and Charleston were insignificant villages compared with it. There lived most of the brilliant writers; there was the meeting point of our best minds. Naturally it became the production centre of most of the books and pamphlets published at the time.

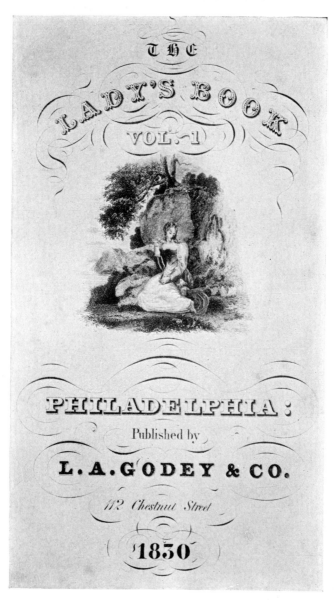

THE

LADY'S BOOK

VOL. 1

PHILADELPHIA:

Published by

L. A. GODEY & CO.

112 Chestnut Street

'1830'

TITLE PAGE OF THE FIRST NUMBER OF *THE LADY'S BOOK* AS
FOUNDED BY LOUIS A. GODEY

Previous to the Revolution and for a decade afterward it was the political as well as the actual capital of the nation. The opening of the western lands that followed the Revolution promised also to bring the city great wealth and give it an enviable reputation as a centre of finance.

But in these affairs it was soon outstripped. With the moving of the capital to the newly founded city of Washington, its political prestige took a sharp decline. Its geographical situation did not aid it in reaping all the benefits it might have derived from the western development. And since it seemed content with its ways, the newer generation of writers were not attracted to it—they preferred the more lively taste of Boston and Charleston which were then undergoing an intellectual and cultural renaissance. Gradually Philadelphia "succumbed to the taste of Victorianism" says Parrington in "The Romantic Revolution in America" and became "the acknowledged home of 'female genius' that for years fed the American reading public on cambric tea."

The movement began with Thomas Cottrell Clarke resigning from the editorship of *The Saturday Evening Post* to establish in 1828 *The Album and Ladies' Weekly Gazette*. Two years later Louis A. Godey, a New Yorker by birth, and self-educated, who had served as clerk for a Philadelphia newspaper publisher, ventured on his *Lady's Book*. He bought up some old plates from a defunct publication, clipped articles from English magazines, and thus equipped, started his publication. Prosperity came at once. He could buy out his Boston competitor and hire the most promising woman editor in the country.

These plunges into the depths of female journalism encouraged the establishing of several other women's publications, which bore names reeking with the sentiment of the times—*The Ladies' Literary Portfolio, The Casket, or Flowers of Literature, Wit and Sentiment, The Ladies' Garland, The Ladies' Companion,* Peterson's *Ladies' National Monument,* and *The Lantern.* All these were cut from about the same cloth. Some lived only a year or so; others dragged on to the inevitable grave of unsupported magazines. The one that best withstood the vicissitudes of time and the vagaries of the reading public was *Godey's Lady's Book,* for half a century the *Vogue* of American taste.

In addition to creating the type of magazine that appealed most to the taste of women of the day, Mr. Godey set a fashion in publishing which still persists —he incorporated his own name in the title of the magazine. This personal assertion of the owner may be due to vanity or to a belief that he is sufficiently known to the reading public to attract it, once his name is attached to a publication. It has not always been successful.

However, *Godey's* had its keen rivals. The publisher of the Philadelphia *Album,* determined to capture good editorial talent, offered Mrs. Felicia Hemans $1500 a year and a house rent free and fur-

WALKING DRESS.

Nº 1 of the Ladies Book.

*Published by L.A.Godey &c. 112 Chestnut St. Phil*ª

THE FIRST FASHION PLATE PUBLISHED IN VOLUME I, NO. 1, OF
THE LADY'S BOOK, BY MR. GODEY

nished, a tempting offer for 1827. There was also
Hearth & Home, appearing about the middle of the
century, with Donald B. Mitchell for editor and
Harriet Beecher Stowe on the staff. By this time,
1868, Mrs. Stowe had reached that proficiency in
letters and that following where she could write (and
be believed) on almost any topic. In one volume of
this magazine she writes with equal ease and fluency
on the care of babies, the cheapness of beauty, how
to use matting, travel, and good manners! ([24])

III

Today *Godey's Lady's Book* is a happy hunting ground for interior decorators. They descend
upon it with knives and scissors, like Indians on a
scalping raid, and ruthlessly strip it of its colored
fashion plates wherewith to make lampshades, port-
folios, scrapbaskets and such other innocuous acces-
sories of decoration which they can palm off on un-
suspecting customers as "Early American," and at
highly remunerative prices. Had Mrs. Hale been
able to foresee this end of her endeavors, she doubtless would have contemplated it with horror. For
though the fashion plates in *Godey's Lady's Book*
were a feature that brought the magazine popular
support—its circulation reached 150,000 a month, a
staggering total for that time—Mrs. Hale's great
work lay in the text. That was her true *metier*.

The descriptions of the early fashion plates occupy
only a small block of text at the back of the book,

rubbing elbows with such pretty household hints—
"Pleasing Experiments" she called them—as changing the color of a rose, reviving dead plants, the singu-
lar effect of tears on a dry piece of paper stained with
the juice of violets. The major part of each issue
was given over to stories, poems, essays, little moral
"fillers" and the editorials in which Mrs. Hale pursued her female propaganda.

Now and then in these early issues Mrs. Hale's
pen was moved to write of fashion but always in the
most restrained and proper tone. In an issue of 1837
she says of one of the figures on the fashion plate:
"her heart has already imbibed the poison of vanity."
In that same year Emma Willard assures us that:
"The greater portion of the elegance and refinement
of this country is now found within the limits where
the authority of virtue and religion is acknowledged
to be paramount." "True taste in dress," we are
sententiously told, "is an intellectual accomplishment" . . . "Some attention to fashions is not in
itself unwise or injudicious." However, later on we
find frivolous tidbits of fashion news given space—
that lace is everywhere, flounces general, shawls in-
dispensable, and that high-heeled shoes are being
revived.

Thus Mrs. Hale kept one eye on the subscription
list and one eye on the devil of vanity. Even in
those days the business office lay very close to the
editor's sanctum. In fact, Mr. Louis Godey located
his "column," in which he conducted the reader be-

EDITOR OF THE LADY'S BOOK

Yours Truly

L A Godey

MR. GODEY IN HIS PRIME, WHEN HE WAS CONSIDERED ONE OF THE LEADING
MAGAZINE PUBLISHERS OF AMERICA

hind the scenes, to immediately follow Mrs. Hale's editorial.

Just as Mrs. Hale was purposeful and enterprising in her editorial policy, so was Mr. Godey in the business management of the magazine. Hitherto authors had hid modestly under classical pseudonyms. This shrinking delicacy he swept away with one stroke. Thereafter authors were to sign their names to contributions in *Godey's Lady's Book*. Moreover, they were paid for their contributions! Thus was authorship raised to a respectable profession in the magazine world.

But his greatest stroke of publishing genius was the use of colored fashion plates. In those issues of the 30's one plate sufficed. Mrs. Hale writes in defense of them, that they cost $3,000 a year to hand-color and that they give constant employment to twenty women. And just to show how valuable was this coloring, she publishes side by side tinted and untinted plates. By 1850 the circulation has attained eighty thousand; by 1860 one hundred thousand. Mr. Godey tells his readers that in one year he has spent over $100,000 to produce *Godey's Lady's Book*, and the cost of coloring the fashion plates rose to $8,000.

His enterprise pushes this fashion news idea to its furthest limits. He sends fashion artists to Paris and has society reporters attending social functions to jot down notes on the dresses. Starting with dress fashions, the plates were multiplied to include all manner of female interests—patterns for needlework, plans and drawings of houses, furniture, children's amusements, music. He arranges with Stewart's in New York to furnish dress models—he even sees to it that Mrs. Hale devotes her first article in one issue to a description of Stewart's department store. By 1863 the issues were running two fashion plates in color, fourteen pages in black and white and nine others with descriptive text. For these we can scarcely say that Mrs. Hale was responsible; in fact, in each issue Mr. Godey's column clearly states that Mrs. Hale was *not* the fashion editress. To her belonged the more rarified air of domestic ideals and women's advancement.

The editorial candor that Mrs. Hale first manifested in the *Ladies' Magazine* took a different tack in this new publication. She now opened up her columns to a discussion of the manuscripts submitted to her and why she rejected them. Of "My Mother's Grave," for example, she remarks, "the author, should he live ten years longer, will thank us for declining to publish this article." Often she quotes the choicest tidbits of these rejected manuscripts. Present-day editors could have a lot of fun doing that—in fact, it would make an amusing department run at a minimum of expense.

Paging over the forty-seven years of this magazine one can view the literary output of America in fine perspective. Here are the earlier compositions of Longfellow, Holmes, Poe, Bayard Taylor, Lydia

H. Sigourney, and Frances Osgood. The writings of George Gilmore Simms, Bayard Taylor, Hawthorne, Charles Godfrey Leland, N. P. Willis and many of Mrs. Hale's books ran serially through its pages. So did some of Harriet Beecher Stowe's and the articles of Horace Greeley. To appear in *Godey's Lady's Book* was to be "made." Aspiring authors dreamed of the day when they would receive a letter of acceptance signed "Sarah Josepha Hale."

From her "own quiet study," as she called her office, the spate of Mrs. Hale's propaganda poured undiminished—how to educate children; motherhood in its multifarious aspects; growing old gracefully; taking country walks—but be sure, girls, you wear thick-soled shoes!; the evils of naughty French fiction. But always her feminist propaganda crops out. Let the other pages display vain mantillas and Niagaras of flounces; she sits alone to write sweetly of "Woman's Moral Destiny."

Mrs. Hale also was the progenitor of that type of editor of women's magazines who today leaps to fame on the tail of righteous causes. As can be noticed by glancing through them, it is a pretty poor woman's publication that isn't thundering away at some desirable improvement for the race. In Boston she helped lead the movement, as we have seen, to finish the Bunker Hill Monument, and she had a hand in founding the Seamen's Aid Society, which apparently undertook to swamp lusty tars with Bibles, moral tracts and other inducements to make them shun the flesh-pots when they got shore leave. In *Godey's Lady's Book* one of her public benefactions was the establishment of Thanksgiving Day as a national feast.

In 1846 she first proposed the idea of a national Thanksgiving Day and for eighteen years thereafter she besieged Presidents to do something about it. The day had been celebrated in a hit-or-miss fashion for years, each state picking out its own date. In her September 1863 issue she suggested the last Thursday in November as the best date, and November of the following year saw President Lincoln finally succumbing to her zealous entreaties. Mrs. Hale rejoiced over this conquest in a well-mannered editorial, belittling her part in it, although everyone knew she was responsible for the national adoption of the holiday. Among her other labors she could be proud of the assistance she gave the founding of the first medical college for women. This was started in 1850 in Philadelphia and was designed to give medical education to women missionaries. Equally enthusiastic were her endeavors for foreign missions: for nine years she sat as president of an organization that labored under the name of "The Woman's Union Missionary Society for Heathen Lands."

The other-worldliness that possessed Mrs. Hale occasionally caused her to be duped by leaders of reforms who themselves were not above reproach. Witness her championing in the *Godey's Lady's Book* of the notorious E. Z. C. Judson, who, under

the name of Ned Buntline pretended to lead all
manner of reforms. In New York this lurid reformer
published a sheet called "Ned's Own" or "Bawdy
House Directory," apparently designed to reveal the
evil of these lewd rendezvous in New York. He also
championed temperance, the underpaid seamstresses
of the metropolis and the Know-Nothing Movement.
For a long time he "gammoned the public with his
lachrymal whinings of Reform" and attained quite a
following. His real character, however, was soon
revealed. A prodigious hypocrite, he had "been
hunted out of Florida, kicked out of Pittsburgh,
drummed out of Nashville, disgraced in Philadelphia"
and was eventually exposed in New York after James
Gordon Bennett attacked him in the *Herald* and
his own wife sued him for divorce. An account of
Judson's travels "through all the signs of the immoral
Zodiac" is contained in a quaint pamphlet, published in New York in 1849, of which the title deserves
repeating. It reads: "The Private Life, Public
Career and Real Character of that Odious Rascal
Ned Buntline, as Developed By His Conduct to His
Past Wife, Present Wife and His Various Paramours!
Completely lifting up the Veil, and Unmasking to a
Horror-stricken Community, his Debaucheries, Seduc-
tions, Adulteries, Revelings, Cruelties, Threats and
Murders!!!"

IV

Despite the patriotic and religious ardor with
which Mrs. Hale labored to have Thanksgiving Day

made a national event, and to institute reforms that
threatened a general housecleaning of public morals,
we find her pursuing the course of feminism without
regard for great national events going on about her.
True, the Civil War and the events leading up to it
and from it could not help captivating the imagination of even the most ardent feminist, yet these
worthy ladies often used the national crisis for for-
warding their own dearly dreamed ideals. Turning
the pages of *Godey's Lady's Book* issued during
the Civil War years, one would never suspect that
the nation was being torn asunder by a great struggle.
Lee may be battering at the gates of Pennsylvania;
Mrs. Hale writes calmly on the sin of extravagance
among women. Lincoln signs the Emancipation
Proclamation; Mrs. Hale rejoices that her work for
the education of women by women has been attained
in the founding of Vassar College. Peace may come;
she is interested alone in the revival of deaconesses
and in the medical training of women for work in the
mission field. This is the quiet harbor that *Godey's
Lady's Book* offered its distracted 150,000 women
readers in the hectic year of 1864.

Her oblivious attitude toward current events is
quite characteristic of the history of feminism in this
country. Once it got under way, these ladies considered their cause always above all others.

The beginning of the feminist movement in
America was inseparably intertwined with the cause
of temperance. Almost invariably the advocates for

woman suffrage and equal rights started their careers as temperance lecturers. In another chapter of this book it will be seen how Anne Royall, the journalist and traveling-reporter, made drinking one of her chief objects of attack. Lucy Stone, Elizabeth Cady Stanton, Susan B. Anthony, Amelia Jenks Bloomer—all these evolved from the evils of intemperate drinking by men the idea that the world's salvation lay in giving to women suffrage and equal rights. Fanny Wright D'Arusmont alone seemed to be more interested in rationalism than in temperance.

By the middle of the century, however, temperance had become a secondary issue. Some of the feminists even appear to have jettisoned it. Elizabeth Cady Stanton was summoning the first Woman's Rights Convention at her home in Seneca Falls, New York. Lucy Stone was lecturing boldly on the subject. Susan B. Anthony was agitating for the coeducation of sexes and equal suffrage. Scarcely had the smoke of the Civil War battles blown away than she started editing *The Revolutionist*, a magazine devoted solely to woman's emancipation. Amelia Jenks Bloomer had been publishing the same doctrine in her *Western Home Journal* in Ohio, and was repeating it in *The Lily*. It was at the Woman's Rights Convention in '61, however, that she had assumed the Turkish plus-fours that were to send her name rolling down to posterity. Nor had

Lucy Stone yet run afoul of the authorities for non-payment of taxes and keeping her maiden name.

While these women were traveling about the country lecturing and preaching their ideas, Mrs. Hale kept busily engaged at her *Godey's Lady's Book* and at divers literary endeavors. However strongly she may have felt about the emancipation of her sex and however persistently she wrote in its behalf, one always feels that Mrs. Hale never forgot that she was a lady, never forgot that among those 150,000 subscribers many there were who did not share the heterodox and advanced notions of the itinerant, unbridled feminists. If the emancipation of women took them out of the home, Mrs. Hale feared for its future. She preferred the middle of the road. Sentiment was a safer course, and into that channel she steered her way.

Without cessation, books poured from her pen once she was located in Philadelphia:—"The White Veil, A Bridal Gift"—a collection of poems and edifying observations on the married state, assembled from various sources; "Alice Ray, a Romance in Rhyme"; "Harry Gray, the Widow's Son," a sea tale; "Three Hours, Or the Vigil of Love," "The Ladies' New Book of Cookery"—in which advanced notions of diet and health and food values are put forth, and in which Mrs. Hale writes also on etiquette and the behavior and dress of servants in the most approved Emily Post fashion. "The New House-hold Receipt Book" followed on the heels of this

laſt. But the great work, one that ſtill holds its
authoritative position, appeared in 1854,—"Woman's
Record, or Sketches of All Diſtinguished Women
from the Creation to A.D. 1854." This encyclopedic
work is dedicated, not without pointed irony, to
the men of America! The following year appeared,
"A Diĉtionary of Poetical Quotations," another
ſtupendous anthology. One almoſt suspeĉts there
were several Miſtresses Hale, so speedily did these
great works follow one another.

Having accomplished this much, in addition to
her day's work as editor, she simply could not ſtop.
The writing momentum carried her on into "The
Judge, a Drama of American Life"; several annuals,
such as "The Opal" and "The Crocus," edited for
the Chriſtmas trade and, to make the measure good
in 1856, editions of the letters of Madame Sevigne
and of Lady Mary Wortley Montagu.

This brought her up to the Civil War. She was
then seventy-three. The war over, we find her
writing "Manners or Happy Homes and Good
Society," and "Love or Woman's Deſtiny," a
volume of poems. Even now we have not named all
her books, but these will suffice to show the output
of this ſturdy New England widow.

Moſt of these books were firſt serialized in the
magazine. Mrs. Hale threw her odd bits of editing
and writing into its pages much in the way a good
cook tosses choice scraps into the ſtock pot. Nothing
of her sedulous endeavors is ever waſted. If she

writes a poem, in it goes. If she is editing an anthology, in go the selections. If she writes a biography, or a sketch, or sets down a casual sentiment
—plop! into the pages! Good soup is made that
way and so is a good magazine of this kind.

When she reached eighty-nine, having been a
magazine editor for nearly half a century, she retired
from active labors. The pen that had been taken up
to support and educate her children had seen them
attain age and worthy places in their respective
callings. At last it lay idle. But an editor can never
really retire; when he or she does, life loses the worth
of living. Mrs. Hale survived her retirement only
two years. The thirtieth of April, 1879 wrote the
last "Finis" to her copy.

V

Sarah Josepha Hale and her half century of
editing and writing present an interesting type of
endeavor. It was a conquest that ended in defeat.
Whereas it begins as a crusade for woman's rights and
woman's place in education, the years pass and the
shouts of the world drown the sweet persuasion of
her who led it. The cause gets beyond her. The
especial things she battles for come to pass. She
accepts their attainment with self-effacing grace.
Her more militant sisters are making a great to-do;
Mrs. Hale's pace, her tone, her cadence remain
constant. The bloomered battalions sweep by her
with fiery gusto; she sits there—a cheery face ringed

THE LAST FASHION PLATE IN *GODEY'S LADY'S BOOK*
PUBLISHED UNDER THE EDITORSHIP OF
SARAH JOSEPHA HALE

about with pendant curls—gracious, cautious, imperturbable, setting down her sentiments about women in the Bible, women as mothers, women as housekeepers.

She never quite surrendered the old-fashioned idea, held before the Civil War, that by constitution woman was physically weak and helpless and that "delicacy was her chief characteristic." This was indicated by the clothes fashionable at the time. Woman's diminutive waist symbolized her ethereal quality.

A writer in *Blackwoods* of April 1865 states the relation between fashions and feminine nature thus: "The hoop and sweeping skirt are an admission that they are very women after all, unfitted by nature and constitution to move easily or to feel in their place in the bustle of crowds and the stir of active, outdoor life." This delicacy "was sought and attained at great price because it was considered as the visible sign of an ethereal, spiritual nature, a moral sensitiveness and purity superior to man's." These sentiments are echoed in an editorial in *Godey's Lady's Book*—"Woman's spiritual strength seems perfected in her physical weakness, by the gift of intuitive sympathy with the Divine Goodness, which, after the Fall, mercifully exalted her sex to conserve the moral virtues of humanity and thus become 'the glory of man'!"

From this dream of "lady-like uselessness" women were rudely awakened by the shock of the Civil War.

The fainting female began to wind bandages and forget her "gift of intuitive sympathy with the Divine Goodness." So far beyond the idea of helplessness did women go that the newly-founded Vassar College claimed to send forth its graduates physically well-developed and vigorous. Graduation exercises were held in loose dresses and the girls—imagine it— had discarded their corsets!

Clinging to the pre-Rebellion relationship between clothes and woman's ethereal qualities, Mrs. Hale never quite caught up with this new liberty. Scarcely had she begun her sweet crusade for the education of women by women than arose another movement that was to leave her far behind. Her attitude toward women's fashions, cautiously respectable from the first, was soon swamped by the popularity of those colored fashion plates. More and more of the space she cherished for her female sentiments is given over to them. Inch by inch she retreats before the oncoming tide of female vanity. Beauty hints, with receipts for face creams and lip sticks, burst into her editorial sanctum like a mob of *sans culottes* into a lady's boudoir. A shopping department for out-oftown readers pre-empts the space she used to give to moral observations. It ceased being Mrs. Hale's *Godey's Lady's Book.*

The year after she laid down her editorial pencil and Mr. Godey sold his magazine, ([25]) it was printing fiction that had titles such as "A Trap to Catch an Heiress" and "A Rosebud Garden of Girls." Its

LOUIS A. GODEY, AT THE TIME OF HIS RETIREMENT IN 1877
FROM ACTIVE WORK AS PUBLISHER OF *GODEY'S LADY'S BOOK*

fashion editor was proclaiming an "increase in the luxury and costliness of underwear," and handing down *ex cathedra dicta* on the new tight chemises, and monogram gloves and stockings! In Mrs. Hale's world, underwear was never mentioned and women were not conceded to have legs.

In all the 571 issues of the magazine Mrs. Hale edited, her publisher could boast that never did an immoral idea or a profane word sully its pages. It had served three generations. It had brought its owner great wealth and its editor a good living and a place on the rolls of memorable American women. Beyond that no magazine could go. Beyond that no decent woman editor would dare aspire. The farewell of these two—old Mrs. Hale and old Mr. Godey —as they come before their readers hand in hand in the issue of December 1877, is very touching.

After their departure the magazine became nondescript. For it is an axiom of the publishing world that the personality of a magazine is the personality of its editor. The issue of April 1879, the month Sarah Josepha Hale died, finds no mention of woman's rights and woman's education, no editorial aspiration to lead the race to a higher plane. The old editor passes peacefully away in her sleep while the new one is telling her readers that "dressy wraps for spring will be mantles of Chuddah or plain camel's hair trimmed with fringes."

The Madonna in Bustles had been supplanted by a hoyden in a kilted skirt.

CHAPTER VIII
TWO SWEET LITTLE DEMONS

MARGARET AND KATHERINE FOX, ON INVESTIGATING MYSTERIOUS NOISES IN THEIR BEDROOM, HAPPEN ON THE BEGINNINGS OF SPIRITUALISM IN AMERICA

I

THE 40's and 50's of the past century were a paradise of pitchmen. Towns and cities and the countryside as well became a vast and constant carnival at which venders of all manner of good, medium and cheap-jack amusements, half-baked religions, strange sects, diluted science and novelties in philosophy hawked their wares. The cultured and the misleading, the true and the false mingled with easy grace. From the sublime heights of singing by Jenny Lind and Kate Hayes, dancing by Effie Ellsler and acting by the elder Forrest, it ranged down through the circus under the aegis of Barnum and others, and the itinerant theatre under the cheapest types of barnstormers, to ludicrous but nevertheless solemnly delivered lectures on Mesmerism, Phrenology, Animal Magnetism, and Spiritualism. And America accepted them with the undivided credulity of the neophyte. It was an era of fads.

The sects that arose to grip popular imagination and gain following were legion. The Hydropaths set great store by water in unlimited quantities and the

218

What Jenny Lind and Kate Hayes have to answer for.

THE CARTOONIST OF *YANKEE NOTIONS* THUS DEPICTS WHAT
JENNY LIND AND KATE HAYES, THE TWO SINGERS, WERE
RESPONSIBLE FOR

Vegetarians, eschewing all flesh, hoped to gain Heaven and health by following Nebuchadnezzar's taste for green vegetables. There were those who gravely trailed after Graham and ate only rough whole-wheat bread. The name Graham applied to the bread still reminds us of those days.

Meantime, the followers of Fourier, that innocuous little French traveling-salesman preacher of Utopia, went off into rural colonies to save the world and themselves by communistic living, high thinking and rustic endeavors. "Professors" displayed charts whereon the human cranium was subdivided, like a real estate development, into the bumps of Amativeness, Caution, Combativeness, Self-Esteem, and such, and the wondering populace held that Phrenology had become a demonstrable science. Mountebanks armed with galvanic batteries were making decorous ladies tingle beneath their ample hoop-skirts. Men and women sat around in circles gravely holding a rope wound with wire, and felt the thrill of animal magnetism. The followers of Mesmer demonstrated their skill on their confederates and whomsoever from the audience was bold enough to present himself as a subject. Physicians solemnly proclaimed that even serious operations could be performed without pain on persons who had been mesmerized.

Most of these "professors" and lecturers were charlatans of the worst kidney, cheap showmen with a gift of gab that impressed the credulous. Many of them were not above petty theft and even worse

crimes. Yet America enjoyed them, for the country
had reached that age when it lusted after novelties
and was willing to throw away its pennies, its time,
and its good sense on cheap attractions. It demanded
strange gods—and the charlatans saw to it that the
gods were furnished them aplenty.

Out of all these amusing phenomena the one that
survived many generations and comes down to the
palpitating and incredulous present was Spiritualism.
Like the mighty oaks that grow from little acorns,
it had a humble and obscure beginning, one that
involved two equally humble and obscure young
women—the Fox Sisters. In the Valhalla of Spiritualism, in the burning heart of the celestial Seventh
Circle of the Spirit World, these two little country
girls may still sit enthroned as goddesses of superior
quality. Between that heavenly beatification and
their beginnings in life lay the picturesque path of
their careers.

II

Sometime in December, 1847, John D. Fox moved
his family from Rochester into a house in Hydesville,
a section of Arcadia, Wayne County, New York.
Besides himself and his wife were his two daughters,
Margaret, aged seven, a mild, gentle child, with no
especial cunning in her face, and Katherine, six.
Two miles away lived a son, David, and in Rochester
a married daughter, Ann Leah Fish.

It was an ordinary humble dwelling, but it had

The Forte of a Fashionable Female.

A CONTEMPORARY CARTOON OF THE 50's, THAT PILLORIES BOTH
THE COSTUME AND THE GENTEEL AMUSEMENTS OF LADIES
OF QUALITY

gained a strange reputation under its previous owner. Michael Weekman, who lived in it from 1846 to 1847 had been annoyed with rappings on the outside door about nine o'clock one night. When he investigated the source of the noises, he could find no one around the house, and though the raps continued and he persistently trailed them, he never found out where they came from. So it was really a haunted house that John Fox elected to live in. Of course, the neighbors had heard all about it and John and the girls were soon told its reputation. Being a good Methodist, the father paid no attention to these silly rumors, whereas his wife, a weaker mortal, kept all these things in her heart.

December passed, and after it most of the winter. The Foxes lived the normal, hard-working life of a small country settlement. The neighbors forgot those stories about the rappings the previous tenant had heard, but in the impressionable minds of the two young daughters they remained vivid and unforgettable. One night toward the end of March 1848, after they had gone to bed, the girls said they heard rappings. It was as though someone was knocking on the floor and moving chairs. These sounds varied from a light, clear, metallic ting to a dull, muffled thud like the rapping of knuckles on a cloth-covered partition. The girls called their parents, and the house was searched. No one was found. The next night the same noises were heard and equally unsuccessful was the second investigation. By the thirty-first, things had gotten to such a pass and the family was so worked up, that neighbors were called in.

The noises invariably issued from where the two girls stood. Growing suspicious, a neighbor began cross-questioning them: were they positive that they hadn't been making those noises? To this one of the girls replied in a way that must go down to fame as among our sublime utterances: "We are innocent," she vowed ecstatically. "How good it is to have a clear conscience!"

This assurance from the lips of an eight-year old set at peace all rumors of deception. Verily upon the Fox girls had descended a strange, psychic power. Immediately they were considered to be children set apart from all the other children of the place. The world began making a beaten path to their door. A committee came to investigate—and went away mystified.

It was evident to those who looked into this mystery that the knockings were the efforts of disembodied spirits to communicate with mortals. Before the messages could be decoded an alphabet must be evolved. After a time the mother, the elder sister, and brother David, assisted by the neighbors, decided that one rap meant *No*, two *I don't know*, three *Yes* and so on through a long alphabet and code, that could spell out intricate answers to questions. Neighbors and a host of visitors sat around with the Fox family both at night and by day and listened for messages from the spirits that the two little girls

KATE FOX, THE YOUNGER OF THE TWO FOX SISTERS,
WHO AT THE TENDER AGE OF SIX, DISCOVERED THAT
SHE COULD SNAP HER TOE BONES AND MAKE
SPIRITUALISTIC RAPPINGS

delivered. Thus from this Nazarean Hydesville came the wonder of the spiritualistic séance.

Fame having descended upon them, Margaret was taken to Rochester where she lived with her eldest sister, Mrs. Fish. This worthy matron of thirty-three had been abandoned by her dissolute husband and was obliged to give music lessons to make ends meet. Here the noises were heard again, clearly demonstrating that Margaret was psychic. Katherine, the younger, was taken to Auburn, and here also noises were heard in her vicinity, thus establishing her claim.

On November 14, 1849, in Corinthian Hall at Rochester the two girls gave a public demonstration. An investigating committee from the audience watched them carefully. The noises came as usual. There could be no doubt that they were media for spirits struggling to convey messages.

Naturally the news of these strange occurrences soon spread beyond central New York. From Stratford and Norwalk, Connecticut, Newark, New Jersey, Syracuse, New York, Cincinnati, Ohio, and scores of other places came reports of persons hearing spiritualistic raps. The minister at Stratford attributed them to the Devil, and in Syracuse a house fairly thundered with evil sounds. With such competition arising on all sides, it was evident that if the Fox Sisters were to keep their pristine reputation as psychics they must go on the road and demonstrate their gifts to the entire country.   So they were taken on tour by Mrs. Fish.

At Buffalo where a great crowd of the credulous and curious gathered on Feb. 17, 1851, a committee of physicians from the University was asked to investigate them.   Some of these doctors were assigned the task of watching the girls' faces.   The others placed the sisters in chairs with their feet resting on cushions on chairs in front of them so that the toes were elevated and the feet separated, a position that made the ligaments of the joints tense and gave no chance to make pressure with the foot or to displace or snap the foot-bones.   Result?   No raps.   Then the doctors placed the girls' hands on their knees and stood aside to see the result.   Again no raps.   But immediately their knees were not held or their feet were taken down from their tense positions on the chairs, raps were audible.   From the expressions on their faces it was evident that the making of these noises involved an effort even though the girls strove to conceal every indication of voluntary effort.   Also they seemed completely exhausted after the demon-stration.

Nothing to it!   The committee handed down a learned report that amounted to the following: "The raps are produced by snapping certain tendons at the knee and ankle joints.   The girls merely snap the tendon of the *posterior tibia* over one of the ankle bones.   If this is done near a table it causes a slight concussion.   Also when they lay their hands on the edge of a table they make raps by pressing againſt the ledge of the table the *os pisciforum*, a bone at the outer angle of that portion of the palm adjoining the wriſt. By slightly contracting the contiguous muscles the bone is displaced and a rap results. This trick of the hands can be done without a perceptible movement."

Having rendered their decision, the physicians ſtepped down from the ſtage. When they reached Boſton a committee of professors from Harvard inveſtigated them, and with equally pronounced reports on their fraudulent methods. However, audiences and the country at large were not to be taken in by professional long words. No amount of scientific explanation could convince these good people that the Fox Siſters were not media for messages from the spirit-world. What if they did make those raps by snapping their *os pisciforum;* indeed these very bones were spiritualiſtic media!

So the Fox Siſters went on their way, gathering adherents wherever they traveled. And their tours took them to all parts of the country, and brought them a tidy and comfortable living. Mrs. Fish ceased mourning for her departed Fish and became Mrs. Brown. She and Margaret gave demonſtrations in New York, firſt in a house at Eighth Avenue and 19th Street and later at Barnum's Hotel where crowds gathered to see them. At this time Margaret was only eleven and Katherine nine. They acquired enough through séances to take a house on 26th

Street, then a thoroughfare of fine residences. In the metropolis they were patronized by such leaders of the time as Fenimore Cooper, George Bancroft, the historian, William Cullen Bryant, Drs. Hawker, Frances, and Griswold, John Bigelow, Theodore Parker, Alice Carey, Bayard Taylor and others of like standing. Horace Greeley entertained the sisters in his house at Turtle Bay, now East 48th Street, and became their devoted follower. It was he who saw to it that the younger sister Katherine was given an education.

III

The success of the Fox Sisters soon brought to light a host of rival media who laid claim to their fame and fortune. Many strove to prove that their venture into the spirit world antedated the Rochester knocking. Countless numbers improved on their style. Spiritualistic mediums became highly specialized and highly diversified callings.

Among the earliest rivals were those two picturesque sisters: Tennie C. Claflin and Victoria Claflin Woodhull. Natives of Homer, Ohio, they claimed to have received spirit messages long before the Fox Sisters trembled in their sheets at Hydesville. At the tender age of fourteen, Victoria fell into the clutches of a gay, young rake by the name of Dr. Canning Woodhull, who treated her abominably. Finally she drifted out to California where, with the assistance of Anna Cogswell, the actress, she was

The Lady who was SO anxious to see Lola Montes.

LOLA MONTES, THE ACTRESS WITH THE VERMILION PAST
WAS PATRONIZED GENEROUSLY DESPITE HER REPUTATION

given a part in "New York By Gas Light," a roaring
comedy of the times. While playing here, she
claimed, she had a spirit summons from her sister
Tennie C., and she flew back to Ohio where, in
Cincinnati, she and her sister put on séances. In a
short time Victoria gained a wide reputation as a
spiritualistic healer, and the halt and the lame and
the sick came to her from all parts of the surrounding country. They lavished their gifts on her and
she waxed rich. In one year her income was said
to have reached $100,000 and up to 1869, she claimed
to have made $700,000.

Victoria Woodhull's reach for fame started early.
As a child she was aware of her guardian angel—a
glistening person in a Greek tunic. Verily "a
majestic guardian," for he later turned out to be
none other than Demosthenes himself. Now a
person who had Demosthenes for guardian angel,
Victoria argued, was intended by the Divine Wisdom
to become an orator. And it was as an orator for
many causes that she won fame and attracted a
following.

The spirit urged her to go to New York; in the
metropolis alone would she find a field worthy of her
talents. With Demosthenes guiding their every
move, she and her sister descended upon the city
and, to the astonishment of conservative business
men, invaded their field by opening a brokerage
office at 44 Broadway. In this case Demosthenes
assumed the human form of Commodore Vanderbilt,

their patron and angel. Having attained this foot-hold, Victoria began issuing learned opinions on finance, national affairs, scientific matters and the condition of the market. Powerful magnetic currents flowing around her, she said, supplied the information for these statements.

Would that some of our captains of industry and giants of finance were equally humble! Victoria attributed her information and right to speak on such profound and diverse subjects to an influence other than herself; these contemporary issuers of solemn *obiter dicta* are not so self-effacing. They really believe that they know something about the subjects on which they speak. Their opinions, save where they impinge on their immediate world, are as valueless, of course, as were the opinions of the Claflin girls.

Their later history is entwined with several movements of national interest. Victoria was elected President of the National Association of Spiritualists. She and her sister Tennie C. started, under the guidance of the great Demosthenes, a paper called *Woodhull and Claflin's Weekly* in which women's rights, among other things, were championed. And Victoria was founder of the picturesque Cosmo-Political Party which in 1872 nominated her for President of the United States. As an advocate of Free Love, she managed to split the feminist ranks. Her name also came into the Henry Ward Beecher-Tilton wrangle. [26]

Much lower in the scale of psychic cherubim was Henry C. Gordon. In 1835 Bridgeport, Connecticut, saw his birth, and invisible hands rocked his cradle. Even when young, mysterious noises gyrated about him and he would fall into trances. Like the boy in "Slovenly Peter," who so misbehaved himself at meals that he upset the table, young Henry would come to supper and immediately his spiritualistic powers would move the table until it came perilously near spilling the food. This must have been very distressing to his parents. As he entered adolescence he began hearing raps, and in Hartford in the Year of Grace 1851, his eyes were astonished to see the form of a beautiful young woman arise through the leaves of a table at which he was seated. Strange things, indeed, may happen in Hartford, but this occurrence deserves a place at the head of the list.

Mr. Gordon's claim to the remembrance of posterity lies in the fact that whereas the Fox Sisters were the first American female mediums, he was the first male to follow that calling. And follow it he did, through a stormy and bellicose career. For six years, from 1852 to 1858 he traveled about the country doing levitation, ringing spirit bells and performing the miracle of "full form materialization." He had "demonstration rooms" for a number of years in New York at Fourth Avenue near 27th Street, to which both the curious and the believing flocked.

But the way of the medium is hard. In 1873 a

female patron of his séances lured him into marriage.
Having accomplished this, she turned his "circle"
against him, and gave him poison to drink. However,
the stupor from the poison was only temporary, but
in the meantime she had managed to depart with his
furniture and his paraphernalia and saw to it that he
was bundled off to an insane asylum. Released three
months later, he came back, like Enoch Arden, to
find her posing as a widow and engaging the attentions
of an ardent lover. Gordon punched the lover's nose
and then started on the wife's, whereupon she had
him arrested. On another occasion in Philadelphia,
one of his patrons at a séance, dissatisfied with what
the spirits told him, started to wreak vengeance on
Mr. Gordon's anatomy. The police had to be called,
and the judge sentenced them both to sufficient time
in Moyamensing Prison to soothe their injured feelings.

Though Gordon advertised himself as "Medium
for Personification, Transformation and Materialization," and though he and his works have been im-
mortalized in a biography, we must bow before the
unrelenting fact that he belonged to the rowdy
charlatan class. And that—to cite him as a type—
is the sole excuse we have for including him in the
pages of this eminently respectable American Family
Album.

A third type is represented by the Davenport
Brothers, the play-boys, the vaudeville artists of the
Spiritualistic World.

So many of these mediums were frank imitators of the Fox Sisters that it is amusing to see just how the influence of those two girls worked. Thus the Claflins were quite emphatic, indeed, snobbish, in their claim to antedating the Daughters of Hydesville. From the obscurity of Dixboro, Washington County, Michigan, arose a bold soul who saw ghosts nine times and three angels as early as 1843. These angelic and ghostly visitations antedated the Foxes by three years. The Davenport Brothers, on the other hand, made no claim to priority; they were satisfied to elaborate the simple creed and ritual of the Hydesville demon-stalkers.

The senior Davenport was a painter by trade, resident in Buffalo. He had gone to lectures on Animal Magnetism, Phrenology and Mesmerism, he had drunk abundant water with the Hydrophants and gnawed raw carrots with the Vegetarians and munched rough bread with the Grahamites. He had seen and heard the Foxes. In fact, he had run the gamut of extraordinary religions, beliefs, sciences, and experiences; and he saw no reason why he should not capitalize it. So he went home and experimented with tipping tables. Sure enough, he could make tables move. Then he turned out the lights and by projecting his spiritualistic powers, he could make a violin float around the air like a bird, and strum its strings. A man with such capacities should not hide his light under a bushel. Mr. Davenport was highly gratified when the public began coming to his séances.

There were two sons in the family—Ira E., the elder, and William. Both followed in their father's spiritualistic footsteps. In trances William would speak a strange tongue. These two burst upon the credulous world as full-fledged mediums in 1855, at the respective ages of sixteen and fourteen—small statured, heavily-built, exuberant lads. A sister, Mrs. E. Davenport Colie, joined the troupe and together they began touring the country, giving demonstrations and constantly running up against the authorities because they lacked the license of show-men.

Their act, for it was a vaudeville act, added lustre to the fast-growing diversion of *diablerie*. It consisted of the following: The curtain rose revealing a cabinet about six feet high, six feet wide and two and one-half feet deep with three doors on the front that opened out toward the audience. In the upper part of the middle door was a diamond-shaped opening covered with a black cloth. The middle door could be bolted from the inside. On each side were two seats and holes on each side wall gave room for ropes to be passed through by which the boys were tied. A table stood between these seats, on which were various stringed instruments.

The boys appeared on the stage and entered the cabinet. There came a sound of ropes rattling. From the audience was summoned a committee of investigation who attested that the boys were tied so close to the side walls that they couldn't move, and their hands were closely bound together. Then a member of the committee bolted the middle door by reaching through the opening. The lights were lowered. A moment of suspense came, followed by a loud noise from the cabinet. This brought the audience to the edge of its seats. Everyone listened intently and peered on to the darkened stage. Gradually there drifted out over the audience the sound of a guitar, a violin, a zither, and the tinkle of bells. Now strumming furiously, now gently, the music kept up for a long time. The lights went on. The committee stepped on the stage. The boys were still bound as they had been. They were unleashed and stepped out before the footlights, amid gasps and applause.

Sometimes the committee did the tying, which certainly carried conviction, but usually, so the brothers attested, it was done by spirit power. Spirits, of course, strummed the instruments.

What actually happened was this: the ropes were so arranged that even if the most skeptical investigator did the tying the boys could slip out of the knots. They usually tied themselves in and the knots were made to appear solid.

They also could make the spirits play instruments without the aid of the cabinet. Here a confederate was usually employed, although even an innocent bystander could be dragged on to the stage and mystified. A table was placed on the stage to hold the instruments. One of the boys sat with his right side to the table, the other took a seat across, at the left. The investigator sat in front of them and placed a hand on the head of each. Then, reaching up, each boy put his hands close together on the investigator's arm. The audience saw them posed: both their hands were placed and their heads were held. Lights down. Without moving their heads or showing any movement of the body, each boy took from the investigator's arm the hand farthest from the audience, strummed an instrument, and then put his hand back just before the lights went on.

Both these stunts they did in New York at Cooper Union and at Union Hall on the Bowery. Committees of the clergy and eminent citizens sat on the stage and pretended to investigate them. James Gordon Bennett was so fascinated by these musical spirits that he invited them to his house for private séances. Of course, time and again they were proven to be frauds, but there was always enough of the audience which believed them. This is the phase of mob psychology on which all conjurers depend for their support and reputation. Barnum, of course, was on to their trick in a minute. "Well, boys," he said, "you are greater humbugs than I am. You may take my hat!"

Although the Davenport Brothers traveled the Atlantic coastal towns and cities, the business was too productive for the family to part with. So the western towns were assigned to the sister, Mrs. E. Davenport Colie, who was assisted by a Mrs. M. A. C. Lamb in the old cabinet trick. Meantime Papa

TABLE-TIPPING AND ALL FORMS OF SPIRITUALISTIC SEANCE ENGROSSED THE CREDULOUS OF THE MIDDLE PAST CENTURY

From Yankee Notions

Davenport toured with the boys and gave lectures on spiritualism.

IV

By no means do the three kinds of mediums cited in the previous section represent all types that flourished, gulled the public and took their money in those years.

As Spiritualism developed it evolved six distinct types of mediums, viz: Rapping, Tipping, Speaking, Singing, Writing, and Impressible, *i.e.*, mediums whom the spirits impressed to think as they, the spirits, wished. The number of people who claimed to be either one or another of these was amazing. In 1852 it was estimated that there were over two thousand writing mediums in the United States. In that year Boston—the hub of Spiritualism—held a convention of Rappers, and quite a noisy convention it must have been. Over a million followers in this country were the figures the *Spiritualist* gave. In New York City alone it is said that fully forty thousand people, many of them otherwise intelligent specimens of humanity, solemnly believed in messages sent by spirit rapping. One New York cabinet-maker did a tidy trade in constructing special rapping tables, with concealed machinery for producing the raps for those who, lacking the agility of the Fox Sisters, couldn't snap their *ossa pisciforums*. At one time the medium business proved so profitable that the *New York Telegraph* carried an advertisement offering work to those endowed with psychic power and, of course, practically all newspapers printed advertisements of séances, at which the admission ranged from 25c to $2.

Had this credulity been limited to the lower classes, it would have caused no surprise, but men and women in the highest walks of life gathered at séances night after night in a state of spiritual elevation awaiting messages from the departed.

Robert Hare, professor of chemistry in William and Mary College, and a man of high standing in his line, strove to prove the reality of spiritualistic communication by science. He wrote a learned book on the subject, in which his theories are demonstrated by charts. Robert Dale Owen, who helped his father and Fanny Wright found the Fourier Colony at New Harmony, Indiana, and was an active leader in the feminist cause and in abolition, wrote two dreary books on the subject of Spiritualism. Robert S. Shaw, one of the prominent Boston Shaws, proclaimed himself to be the especially adopted medium of Daniel Webster.

Harriet Beecher Stowe, certainly a favorite among the female geniuses of the time, took to Spiritualism as a duck to water after she lost her second son by drowning. She went about from séance to séance frantically listening for messages from the boy, and she insisted on her husband's—who didn't believe a word of them—being dragged to these performances. On one occasion the poor dear's faith wavered. She doubted if it was her son Henry who twanged the guitar. Perhaps it was her husband's first wife, Harriet! She counseled him to keep a guitar in his bedroom so that he might have it handy for her spirit when she wanted to communicate with him!

The experiences of Judge Edmonds, Dr. Dexter, and Governor Tallmage were even more incredible. John W. Edmonds was a New York State judge of unquestioned repute, who was initiated into Spiritualism by rapping, then took to consulting clairvoyants and for three years studied Spiritualism in all its phases until he was thoroughly convinced of its verity and worth. Dr. Dexter was converted at a séance in 1851 where he claimed he heard an illiterate mechanic speak Latin, Greek, and Chaldaic—this man was a speaking medium. Governor N. P. Tallmage of Wisconsin was also an easy convert. These three men kept careful notes of their experiences and corresponded constantly on them. Their letters are ludicrously like the letters of small boys and other radio fans today who correspond on the stations they are able to reach. Dr. Dexter would solemnly report that he "got" Swedenborg and Francis Bacon, whereupon Tallmage would counter with Tom Paine, Calvin, and John C. Calhoun, and Edmonds would finally take the trick with Henry Clay and Elias Hicks, the Quaker who caused the modernist split in the Society of Friends.

These three men wrote books together on Spiritualism, books that are still standard for believers in occult religion. But more than once they had their legs pulled. The Ewer case was a notable example.

John F. Ewer, editor of a California magazine called *The Pioneer*, published an article of his own composition entitled "The Eventful Nights of August 20 and 21, 1854" in which he claimed that he had had spiritualistic communication with a John J. Lane. Ewer saw that this article came into the hands of Judge Edmonds and the Judge gave it his mediumistic *imprimatur* in the *Sacred Circle*, a Spiritualistic magazine he was editing at the time. Then Ewer exposed the whole hoax in the New York *Herald*, much to the discomfort of the Judge and his followers, and the delight of the public.

From such social and intellectual heights belief in Spiritualism percolated downward through all classes and orders of intelligence. Ministers who felt it luring their congregations away thundered against it as the "infidelity of the times." The press ridiculed it in every issue. Nevertheless it captivated public imagination to an amazing extent, and with good reason. The spirit of the age was materialistic, so its apologists said: it needed religion: Spiritualism was created to satisfy this need. Well, all ages are materialistic in the minds of those who oppose them. Andrew Jackson Davis, one of the high priests of the new sect, attributed its rise to the fact that the age was one of unparalleled mental activity.

The flood of books, tracts and letters that early Spiritualism produced and the publicity it was accorded make one of the strangest phenomena in American history.

It supported its own newspapers and magazines. There was Edmonds's *Sacred Circle: The Spiritual Telegraph* had a large subscription list: *The Anthropologist* was published in Milwaukee to further the interests of Mesmerism: *The Banner of Light*, a weekly, was read by a huge following: *The New England Spiritualist* and *Tiffany's Monthly*, also found support. In these journals all manner of spiritualistic experience and discussion filled the pages, ranging from spirit messages of intriguing interest to grave arguments on the toe bones of the Fox Sisters.

It would require many more pages than are available here to set down all the books and articles that were written under the guidance of the spirits in those years. Harriet Beecher Stowe claimed that some of her literary output was directly traceable to psychic influence. The Rev. C. Hammond, a medium of twenty-two years' standing and author of two books, wrote a fascinating series of experiences around Tom Paine in Heaven in which Tom is converted from his infidel ways, and pals around the celestial courts with such worthies as Emanuel Swedenborg, Benjamin Franklin, and William Penn.

Fed on such pabulum, the credulous flocked to séances day and night. People who had lost dear ones rushed from table to table frantically hoping for messages. Business men submitted their problems. Lovers their troubles. Married people their spats. Politicians their platforms. Families and businesses were neglected and even runs on banks were started by spiritualistic prophecy.

Out of this welter of strange experiences were evolved the tenets of the Spiritualist religion. The belief amounted to this: that on death the spirit enters into a state of progress in a world of seven spheres, each sphere of which is comprised of seven circles. In this material world where we reside there are likewise spheres and circles. At death a soul goes to that sphere of the Spirit World which corresponds to the one he has attained in this life.

The Spirit World, therefore, is a congenial place filled with all sorts of spirits—good, bad, indifferent, superior and inconsequential, meagre and rich— all advancing, learning, progressing through the various concentric rings until they attain the seventh. There they pause. Beyond the Seventh Circle the progress of the spirit is not known. Through this material world of ours the disembodied spirits wander at will. Consequently the believer can communicate not only with friends and relatives whom he knew, but with any spirit he chooses. Hence the experiences of Judge Edmonds and others with great religious and political leaders who were deceased. On the other hand, some spirits, being not far advanced, will lie to, abuse, and trifle with those of this world.

Communication with spirits was possible only through a medium to whom the spirits took a fancy. The messages were delivered sometimes in rapping, sometimes by the tipping of the table and sometimes in writing. Often this writing was illiterate, illegible and wholly undecipherable, but the medium, under the guidance of the spirits, could readily interpret it.

This body of beliefs soon became organized. "Circles" were formed. To form a circle, Andrew Jackson Davis said, the believers must have "a child-like simple-heartedness, a manly, open, and free mindedness, combined with an honest love for truth." They should not meet more than once a week, the séances should be accompanied by music, held in a private room free from outside noises and disturbances, and those who attend the services should dress simply for the occasion. This was to be a thoroughly democratic and catholic religion.

New York City became a bedlam of spiritualists. One writer describes it vividly: "Could New York be unroofed, either in the day or at night, a spectacle of Spirit Rapping would be exhibited which would astound the public by the magnitude of its extent and almost ceaseless continuance. From morning till noon, from noon till night, and from night until morning again, in parlors where flashing mirrors reflect rosewood and velvet and silver and gold; in humble rooms where the floors and walls are bare, the tables are placed, and around them men and women with their hands spread out, and eyes fixed as if on vacancy, are seated, waiting for communications from the Spirit World."

But it had its darker side. An investigator of the mediums of New York calculated that of the nineteen "she-prophets" practising in that city in 1858, selected out of several score, each was visited at the rate of a dozen customers a day; that of these visitors probably two-thirds placed implicit confidence in what they heard and paid for. Many of the clients were ignorant servant girls, unfortunate girls of the town, and uneducated and over-grown boys, as well as respectable men and women. Most of the sorceresses were prostitutes or had been prostitutes. Their darkened rooms were, in reality, places of assignation and stations for the white slave traffic of the times. Some of the mediums were professed abortionists.

Facilis descensus Averno!

Evil reports soon began to spread regarding the effects of Spiritualism. Wardens of insane asylums and physicians were alarmed by the numbers of people whose reason was unhinged by these séances. In 1852 alone no less than ninety patients were admitted to asylums in various parts of the country for these reasons, and it was estimated that over a period of five years, fully five hundred persons had

gone mad or committed suicide, due to attending
séances and reading books on Spiritualism.

V

It may seem incredible that from the mischievous
snapping of their toe bones and their childish fibs
two obscure country girls could start on its way a
body of strange belief that was destined to engulf a
nation and send its ripples to England and the Continent. And yet they—the Fox Sisters—were the
progenitors of this vast movement. So long as they
practiced at their séances, they remained the high-
priestesses of the religion, but the time came when it
got beyond them and when both of them renounced
it altogether. In the inevitable contest between
Romance and Spiritualism, Romance won. The
death blow to Spiritualism was dealt by a love affair.
The story is as tender a page of sentiment as one
could wish.

Among the men who fired the imagination of these
times was Elisha Kent Kane, Arctic explorer, who
had gone to the relief of Sir John Franklin and who
headed a famous expedition to Grinnell Land in 1853.
A native of Philadelphia, his reputation was jealously
held by all citizens of that city.

In the autumn of 1852 Mrs. Fox and Margaret
happened to be at a hotel in Philadelphia for a course
of Spiritual Manifestations. They were the object
of much patronage. One day Dr. Kane entered their
parlor for a sitting. He had never seen Margaret

Fox, and he was astonished to find her a girl of twelve who, at the moment he entered, happened to be deep in her study of French. Her extreme youth and innocence arrested him. "This is no life for you, my child," he said, "you ought to go to school." From that moment an intimacy sprang up between them, an intimacy which eventually flowered into full-blown romance. Kane became a daily visitor. He took her driving. He was seen walking constantly with her. He showered gifts on her. Their names soon were coupled by the gossips of the city, although it could have meant nothing since she was twelve and he thirty-two.

At the time he was preparing for his second expedition to the Arctic and amid all the exacting preparations he found time to write her constantly. When she went to Washington he followed there and took a room in the same boarding-house; when she settled in New York and the Foxes took the house on 26th Street, he managed to slip over to see her. There was a third-storey room that they reserved for their meetings. Here they would sit when she was not busy with clients. And this gallant young explorer used to champ at the bit when their tête-à-tête was interrupted by people who came for sittings. Margaret would rush down, snap her bones, deliver the messages, and rush upstairs again. No, it was no life for a child.

Finally, he prevailed on her to go to school and he placed her in charge of his sister, Mrs. Leiper.

Margaret went to Crookville School, which is near Ridley Park, eighteen miles from Philadelphia. While she was here a constant stream of letters and presents passed between them—playful letters from an older man to a child. Among the many touching sentiments, he counseled her to remember, "as a sort of dream, that Dr. Kane of the Arctic Seas, loved Maggie Fox of the Spirit Rappings." To the little sister Katherine, then in school in New York and under Horace Greeley's eye, he wrote adorable letters addressing them to his "Incomprehensible Kate." Mrs. Fox beamed upon the growing friendliness of the great man, but her elder daughter, the erstwhile Mrs. Fish, opposed Kane strenuously since his insistence on Margaret's education and his persuading her to give up Spiritualism were threatening the income that the séances produced.

Gradually these two strange companions came nearer the day of their separation: Kane's expedition was ready. He must sail very soon. He prevails on Margaret to sit for her portrait, and when it is finished, the picture is safely stowed away in his gear for the expedition. It was this painting of Margaret Fox which Kane carried strapped to his back through his entire wanderings in the Arctic. Nor did he permit it out of his sight night or day. Such was the devotion he offered this girl who intrigued him—this "strange mixture of child and woman, of simplicity and cunning, of passionate impulse and extreme self-control."

On his return he was acclaimed by the nation. He had become a public figure. He was hedged about with all manner of restrictions and ceremonies. His family and many of his friends, knowing of his attachment to Margaret Fox, did everything in their power to break it up and to prevent his seeing her. Ann Leah Brown enthusiastically aided them. Nevertheless he managed to overcome their guard and the romance started once more. They had their lovers' quarrels, their separations and reconciliations, but the affection of the girl for him and his for her cannot be doubted. He was constantly with her and she constantly in his mind. The newspapers printed rumors of their impending marriage. Denials and affirmations came fast and thick.

Due to his arduous work in the Arctic, Kane's health began to fail. His doctor ordered him to England for a rest, thence he was to go to Havana. Before he left, according to Margaret Fox's statement, she and he stood together in the presence of her mother, a servant and a young woman who was calling at the time, and plighted their troth in a Quaker marriage ceremony. This ceremony was undertaken at the suggestion and express wish of Dr. Kane. His letters to her thereafter were addressed to his "wife." They planned to meet in Havana.

After a short stay in England, where he was again acclaimed, Kane went to Havana to await her, but a few days before Margaret and her mother were to sail, he died. The date was the sixteenth of February, 1857. He was aged thirty-seven. Margaret at the time was seventeen.

His death caused a profound change in the girl. She put on mourning and wore it for the subsequent fourteen years. Everyone seemed to accept her story of the marriage; she signed herself with Kane's name and was addressed by all as Mrs. Kane. Following his urgent request, she gave up Spiritualism and, a year after his death, was converted to Roman Catholicism, being baptized in old St. Peter's Church in Barclay Street.

In his will Dr. Kane left a trust for Margaret, putting it not in her name but in the name of his brother, with instructions for him to pay it to her. So bitter was the family feeling against her that the brother refused to pay over the money, although he did allow her interest from it for a time. Knowing that she possessed letters and many other evidences of his famous brother's attachment, he offered to pay over the trust if she would surrender the letters. This she refused to do, and the case was eventually thrashed out in the Philadelphia courts. To establish her claim, Margaret permitted the whole story and the letters to be published in a book called "The Love Life of Dr. Kane," a volume that appeared in 1865 and caused a furore. It is one of the rare and beautiful curiosities of the literature of American romance.

VI

After the Civil War, the fortunes of the Fox Sisters were cast in diverse lines.

Margaret's good resolution to eschew Spiritualism soon encountered the stern reality of bread and butter and she went back to it again. Her oldest sister Ann Leah Brown, who directed the séances, came up in the world and was espoused to Mr. Underhill, a prosperous insurance broker, but she still gave séances and as late as 1888 stated her belief in them by writing a book, "The Missing Link of Spiritualism." Katherine married a Mr. Jencken and bore him two healthy sons, the first of whom, "Ferdie," at the tender age of six months demonstrated psychic powers, although he never manifested them in later life.

Obliged to continue with the séances, Margaret accepted a position in Philadelphia with Henry Seybert, who planned to found a Spiritual Mansion. She was hired, at a satisfactory honorarium, to be high priestess. This was in 1870, after she had left off her mourning for Elisha Kane. In this esoteric job she managed to evoke spirits that hitherto had been silent. Doubtless her experience in being converted to Catholicism furnished her with new spirit fields to wander in. She became on speaking terms with saints and church fathers, and even received communications from St. Paul, St. Peter, Elijah, and the angel Gabriel!

When Seybert died he left a fund to found a chair at the University of Pennsylvania and stipulated that part of it should be expended for psychic research. This gave birth to the Seybert Commission which functioned for a time in Philadelphia. At the head was the eminent Shakespearian scholar, Dr. Horace Howard Furness. His first subject of investigation was Margaret Fox (whom by the way, he entertained at his house and always addressed as "Mrs. Kane"). The report of the committee, delivered in November 1884, pronounced her to be unquestionably a fraud.

Thereafter both Margaret and Katherine dropped out of sight for a time. Both of them took to drinking heavily and Katherine managed to incur the displeasure of the New York Society for the Prevention of Cruelty to Children.

The next we hear of them, Margaret is returning from England. Scarcely had she arrived when she announced in the press that she was about to expose Spiritualism. This threat from its very progenitor struck terror into the hearts of believers. Shortly afterward Katherine also appeared from England and set about to aid Margaret in her revelations. On October 21, 1888, in the Academy of Music at New York, Margaret Fox Kane exposed all her tricks. An investigating committee was on hand to check her up and she made no effort to deceive them—she took off her shoes and showed how the raps were produced.

In the next few weeks the whole sordid story was revealed.

The original noises that their mother had heard in the little house in Hydesville were begun as a lark by these two children. They each tied an apple to a string and after everyone was in bed, they would bounce them on the floor. When their mother came to investigate the noises, they pulled the apples into the sheets and looked innocent. Soon Katherine, the younger, discovered that she could simulate these noises by snapping her toe bones. Margaret could do it too. It was lots of fun. They even let into the secret their little niece, Mrs. Fish's daughter, who lived with them.

Being a superstitious person, and remembering the legends about the house, Mrs. Fox was easily fooled by the children, and it became their own secret game they played on her. When she asked questions of the spirits, they would answer. By and by the neighbors heard of it and they too were mystified. Soon the oldest sister, Anne Leah Fish, got wind of the noises and came down to investigate them. By this time the girls had gotten proficient in rapping.

Now Ann Leah was thirty-three. She had been deserted by a drunken husband whose association had lowered her scruples considerably. When she came to Hydesville, saw the mystification of the neighbors and heard the raps, she was not above taking advantage of the situation. The first thing

she did was to talk to the children in private and find
out how the noises were made. Then she insisted on
their being allowed to live with her in Rochester.
She herself began to develop mediumistic powers,
although she was not able to make such distinct
raps with her toes because her bones, being older, had
set. Meantime she impressed on the children the
idea that they had supernatural powers and were
founders of a new religion. With the aid of her
brother David, she worked out the Rapping Code
which was taught the two girls and which became the
basis for all mediumistic communications.

When they were eleven and nine respectively
Mrs. Fish displayed them in Corinthian Hall in
Rochester in their first big public demonstration and
she took care to dress them in long gowns lest the
investigating committee should see the children's toes
wriggle. She also worked out a tariff of prices for
séances.

From this point on, the story is as we have told it.
These two poor little girls were dragged about the
country by their ignorant mother and scheming elder
sister, forced to go through séances, forced to snap
and rap when they wanted to play, forced to work so
that the money would keep coming in. Even though
they knew that they were the sources of the noises,
even though they could well remember the larks that
started them, so fiendishly had their minds been
warped that not for a moment did it occur to them
to reveal their secret. They were carried away by

the awe in which they were held.   Only when a man
of such calibre as Elisha Kent Kane opened Margaret's eyes to the folly and evil of her life did the
children begin to have a glimmer of what they were
doing.   Nor were they aware of the extent to which
their naughty, hoyden tricks had swept the country.

Here was a vast religion built up on the slim and
ridiculous fabric of two little girls thumping apples
on a bedroom floor!

Considering how much trouble Eve is supposed to
have caused with an apple and what these two Fox
Sisters, in their time, managed to do with that particular fruit, one is almost tempted to believe that
apples should be kept out of the hands of women.

CHAPTER IX
LA BELLE REBELLE

THE VIRGIN SPY, BELLE BOYD, CONFOUNDS HER ENEMIES IN WAR AND LOVE AND BECOMES THE JEANNE D'ARC OF CONFEDERATE MAIDENS, WHILST STILL REMAINING A PRETTY LITTLE EXAGGERATOR

I

THE pursuit of the female prevaricator, however ungallant an occupation it may appear, turns up some amusing episodes and throws a revealing light on character. In a previous chapter, "The Damosel of the Slate Pencil," we considered a religious prevaricator and the sad results her prodigious falsehoods brought to pass. In this final study we consider prevarication under arms, under stress of war, a circumstance that is apt to make small events cast huge and grotesque shadows.

Since it concerns the Confederate side of the Civil War and a Confederate girl, let us first make the gesture that is customary when any Northerner speaks of Southern women—

These women, reared in the legendary luxury and ease of Southern environments, developed a stiff, hard fibre under the exactions of a cruel warfare, and yet appeared to lose none of those alluring qualities that made them desirable among the women of the world.

Thanks to the indulgence of sentimental America,

this pleasant legend of idling, coquetry, and docile helplessness the Southern woman will always boast. And with it will go her background: the equally legendary and picturesque glamour of plantation life, that "mellow, bland, and sunny luxuriance of her old-time society," as John Pendleton Kennedy describes it in "Swallow Barn"—"its good fellowship, its hearty and constitutional companionableness, the thriftless gaiety of the people, their dogged but amiable invincibility of opinion, and that overflowing hospitality that knows no ebb."

Those ante-bellum days were America's Golden Age. No section of the country, save perhaps Monterey in its isolation of the early Spanish settlements, can point back to so romantic and idyllic an era. In no phase of our national evolution did women attain quite the place they are said to have won in the South before the Civil War.

Amorous and innocent philanderers alike, they knew their men and exacted from them the satisfaction of their whims. And once they were thrown into the gross realities of war, they turned their attractions to good account. Skirmishes of restless eyes, ensnaring turbulence of lips, flirtatious forays and laughing retreats, ambuscades of virginal seduction—such wiles practised by these women, accustomed to reduce their men to willing servitors, more than once proved overwhelming when directed at officers and men from the North. That some of them also proved capable of incredible brutality to

BELLE BOYD, THE CONFEDERATE SPY, IN HER LATER
YEARS AS AN ACTRESS
From the Albert Davis collection

their foes is an established fact which, fortunately, need not be expatiated upon here.

Not the least of these wily daughters of the Confederacy was Belle Boyd, famous as a spy, and remarkable for serving her cause with success and for managing, under difficult circumstances, to maintain the maidenly reputation of Young America in espionage.

On the Continent the professional woman spy is commonplace. Her name creeps into the records of all wars and into the *dossiers* of all Bureaux of Intelligence. She wears both her profession and her flag on her sleeve; she exercises the palpable lure of the *demi-monde*. But the amateur spy is an *espion* of a different color. The more youthful she is, the more effective her methods. Her virginity is disarming. With the innocence of the dove she wields the rapier of devilish evasion, which is ever the weapon of the untouched.

It is not to be expected that a nation founded on Puritanism should stoop to employ, even in the exacting exigencies of war, the obvious and practising prostitute. For that reason the annals of American wars do not afford the colorful and mysterious interludes that European wars purvey to fiction writers. Our great feats of female espionage have been accomplished by rank amateurs, without sacrifice of virtue. The golden-haired lass whom Washington and his generals dandled on their knee and told military bedtime stories; Pauline Cushman, the actress, who hunted Southern sympathizers and spies in Louisville and confounded the plans of General Rosecrans; Emma Edmonds, whose disguises carried her safely past the Confederate lines; the three Cuban girls, Lola, Eugenia and Panchito Sanchez, who made names for themselves on Southern fronts; and "La Belle Rebelle," Belle Boyd—such are the young women to wear the unsullied robes of our espionage.

III

Scarcely had Belle Boyd turned seventeen, scarcely had she passed her final year at Mount Washington Female College in Baltimore, and survived the round of parties marking her debut in Washington, than the peace of the Shenandoah Valley was broken by the tramp of Northern forces under General Patterson, a veteran of the War of 1812 and of the Mexican War. She was at home, at Martinsburg, Virginia, when the blue army began drifting down the valley to meet the Confederate divisions that guarded the western approaches to Richmond. It was one of the first invading movements of the war, when 1861 was still young.

Martinsburg had had no contact with wars or rumors of wars since those far-off post-Revolutionary days when the three lame-duck Revolutionary generals, Horatio Gates, Adam Stephen, and Charles Lee, used to sit around the tavern and, over their grog, refight the days when one was cashiered for insub-

AMONG THE NORTHERN FEMALE SPIES, PAULINE
CUSHMAN, THE ACTRESS, WON AN ENVIABLE NAME
FOR HERSELF
From the Albert Davis collection

ordination and another for being disastrously drunk before battle. This little town, established in 1778, slept on for many years as a country village until the Baltimore and Ohio Railroad laid its tracks down the valley and built its round houses and repair shops there. In the calculations of military leaders this center of transportation assumed great value. Martinsburg was an objective worth holding.

By the middle of June, 1861, General Joseph E. Johnston's Confederate Army of the Shenandoah had occupied Harper's Ferry, burned the railroad bridge there and withdrawn to Winchester. General Patterson was advancing from Pennsylvania through Maryland with Virginia for his objective. General McClellan was also on his way through Western Virginia headed for the valley. On the other side, advancing to meet them and anticipate their activities, Stonewall Jackson had sent a brigade to the neighborhood of Martinsburg to aid Stewart's cavalry which was busy destroying the Baltimore and Ohio stock and repair shops. The opening of July saw Jackson's pickets withdraw, allowing Patterson's column of 20,000 men to stream into the town.

Being prominently located, the Boyd house was soon visited by a band of Union soldiers who demanded that the Northern flag be displayed. Besides, officers had their eye on it for headquarters. The women of the household, headed by Belle Boyd's mother, met the invaders and refused their demands. If any flag was to be flown it would be the Confed-

erate flag. The argument waxed hot. One of the
soldiers rudely pushed past Mrs. Boyd. From the
other side appeared a young girl—a slight, lithe
figure in cool pink muslins, with blond braided hair—
who pulled a revolver from her dress and shot him.

She was immediately seized and taken to headquarters. The soldier was carried to the hospital,
where he died a few hours later. Serious charges
were preferred against her.

What conversation passed between Belle and the
commanding officer, what wiles she practised on him,
neither she nor local history records, but in her first
round this seventeen-year-old Rebel appears to have
finished with all points won. The commander was
gallant. He agreed that she had done the proper
thing under very trying provocation. And to assure
her of his sincerity, he presented her with a neat
little revolver that she might use when other like
circumstances arose. So far this was a gentleman's
war!

Having thus had coals of fire heaped on their
heads, the Boyds readily assented when the commander's staff came to take over their house for
headquarters. They were billeted on the first floor,
choosing the parlor for their council room. And the
parlor was directly below Belle's bedroom. A quixotic Nature had seen to it (as she always must in spy
stories) that the floor boards in Belle's bedroom
closet furnished a generous knothole through which
came up, to the young miss sprawled on the floor

with her ear glued to the hole, all the projections
and plans for military activities.

And the activities thereabout soon commenced to
be lively indeed.

The North was demanding that the South be
given an overwhelming blow and the war ended.
"On to Richmond!" was the cry. General Mc-
Dowell planned to strike Beauregard at Manassas
Junction. At the same time Union forces under
Patterson in the Shenandoah Valley would prevent
General Joseph E. Johnston, who was there, from
joining Beauregard. This was McDowell's scheme,
offered to placate the demands from the North. It
was adopted.

McDowell pressed forward. The Confederates
withdrew to Bull Run and Beauregard wired President Davis at Richmond to send Johnston's troops to
his support. By an overnight march and by Patterson stupidly maneuvering in the wrong direction so
that an opening was given him, Johnston escaped a
trap and joined Beauregard. At the opening attack
the Confederates fled, all save the brigade of General
Thomas J. Jackson, which stood there "like a stone
wall." Beauregard and Johnston rallied their men
and the tide of battle began to turn. Luck swung
from one side to the other. At a crucial moment the
remaining troops of the Army of the Shenandoah
that had followed Johnston came into action. Panic
seized the Union forces. Their lines began to break.
Completely demoralized, the rout started, each man

for himself—and some of them never stopped running until they reached the Long Bridge into Washington, thirty-four miles away.

Bull Run was a complete and disastrous Union defeat, a terrible ending to the scheme that was to end the war at one blow.

To the east, secure behind entrenched Confederate lines, Richmond rejoiced over the victory that spelled freedom to them. Here was Davis issuing his rebellious mandates as commander-in-chief. The Rebels had not yet seen the *generalissimo* timber in Robert E. Lee.

While these solemn and serious events had been happening Belle Boyd, if we can take her word for it, had been doing her bit. Her ear was glued to that knothole every time two or three officers gathered together in the room below. As regularly as they held conferences did Belle listen to their plans and immediately sent messengers, protected by stolen passes, to the Confederate pickets with her reports. When she wasn't busy at that, the little minx used to amuse herself stealing their revolvers and sabres, and shipping them across the lines. Time and again she was almost caught, and invariably she managed to flirt her way out of the dilemma. The girl's technique with officers was uncanny. Her youth, her innocence, completely disarmed them.

From her accounts of these activities it must not be inferred that she was a figure in shining armor. Her self-elected role, valuable as it may have been, could boast no such brilliance. It was obscure and infinitesimal. Amid the swirling masses of troops and their gear she was scarcely to be seen. Her part in the valley warfare was like a mouse darting across the floor of a theatre lobby or a station waiting-room— darting, causing a minor panic among women, and disappearing again. And how she could cause a panic is easily to be seen.

On one occasion she went to Winchester under passes from the local Union provost marshal, and while there was slipped some letters, one of which was for Stonewall Jackson. She took a carriage, and encountering a Union officer on the way, offered him a lift. The letter to Jackson she secreted about her person, the others she asked the officer to hold. When they were stopped at the Union lines the sentry found the incriminating letters on the officer, but in the confusion Belle managed to slip away. Jackson received the letter.

III

Since the defeat at Bull Run the previous July there had been activity along other fronts, but very little to disturb the peace of the Shenandoah Valley. Fort Donelson on the Cumberland had fallen, the Battle of Shiloh had given the North an encouraging command of Tennessee, and New Orleans had capitulated. In the Shenandoah there was a small army under command of General Banks. Fremont headed the Mountain Department in Western Virginia. In the wind was a scheme whereby these armies should converge and capture Stonewall Jackson, thereby releasing these Northern forces which could then march toward Richmond.

However, early in May, Jackson anticipated their schemes. He had a force of only 20,000 men, as against the combined forces of Generals Banks, Shields, Fremont, and McDowell which outnumbered him two to one. With plans worked out under General Lee's supervision, Jackson began a series of brilliant raids up the Shenandoah. At Front Royal he defeated a force of Federal troops under Banks, who withdrew. Jackson pursued him to Winchester. The Northern withdrawal soon assumed the proportions of a rout. At Winchester, Jackson struck at Banks again, defeated him and drove him across the Potomac. Terror struck the Northern forces. Washington stood aghast. This well-laid scheme to capture Jackson had been turned into a defeat. Even the safety of the capital itself was threatened.

It was in this campaign against Banks that Belle Boyd performed her greatest exploits. The correspondent of the *Philadelphia North American and United States Gazette* (31 May 1862) attributes the Northern retreat to her activities.

"At the hotel in Front Royal, on the night of the eighteenth, your correspondent saw an accomplished prostitute, who has figured largely in the Rebel cause, and having seen her but a short time previous at Martinsburg, her presence at Front Royal at a time

WAR IN THE SHENANDOAH VALLEY—FRONT ROYAL, MANASSAS GAP RAILROAD—BLUE RIDGE MOUNTAINS IN THE DISTANCE—THE FEDERAL ARMY ENTERING THE TOWN.—Sketched by our Special Artist, Edwin Forbes.—See Page 322.

FRONT ROYAL, IN THE SHENANDOAH VALLEY, THE SCENE OF MUCH CIVIL WAR FIGHTING AND OF BELLE BOYD'S
ACTIVITIES AS A SPY

when the Rebels were surrounding it, aroused sus-
picions that she meant mischief. She was pointed
out to the military commanders there, and her arrest
advised. It is now known that she was the bearer
of an extensive correspondence between the Rebels
inside and outside our lines. I have the following
statement from an officer who participated in the
battle at Front Royal: 'After you left Front Royal,
Belle Boyd made a trip to Winchester in company
with a cavalry officer. While there she was arrested
by the military authorities, but with her usual
adroitness and assumed innocence, she got clear of
any charge of treachery, and returned to Front Royal
again. An hour previous to the attack on Kenly,
Belle went out on a rise of ground south of the town,
and was seen to wave her handkerchief toward the
point from which the centre of the attack was made.'

"Your correspondent cannot vouch for the strict
accuracy of all of the foregoing, but undeniable proof
exists of her treason. Belle now reposes on her laurels
in the Confederate camp."

The correspondent wisely left himself a way of
escape in that last paragraph. The handkerchief
episode is legendary, but the Confederate reports
tell more.

She was said to have given out invitations to
General Banks and his officers for a ball to be held
several days later. Then she took a fleet horse, and
rode to Stonewall Jackson. Together they fixed the
night of the ball so that it should coincide with

Jackson's arrival. Belle then rode back, completing
120 miles in all. During the ball, she "played the
part of Delilah" to General Banks, lavished all her
charms upon him and covered him with a large and
elegant Confederate flag. Jackson attacked, and won
the day.

Elwell's Brigade was near Fort Royal at the time,
and according to a diary kept by one of his staff, she
rode up at great speed to officers sent out by Jackson
to meet her, saluted them in precise military fashion,
and reported that if they hurried they could trap a
whole Yankee regiment. Her costume for this ride
—the little ninny!—was a bright blue gown and a
fancy white apron! It was for this information that
Stonewall Jackson is said to have written her, "I
thank you for myself and for the army, for the
immense service you have rendered your country
today."

Fortunately for the peace of mind of those in
Washington, Jackson found that he stood in danger
of a flanking movement and began to retreat. Fremont, McDowell, and Shields, who naturally should
have pursued him, failed to take advantage of their
opportunities. Jackson escaped after fighting two
more battles. Thus in one month in the Shenandoah
Valley Stonewall Jackson managed, by rapid marches
and quick blows with only 20,000 men, to prevent
40,000 Union troops joining the Northern forces
before Richmond. In these sallies he took vast spoils,

made many prisoners and kept Washington in a constant turmoil of terror.

News of Belle Boyd's activities soon filtered through both lines. To the South she became a vague, legendary heroine, a spotless Jeanne D'Arc; to the Northern camp, anathema. And yet this young lady was a very palpable *ingenue*. Her fearless way of constantly returning home to Martinsburg after a foray of espionage confounded the officers in command there. Finally the reports of her drifted up to the powers in Washington. That a young girl could so easily confuse and twist the young gentlemen in command was more than the authorities could tolerate. This had ceased being a gentleman's war. Intelligence officers grew deadly in earnest. They ordered a trap to be set for Belle and when, with a blithesome air she walked straight into it, she was placed under arrest. On July 30, 1862, Brigadier General Julius White reports her arrest at Winchester to C. P. Walcott, Assistant Secretary of War. What shall we do with her? The reply read, "to come immediately to Washington with Miss Boyd, in close custody."

On searching her she says they found a neat little revolver, loaded and ready for service—the same that had been presented to her by the Union commander on the occasion of her first killing a Union soldier. This was dispatched, so she tells, to Washington and put in a glass case in the War Department where the populace came to gaze upon the lethal weapon used by this deadly Confederate minor.

From these reports one would gather that Belle was really a terrible young woman. Yet never is she said to have acted other than well-born. Although not beautiful, she was lithe and pleasing.

According to her story, General White took his orders seriously—450 cavalrymen escorted her carriage from camp, 450 men at arms to watch over one young slip of a girl in a muslin dress, lest she escape! Close custody indeed! Thus, heavily escorted, she entered Washington where, following the orders of the Secretary of War, she was confined in the Old Capitol Prison, a favorite local jail for dangerous Confederates. With her entrance there she added to her laurels.

"Close custody" under the circumstances of war, would be interpreted as solitary confinement, but apparently no such cruel treatment was given her. She was allowed to have the door of her cell open and to sit outside of it in a hall or stair landing. This exposed her to the curious gaze of the other prisoners —Confederate officers mostly. With some she was on the terms of greatest friendship and when not allowed to speak with them, she would write messages on tissue paper, paste them around a marble and, when the guard was not looking, roll the marble down the corridor. Finally apprehended at this, she cut a hole in her floor and communicated to the officers below.

On Sundays she was permitted to go into the yard to religious service. She always wore a small Confederate flag pinned to her bosom. Her appearance was the signal for a noisy reception. The men would try to get near her, and if she favored them with a look or a smile, they were set up for days.

Her position in the jail was peculiar. It was scarcely equipped to hold a girl so young or so innocent. If she stayed in her cell, she would fall sick. If she sat outside, she was exposed to the curious gaze of a hundred other prisoners and had to endure their remarks about her, some of them unbearably crude. Her cell fronted on A Street and she would sit at the window when troops passed and shower them with her most sarcastic maledictions. "Hurrah for Jeff Davis and Stonewall Jackson!" "How long did it take you to come from Bull Run?" Such pretty remarks she passed out the window, and the soldiers returned the compliments!

When she first entered the prison, local papers took up the cry against her. She was painted a vile creature. The New York *Herald* correspondent is said to have described her as having "a freckled face, red hair, and large mouth." Since she was a blonde, the red hair attribute was evidently intended as the mark of his scorn. The Washington *Evening Star* attacked her savagely and criticized the lax treatment being accorded her. Local patriots wrote indignant letters to the papers. The War Department started an investigation. All this pother over a mere child in her teens! How could she be so dangerous and so vile as her foes were painting her? Indeed, her accomplishments and innocent demeanor bore such a sporting air that she soon threatened to become a heroine.

Perhaps her most dramatic offense while in the Old Capitol Prison was her habit of singing. The first night she was there the other prisoners heard a girl's voice singing "Maryland, My Maryland." At the sound of it the prison was hushed. And thus each night she sang. One of her fellow prisoners reports, "I have seen men, when she was singing, walk off to one side and pull out their handkerchiefs and wipe their eyes."

Realizing that further incarceration would have doubtful effects, the authorities on August 29, ordered her sent across the lines. Though she had been arrested on suspicion of having communicated with the enemy, no specific charge or information was lodged against her. Before she left, her fellow prisoners showed their esteem by presenting her with a gold watch. She was then put on board the transport *Juniata* and sent to Fortress Monroe where Major General Dix, in charge of the fortress, was directed to place her over the lines by the first flag of truce.

Her return to the Confederacy was made an occasion of great rejoicing. As she entered their camp, the Richmond Blues presented arms and Richmond put on gala dress. She was made honorary captain and aide-de-camp to General Jackson. At reviews, sitting on her horse beside Lee and Longstreet and Lord Hartingdon, the British military observer, she helped take the salute.

IV

After the reception at Richmond, she started a tour of the Confederate States, a tour that did much to stiffen the morale of the South. Publicly acclaimed wherever she appeared, she soon became the idol of the Confederacy, the Great Rebel Spy, the Virginian Heroine! At Charleston, General Beauregard and his staff gave her a dinner, and town after town serenaded her.

Her modesty on these occasions was notable. The diary of a Confederate officer reports her as being "embarrassed by the novelty of her position." She was "pleasant and ladylike in appearance." She seemed incapable of realizing that she had accomplished great things or showed any quality of courage above the average. Moreover, she was unwilling to rest on her laurels, unwilling to be satisfied with one or two brilliant exploits. Her triumphant tour of the South completed, she calmly returned to her home in Martinsburg, still in Northern control, and calmly placed herself once more in the hands of the enemy.

Naturally Northern officers viewed her with suspicion. A new outfit, they had heard of the charms of this young lady and were determined to steel their hearts against them. For by this time her reputation as a dangerous character had grown to startling proportions. She was a houri, a vixen, a dangerous and undefeated foe. No method was too fearful for her to adopt, no crime too terrible for her to commit. Sentries posted around her house were warned to watch for the knife in the back and the sudden dose of chloroform, at administering both of which this innocent little flirt was said to be adept. Like cenobites resisting the fleshly allure of their dreams, all ranks avoided her ingratiating smile. To Belle, as to any woman under such circumstances, this stern self-denial of her allure must have been highly amusing. Sooner or later, if she were permitted to remain in Martinsburg, some valiant heart would melt before the warmth of her glances.

The Secretary of War must have felt the same. What? That girl back again? Fearful for the morals and reputation of his staff at Martinsburg, he determined to rid them of temptation. Once again he ordered her arrest. And once again Belle Boyd in her pretty muslins went through the farce of being conducted to Washington under heavy guard. She is said to have looked a little sad on departing. Well, what girl wouldn't be? Privations were beginning to make life tense in the South. From its womanhood were being exacted terrible and ever-increasing penalties. One jail sentence more or less could not dim her ardor. But it was sad to

"The outrages upon the dead will revive the recollections of the cruelties to which savage tribes subject their prisoners. They were buried in many cases naked, with their faces downward. They were left to decay in the open air, *their bones being carried off as trophies,* sometimes, as the testimony proves, to be used as personal adornments, *and one witness deliberately avers that the head of one of our most gallant officers was cut off by a Secessionist, to be turned into a drinking-cup on the occasion of his marriage.*

"Monstrous as this revelation may appear to be, your Committee have been informed that during the last two weeks the skull of a Union soldier has been exhibited in the office of the Sergeant-at-Arms of the House of Representatives which had been converted to such a purpose, and which had been found on the person of one of the rebel prisoners taken in a recent conflict."—*Report of the Congressional Committee on the Conduct of the War.*

THE REBEL LADY'S BOUDOIR.

LADY (reads)—"*My dearest wife, I hope you have received all the little relics I have sent you from time to time. I am about to add something to your collection which I feel sure will please you—a baby-rattle for our little pet, made out of the ribs of a Yankee drummer-boy." &c., &c.*

THROUGHOUT THE CIVIL WAR SOUTHERN WOMEN WERE BITTERLY CARTOONED IN NORTHERN PAPERS, AS WITNESS THIS EXAMPLE FROM *FRANK LESLIE'S WEEKLY*

have to leave her mother alone with the burdens of a beleaguered household.

This time they lodged her in the Carroll Prison, another favorite corral for dangerous Rebels. And scarcely was she there than the news leaked out to the Washington populace. Crowds gathered around the prison at night to listen to her sing "Take Me Back to My Own Sunny South" and "The Bonny Blue Flag." When she was permitted to exercise in the park that faced the prison gaping crowds lined its rim to watch her. Into her windows ardent beaux shot arrows with messages of sympathy. Washington took Belle Boyd to its heart.

By no means was the Carroll Prison an ideal spot, and Belle soon fell ill with typhoid. Washington heard of it and read with unconcealed anxiety the bulletins of her progress. By the time she recovered, the authorities found themselves with an embarrassing incubus on their hands. Both secretly and openly the populace sympathized with their young captive. And yet she was a thoroughly dangerous person. Time and again had she been caught giving aid and comfort to the enemy. Time and again with smile and flutter of eyelid had she worked her way out of the most dangerous situations. If they harried her, if they persecuted her, they stood a good chance of bringing down on their heads the disfavor of the people. Finally they determined to come to grips with the situation. Belle was haled before a court-martial headed by Judge-Advocate

L. D. Turner. By order of the court she was banished to the South. The New York *Tribune* reports on Dec. 2, 1863, that "Captain James B. Mix of General Martindale's Staff, left this afternoon for City Point with the notorious Belle Boyd, who is to be delivered to the Rebel authorities at that place." The next time she stepped across the lines would mean a firing squad. This, of course, was an empty threat, because neither side shot a woman spy during the entirety of the war.

V

Once more Richmond turned out to acclaim her, but it was a different Richmond from the one she had known before; already the thongs of war were beginning to tighten around the city. Northern armies were drawing their lines closer and closer. The city itself had changed. Vice was rampant; all sorts of riff-raff flocked there.

Several arrests and two terms in Union jails had about ended her services as a spy. That line of activities would have to be abandoned. Consequently, she offered herself as dispatch-bearer, and President Davis, mindful of her services to the cause and her place in Confederate esteem, saw that no mean task was assigned her. She was to carry important papers to England.

To the incredulous this may seem to have been a big order for one so young and yet the exigencies of war throw all things out of perspective. Besides we are depending on Belle Boyd herself for much of this story, as she tells it in her book, "Belle Boyd in Camp and Prison."

The local historian of her native town, writing several years after the War, does not even condescend to name her among the illustrious daughters of Martinsburg: he merely states that while that town was the hub for local military activites certain persons, "self-appointed detectives and spies" found a chance to "gratify their spite against their neighbors or cover themselves with glory and obtain great credit as patriots." Such persons, he assures us, the officers on both sides treated with contempt. Well! Well! This local Josephus could not have come from the gallant stock of old Virginia: he must have been a carpetbagger! For has not Belle Boyd related all these breathless and courageous exploits herself? And did not so late a writer of tales as Robert W. Chambers compose a whole book of stories—"The Special Messenger"—on the facts of Belle Boyd's adventures? And were not the papers of her day filled with detailed accounts of her coming and going? Tut! Tut! Mr. Historian! Let the miss have her crowded hour of glory!

Having taken our fling at the author of "A Full and Complete History of Martinsburg and Berkeley County, West Virginia," we too can allow this gallant and colorful young woman to proceed on her way.

At Culpepper, Virginia, while awaiting orders

she puts up at a boarding-house where there are a number of Confederate officers. Belle is the centre of attraction all evening. She amuses everyone with her conversation and stories of her experiences. That night she shares the bed with a Virginia girl who later, in her diary, reports the episode. The incident that impressed her most was that the following morning before Belle stepped into her bath, she poured an entire bottle of cologne into it! Ah well, even heroines must have their little vanities!

Finally her chance comes. Under the thin alias of "Mrs. Lewis" Belle boarded the *Greyhound*, a boat flying the British flag, and one dark night it slipped out of the harbor of Wilmington, North Carolina. That part of the coast was heavily blockaded. It was a ten-to-one chance if the *Greyhound* got through. Her master had no illusions about the dangers he would encounter or the perilous errand his illustrious passenger was on. His cargo of 800 bales of cotton was contraband enough. Nor did he know just how efficiently Northern espionage was functioning those days. Before she sailed the Yankees were aware of the real person of "Mrs. Lewis" and the intent of her errand. The U. S. *Connecticut* began chasing her. It made short work of heading off the *Greyhound*. Before dawn the boat was in Northern hands and a prize crew was put aboard. This crew was in charge of Captain Sam Wylde Hardinge, U. S. N.

Southern apologists for Captain Hardinge claim that, although he was a native of Brooklyn and by

birth consequently a Northerner, and that although
he was an officer in good standing of the United
States Navy, capable of undertaking his duties with
dispatch, skill and dependable fidelity to the cause
of his country, he was, nevertheless, a secret sym-
pathizer with the cause of Secession. This is difficult
to believe. We prefer to feel that the hole in Captain
Hardinge's armor was due to Cupid's arrow rather
than to any inherent weakness in the armor itself.
That is Belle Boyd's theory, and in this account we
are going to be gallant enough to take her word for it.

The simple facts as related by Belle are these:
scarcely had Captain Hardinge laid eyes on his prize
captive than he fell in love with her. The boat was
headed for New York. Twice on the way there he
proposed to her. What wiles she used on him she
does not say, but the gallant young captain fell hard
and speedily. The first proposal she scorned: the
second she thought better of, and accepted him. By
the time the *Greyhound* entered the Narrows—a few
short days since it crept out of Wilmington Harbor
—Belle Boyd had made her captor captive.

They stop in New York long enough to do some
shopping. The papers acquaint the populace of her
presence in the metropolis. They go to Niblo's
Theatre and see a performance of "Bel Demonio."
This pleasant little call over, the *Greyhound* heads
for Boston and there Belle becomes a *cause celebre*.

By clever conniving she manages to help Captain
Hall, the Confederate master of the *Greyhound*, to

escape in Boston Harbor. He heads for Canada—
and then she lands on the Boston wharf. Just how
the newspapers of the day handled her story makes
amusing reading. Each day over its matutinal
codfish balls Boston followed Belle Boyd's activities.
Did she go into a shop? That was jotted down. Did
she attend church? That was made a topic for
comment. This dangerous young woman was accorded the same full measure of publicity that our
tabloids now give to female murderers, abductors,
and national heroes.

On May 20, 1864, the Boston *Post* reports the
arrival in Boston harbor of the British steamer
Greyhound which had been captured off Wilmington, and that among its passengers was "the somewhat famous Miss Belle Boyd," whose deportment
on shipboard was described by the officers as being
very ladylike. The next day its front page broke
out into an extended eulogy of her. She was waited
on by Marshal Keyes and "invited to the lodgings
at the Tremont House until the pleasure of the
Government shall be known respecting her disposition.
She is accompanied by three servants, a white woman, a black girl, and a black boy." She appears
to the reporters to be "a female of intelligence and
quick understanding." She bears herself well. She
is a tall blonde. There is much curiosity to see her.
During the attack on the *Greyhound* it was said she
came on deck, calmly seated herself on a cotton bale,
and watched the fighting. She needed only the

ubiquitous cigarette to complete the picture of the modern, nerveless flapper!

Living thus in what is called "the pitiless glare of publicity," Miss Boyd stayed on in Boston until the authorities announced that she was to be conducted to the Canadian frontier and forever banished from the United States.

The situation was both embarrassing for them and trying for her. This was the second time she had been banished and they wanted to be sure that they made a good job of it. Sending her South would only be an invitation for this impertinent miss to bob up again. Once in Canada, she would probably stay out of the country. Besides she had declared she was going to England. That was the objective she and her fiancé had agreed on. A rendezvous in London—and then their marriage. Apart from Captain Hardinge, she had no one on whom she could rely. Her father had died. No word had come from her mother for many months. She was alone, in the hands of the enemy, in the state that held Ben Butler to be a national hero. And since she was only twenty, no one could envy her lot.

On May 31, the Boston *Post* states: "In accordance with orders received from the War Department that eccentric and not over loyal female, Miss Belle Boyd, has been released from custody by Marshal Keyes. Her conduct while at the Tremont House was quiet and ladylike. . . . She will go to Canada at once. Belle is good looking and smart." As Marshal

Keyes put her on the train for Toronto his parting shot was to the effect that if she set foot in the country again she would be shot.

VI

The next chapter opens at the Brunswick Hotel in Jermyn Street. London, which was ever sympathetic with the Southern cause, took this young lady to its stern bosom once she had landed there. Even this phlegmatic city could not resist the allure of an *ingenue* spy who had twice been threatened with the firing squad and had spent eleven months in jail until her captors were obliged to banish her out of sheer embarrassment. London mothered her, acclaimed her and awaited the impending romance with titillating expectancy.

For in the meantime Captain Hardinge, true to his tryst, had gone to his superior officers and prevailed upon them to accept his resignation from the Navy. It wasn't quite the thing one does in the midst of war, but the authorities probably figured that once an officer had come under the spell of Belle Boyd his services were thereafter useless. So soon as he was released he headed for London, and the happy wedding at St. James, Piccadilly, attended by local Confederate representatives, society and the generally curious, was followed by breakfast at the Brunswick. The date was the twenty-fifth of August, 1864. The bride had just turned twenty-one.

Two months after the wedding Captain Hardinge

left his bride and returned to America, there to arrange his personal affairs. He came to Brooklyn and thence started South with the intention of visiting his newly acquired mother-in-law at Martinsburg. On his way through Baltimore he was arrested as a deserter and sent to Washington. After a short confinement in the Carroll Prison—the same one that his bride had graced—he was shipped to Fort Delaware in Wilmington where he was held as a political prisoner until February 1865. The husband of the celebrated Belle Boyd, he moved in a glamour of reflected glory among the other Confederate prisoners confined there.

Meantime in London his bride was feeling the pinch of reduced circumstances. The first excitement over, the wedding accomplished, London went about its stodgy way and completely forgot the girl. She was obliged to sell her few possessions one by one. Her circumstances grew so desperate that she was reduced to living in a dismal boarding-house (and how dismal a boarding-house in London can be!) where she busied herself writing the book, "Belle Boyd In Camp and Prison."

One day George Augustus Sala, the journalist, known for his outspoken sympathies with the Southern cause, was busy in his office when Belle Boyd was announced. As she came in she exclaimed, "Sir, will you take my life?" Sala was flabbergasted. So beautiful a creature! So soft a voice! So plaintive, so sad a young lady! Take her life? She saw his embarrassment and relieved the situation. From the folds of her shawl she produced the manuscript of her book. Sala took the life. He did more—he wrote a laudatory preface to it. London published it first, and the reading public of New York was palpitating over it in 1865. But even some London critics felt that Belle had pulled Mr. Sala's leg. The *Athenaeum*, for example, in a sarcastic review, says that the narrator is "strangely devoid of definite information although she shows no disinclination to sound her own praises."

VII

In the beginning of this chapter we hinted that the story of Belle Boyd would be a study of prevarication under arms. Our sources for her story have been first, her book, "Belle Boyd in Camp and Prison," then Government Civil War Records, then newspapers of the day, and finally recollections of men who fought in the Shenandoah campaigns in which she was concerned. To what extent did this young lady, writing in the dingy bedroom of a London boarding-house, draw on her imagination?

As we have seen, the local historian of her native town, gives her and her kind short shrift. The opening incident of her career when, appearing suddenly from behind her mother's skirts, she shot a Union soldier, was evidently pure fiction; a search of local records and personal diaries reveals no account of it. The story of the knothole in the bedroom floor is too ingenuous, too much a device of fiction to be considered seriously. We must remember that we are dealing with a virgin in her teens. The knothole is the sort of imaginative incident that a girl of that age would invent.

Her prison experience at the "Old Capitol" does not appear so romantic when viewed through the eyes of Col. N. J. Colby who had charge of the prison during the war. His comments are rather withering—

"Of the secret agents or spies in the service of the rebel government, there were some who achieved notoriety, at least, and they were well represented in the Old Capitol, both male and female. Among the latter was Belle Boyd, who left the impression with those with whom she came in contact of a woman governed more by romance and love of notoriety than actual regard for the Southern cause. Undeniably good-looking, with a fine figure, and a merry disposition, she could have been dangerous had she possessed equal good sense and good judgment. I believe the extent of the damage she inflicted on the Northern cause was in tempting from his loyalty a subordinate officer of the Navy, whom, it was affirmed, she married. He also found his way to the prison, from which he dictated a challenge to the editor of the Washington *Star*, for some rather scornful allusions to himself and wife. They were both 'light weights' in the profession."

In her book Belle relates how at Fortress Monroe she was brought under the strabismic gaze of that prince of misogynists General Benjamin F. Butler, commander of the fortress. The Government records show this to be General Dix. General Butler had been in command of Fortress Monroe, but by this time was supplanted by Dix. Her hitting on Butler was the course natural to any Confederate woman.

This cross-eyed and bombastic general won his spurs of woman-hatred early in the war. During his first command, in Baltimore, Confederate women who persisted in wearing tiny flags pinned to their bosoms riled him into issuing a general order against them. His wrath centred on the lovely Hettie Cary, whose sister Jennie first sang the newly composed Rebel song, "Maryland, My Maryland." Hettie was a tease. She paraded Baltimore streets wearing an apron made of a white field with the crossed red bars of the Confederacy. Butler promptly threw her into jail. Later, as commander of New Orleans, he issued the infamous General Order No. 28 in which he stated that "when any female shall by word, gesture or movement insult or show any contempt for any officer of the United States, she shall be regarded and held liable to be treated as a woman of the town plying her trade." This order, together with other blunderings, soon caused Butler's recall. Because of it he was referred to in New Orleans as "Butler the Beast;" in the wartime parlance of the Southerner "to Butlerize" meant to assault a woman.

Of course, on August 29, 1862, when she was sent

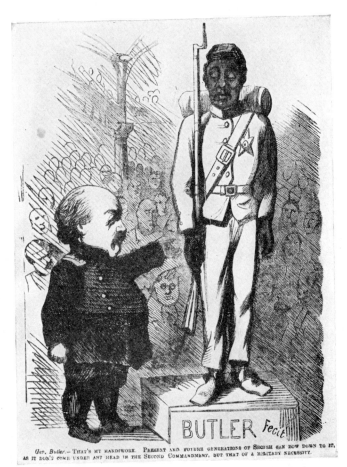

Gen. Butler.— THAT'S MY HANDIWORK. PRESENT AND FUTURE GENERATIONS OF SECESH CAN BOW DOWN TO IT, AS IT DON'T COME UNDER ANY HEAD IN THE SECOND COMMANDMENT, BUT THAT OF A MILITARY NECESSITY.

AMONG THE MANY "OUTRAGES" THAT GENERAL BEN BUTLER
PERPETRATED WHILE MILITARY GOVERNOR OF NEW ORLEANS
WAS ENLISTING NEGROES IN THE NORTHERN ARMY

to Fortress Monroe, Belle Boyd could not conceivably have seen General Butler, since, at the time, he was in New Orleans.

Belle's protestations of love for Stonewall Jackson and her great services to him in the campaign against General Banks would naturally find at least a mention in the various lives of that valiant and noble general. Yet a search of many volumes comprising five lives, memoirs, and letters, etc., of General Jackson does not reveal even the mention of her name. He evidently did not consider his note to her of sufficient importance to record in his official reports or her services sufficiently valuable to make note of.

Belle tells us of a second prison experience, when she was incarcerated in the Carroll Prison, and she gives her good friend George Augustus Sala to understand that she spent no less than eleven months behind bars for her patriotism. On this second sentence the Government records are singularly silent, save for the mention of her being conducted to City Point by Captain Mix on December 2, 1863.

It is also amusing to find that the *Greyhound* episode is treated lightly by one of her contemporaries. On board the boat at the time it was captured was Ed. A. Pollard of the *Richmond Examiner*, author of many books on the Civil War, who also wrote an account of his experiences for two weeks on the *Greyhound* before it was captured. He makes no mention of her. The New York *Tribune*, reporting the capture of the blockade-runner, mentions him as being aboard, "also a woman reported to be Belle Boyd, but the identity of the latter with the famous Rebel spy is doubtful." By the time the *Greyhound* reached Boston, however, her identity is assured, for the Boston *Post* reports both Pollard and her as landing in that city.

We are inclined, therefore, to read "Belle Boyd In Camp and Prison" with the salt near at hand. Undoubtedly she did serve the Confederate cause to its benefit on one or two occasions but not with such persistent and brilliant a series of episodes as she records. Rather she appears as a girl who used her charms to good advantage and obtained valuable information which she was able to carry to the Confederate lines. That she was all the evil things some correspondents say of her may be discounted as exaggerations made in the heat of war.

VIII

By the eighth of April 1865, Grant, Meade and Sheridan had the Army of Northern Virginia hemmed in. Lee realized no other choice lay ahead but to surrender. The next day he met Grant at Appomattox Court House. The cause was lost.

From the dismal London hall bedroom Belle Boyd managed to make her way to America and her husband. There was an affectionate reunion. Thin and worn from incarceration, Hardinge had first to be nursed back to health. The poor fellow never really recovered. Three years later he died. The romance had been more of a dream than a reality, but that is the way with many a war wedding.

Having had this scant taste of married life, Belle Boyd was tempted into trying it again. The following year, 1869, she married John V. Hammond, an ex-British army officer living in New Orleans and went to live with him in California. Thereafter "La Belle Rebelle" followed the decline peculiar to heroines. For a time she was an actress, then as the years went on, she gained local fame as a lecturer at Grand Army Encampments, recounting her exploits to the assembled veterans and their wives.

In 1884 she divorced Hammond and a year later was married to Nathaniel R. High of Toledo, Ohio. Somehow she couldn't remain unmarried more than a year. And why should she? A woman who had packed so much romance into so few years could well be carried on by its momentum for many years to come. She was desirable, for she was still this side of forty. She had had an enviable and a colorful past. Mr. High succumbed to her enchantments without a struggle.

But even to such heroines Time brings the ignominy of the forgotten. In the quiet obscurity of Kilbourne, Wisconsin—a summer resort about fifty miles or so from Madison—in 1900, her chapter came to its inevitable close. Papers of the day reported the fact, recounted her exploits and thereafter we hear no more of her, save that each Memorial Day— the irony of it!—her grave at Madison is decorated by veterans with the Union flag! Mention her name today, and men stare at you blankly. "Belle Boyd? Who was she?"

Death in an obscure little summer resort! To such dismal ends do heroines come. Indeed the heroine who does not come to a dismal end has rarely ever been a heroine. The woman who attains her sole hour of self-importance when she assumes the role of chief actress before the panoply of death, ordinarily has lived her life desperately avoiding the unusual, desperately trying to maintain an even keel. But those who have attained the heights of romance and adventure know the price that will be exacted of them: the only path from the top of the hill leads down to the dismal obscurity of the other side.

BIBLIOGRAPHY

CHAPTER I

BRACKENRIDGE, H. M.—*Views of Louisiana.* Baltimore, 1817.

CHAMBERS, HENRY E.—*History of Louisiana.* New York, 1925.

FRENCH, B. T.—*Historical Collections of Louisiana.* New York, 1851.

GAYARRE, CHARLES—*History of Louisiana.*

"Illinois, Osage and Otoplata Chiefs in Paris, in 1725," in *U. S. Catholic Historical Magazine.*

Jesuit Relations, The, Edited by REUBEN G. THWAITES. Vols. 67 and 68.

Les Indiens Osages. Paris, 1827.

Mercure de France. December, 1725.

PERKINS, JAMES B.—*France Under Louis XV.* Boston, 1897.

SHEA, JOHN G.—*Catholic Missions Among the Indian Tribes of the United States.* New York, 1855.

WOOD, JOHN R.—*A Sketch of the Life and Projects of John Law of Lauriston, Etc.* Edinburgh, 1791.

CHAPTER II

CRAWFORD, MARY C.—*The Romance of the American Theatre.* Boston, 1925.

DALY, CHARLES P.—*The First Theatre in America.*

DUNLAP, WM.—*History of the American Theatre.* New York, 1833.

DURANG, CHARLES—*History of the Philadelphia Stage.*

HORNBLOW, ARTHUR—*History of the Theatre in America.* Philadelphia, 1919.

IRELAND, JOSEPH N.—*Records of the New York Stage.* New York, 1866.

Jamaica Mercury and Kingston Advertiser, 1779-1780.

ODELL, GEORGE C. D.—*Annals of the New York Stage.* New York, 1927.

SEILHAMER, GEORGE O.—*History of the American Theatre.* Philadelphia, 1888.

WILLIS, EOLA—*The Charleston Stage in the XVIII Century.* Columbia, S. C., 1924.

WRIGHT, RICHARDSON—*Hawkers and Walkers in Early America.* Philadelphia, 1927.

CHAPTER III

COKE, DR. AND MR. MOORE—*Life of the Rev. John Wesley.* Philadelphia, 1793.

COULTER, E. MERTON—"When Wesley Preached in Georgia," in *Georgia Historical Quarterly.* 1925.

GAMBLE, THOMAS—*The Love Stories of John and Charles Wesley.* Savannah, 1927.

GREEN, RICHARD—*The Works of John and Charles Wesley.*

JONES, JR., CHARLES C.—*History of Georgia.*

JONES, JR., CHARLES C.—*History of Savannah.* New York, 1890.

LEE AND AGNEW—*Historical Record of the City of Savannah.* Savannah, 1869.

McCALL, HUGH—*History of Georgia.*

Methodist Times. Vol. VII, No. 322.

MOORE, HENRY—*The Life of John Wesley.* 1824.

WESLEY, JOHN—*Sermons on Several Occasions.*

Wesley, John, Works of. London, 1803–13, 17 volumes.

Wesley's Journal, John, edited by NEHEMIAH CURNOCH. 1909.

WHITE, REV. GEORGE—*Historical Collections of Georgia.* 1855.

WINCHESTER, C. T.—*Life of John Wesley.* New York, 1906.

CHAPTER IV

ADAMS, JOHN TRUSLOW—*New England in the Republic.* Boston, 1926.

Asbury, Rev. Francis, Journal of the. 3 vols., New York.

BOUCHER, JONATHAN—*Reminiscences of an American Loyalist.* Boston, 1925.

CHASTELLUX, MARQUIS DE—*Travels in North America, 1780–82.* New York, 1827.

ELLET, ELIZABETH F.—*Women of the American Revolution.* New York, 1848, 2 vols.

Female Review, The, or Life of Deborah Sampson, edited by JOHN ADAMS VINTON. Boston, 1866.

FOWLER, WILLIAM W.—*Women on the American Frontier*. Hartford, 1876.

JAMESON, J. FRANKLIN—*The American Revolution Considered as a Social Movement*. Princeton, 1926.

JONES, THOMAS—*History of New York During the Revolutionary War*. New York, 1879.

MCMASTER, J. B.—*History of the American People*. Vol. I.

NEVINS, ALLAN—*The American States During and After the Revolution*.

RAYMOND, W. O.—"Loyalists in Arms," in *New Brunswick Historical Association's Publications*, No. 4.

RYERSON, EGERTON—*The Loyalists of America and Their Times*. Montreal, 1880.

CHAPTER V

Answer to "Six Months in a Convent," by THE LADY SUPERIOR. Boston, 1835.

Awful Disclosures of Maria Monk. New York, 1836.

BEAN, W. G.—"An Aspect of Know Nothingism," in the *South Atlantic Quarterly*. Vol. 23.

BRAND C. F.—"History of the Know Nothing Party in Indiana," in *Indiana Magazine of History*. Vol. XVIII.

BROWNLEE, REV. W. C.—*Popery*. New York, 1836.

Brownlee, D. D., Rev. W. C., Memorial of the. New York, 1860.

Cases in the Vice Chancellor's Court, 1837.

CONDON, PETER—"The Revivals of Religious Intoleration," in *Historical Records and Studies*. Vol. IV.

DESMON, HUMPHREY J.—*The Know Nothing Party*. Washington, 1904.

Documents Relating to the Ursuline Convent in Charleston. Boston, 1842.

Dublin Review, The. Vol. I.

Further Disclosures of Maria Monk. New York, 1837.

HAYNES, GEORGE H.—"The Causes of Know Nothing Success in Massachusetts." *American Historical Review Quarterly*. 1897.

Herald (New York). 27 and 31 August, 1836.

Interview of Maria Monk With Her Opponents. New York, 1836.

JOHNSON, STANLEY G.—*A History of Emigration from the United Kingdom to North America, 1763–1912.* London, 1913.

Life and Death of Sam, The, by a VIRGINIAN. Richmond, 1856.

Maria Monk's Daughter. New York.

MORSE, SAMUEL F. B.—*A Conspiracy Against the United States.* New York, 1835.

Native American, The. Philadelphia, 1845.

OSBORNE, LAUGHTON—*The Vision of Roberta.* Boston, 1838.

Proselytizing, A Sketch of Know Nothing Times. Cincinnati, 1854.

REED, REBECCA THERESA—*Six Months in a Convent.* Boston, 1835.

REED, REBECCA THERESA—*Supplement to "Six Months In A Convent."* Boston, 1835.

Review of the Lady Superior's Reply to "Six Months in a Convent," A. Boston, 1835.

ROBERTSON, S. Y.—*The American Party.* Frankfort, Kentucky, 1855.

SCHMECKEBIER, L. T.—"History of the Know Nothing Party in Maryland," in *Johns Hopkins University Studies Series XVII, Nos. 4–5.*

SLEIGH, W. W.—*An Exposure of Maria Monk's Pretended Abduction and Conveyance to the Catholic Asylum, Philadelphia.* Philadelphia, 1837.

Sons of the Sires, The. Philadelphia, 1855.

STICKNEY, CHARLES—*Know Nothingism in Rhode Island.* Providence, 1894.

SWINSON, WILLIAM—*An exposé of the Know Nothings.* Philadelphia, 1854.

"Truth About Maria Monk, The." *Watson's Magazine,* May, 1916.

TUSKA, BENJAMIN—"Know Nothingism in Baltimore," in *Catholic Historical Review,* 1920.

WALSH, J. J.—"Keeping Up the Protestant Tradition," in the *Catholic World,* Vol. CI

WISE, GOV. HENRY A.—*Religious Liberty.* Alexandria, Virginia, 1854.

ZWIERLEIN, REV. F. J.—"Know Nothingism in Rochester, New York," in the *Historical Records and Studies of the U. S. Catholic Historical Society,* Vol. XIV.

CHAPTER VI

BLANKENHORN, HEBER—"The Grandma of the Muckrakers."
American Mercury, September, 1927.

Huntress, The.

Illustration of Masonry, by A MEMBER OF THE CRAFT. Cincinnati, 1826.

LANG, OSSIAN—*History of Free Masonry in the State of New York.* New York, 1922.

PORTER, SARAH H.—*The Life and Times of Anne Royall.* Cedar Rapids, 1909.

ROYALL, MRS.—*Black Books.* 3 vols. Washington, 1828–9.

ROYALL, MRS.—*Letters from Alabama.* 1 vol. 1830.

ROYALL, MRS.—*Pennsylvania.* 2 vols. Washington, 1829.

ROYALL, MRS.—*Southern Tour.* 2 vols. Washington, 1830–1.

ROYALL, MRS.—*The Tennessean.* New Haven, 1827.

Sketches of History, Life and Manners in the United States, by A TRAVELER. New Haven, 1826, 2 vols.

Washington Paul Pry.

CHAPTER VII

Crocus, The, Edited by SARAH JOSEPHA HALE. New York, 1849.

FARNHAM, ELIZA—*Woman and Her Era.* 1854.

FISCHEL, DR. OSKAR, AND MAX VON BOEHN—*Modes and Manners of the 19th Century.* Translated by M. Edwarder. London, 1927.

Genius of Oblivion, The, by A LADY OF NEW HAMPSHIRE. Concord, 1823.

Godey's Lady's Book. 1837 to 1887.

HALE, SARAH JOSEPHA—*Boarding Out.* New York, 1846.

HALE, SARAH JOSEPHA—*Flora's Interpreter and Fortuna Flora.* Boston, 1849.

HALE, SARAH JOSEPHA—*Keeping House.* New York, 1845.

HALE, SARAH JOSEPHA—*The Ladies' New Book of Cookery.* New York, 1852.

HALE, SARAH JOSEPHA—*Northwood.* New York, 1827.

HALE, SARAH JOSEPHA—*Poems for Our Children.* Boston, 1830.

HALE, SARAH JOSEPHA—*Woman's Record.* New York, 1852.

HOLLIDAY, CARL—*Woman's Life in Colonial Days.* Boston, 1922.

Ladies' Magazine, The. Boston, 1829.

MUNSEY, FRANK A.—*The Story of the Founding and Development of the Munsey Publishing House.* New York, 1907.

OBERHOLTZER, ELLIS P.—*The Literary History of Philadelphia.* Philadelphia, 1906.

PACKARD, PROF.—"History of the Bunker Hill Monument." *Maine Historical Society Collections,* Vol. 3. 1853.

REED, ANN LOUISE—"Female Delicacy in the Sixties," in *The Century,* 1915.

SAGE, ELIZABETH—*A Study of Costume.* New York, 1926.

SMYTH, ALBERT H.—*The Philadelphia Magazines and Their Contributors, 1741–1850.* Philadelphia, 1892.

TITUS, LILLIE B.—"How The Ladies of Boston Finished Bunker Hill Monument," in the *Massachusetts Magazine.* April, 1908.

WHEELER, EDMUND—*History of Newport, N. H.* 1879.

White Veil, The, edited by SARAH JOSEPHA HALE. Philadelphia, 1854.

CHAPTER VIII

ABBOTT, ORRIN—*The Davenport Brothers, Their History, Travels and Manifestations.* New York, 1864.

Banner of Light, The.

DAVENPORT, R. R.—*The Death Blow to Spiritualism.*

DAVIS, A. J.—*The Philosophy of Spiritual Intercourse.* Boston, 1868.

DAVIS, A. J.—*Principles of Nature.* Boston, 1868.

Dixboro Ghost, The. New York, 1850.

"DOESTICKS," PHILANDER, Q. K.—*The Witches of New York.* New York, 1859.

EDMONDS, J. W., AND DEXTER, GEORGE J.—*Spiritualism.* New York, 1853.

Eventful Nights of August 20 and 21, 1854, The.

HAMMOND, C.—*The Pilgrimage of Thomas Paine and Others to the Seventh Circle in the Spirit World.* New York, 1852.

HAVEN, GILBERT—*Heavenly Messenger.* Washington.

HAZARD, THOMAS R.—*Autobiography of Henry C. Gordon.* Ottumwa, Iowa.

History of the Mysterious Noises Heard at Rochester and Other Places. Rochester, 1850.

HORI, ROBERT—*Spiritualism Scientifically Demonstrated.* New York, 1856.

Love Life of Dr. Kane, The. New York, 1865.

LOVI, HENRIETTA—*The Best Books on Spirit Phenomena.* Boston, 1925.

MATTISON, H.—*Spirit Rapping Unveiled.* New York, 1853.

MORSE, J. J.—*An Apostle of Spiritualism, Biography of.* Boston, 1886.

New England Spiritualist, The. 1855–56.

Rappers, The, or The Mysteries and Absurdities of Spirit-Rapping, Table-Tipping and Entrancement. New York, 1854.

Spiritual Telegraph. 1852.

Tiffany's Monthly. 1856.

CHAPTER IX

Annals of the War, The. Philadelphia, 1879.

ANDREWS, M. P.—*The Women of the South in War Times.* Baltimore, 1920.

BARTON, GEORGE—*The World's Greatest Military Spies and Secret Service Agents.* Boston, 1917.

Belle Boyd in Camp and Prison, written by Herself. With an Introduction by GEORGE AUGUSTUS SALA. New York 1865.

Boston Post. 20, 21 and 31 May, 1864.

EDMONDS, S. EMMA E.—*Nurse and Spy in the Union Army.* Hartford, 1865.

Frank Leslie's Weekly. 1861–1865.

MAHONY, DENNIS A.—*The Prisoner of State.* New York, 1863.

New York Times. June 13, 1900.

New York Tribune. 2 December, 1863.

Official Records of the Union and Confederate Army, Series II, Vol. 4. Washington.

Philadelphia North American and United States Gazette. 31 May, 1862.

Photographic History of the Civil War. New York, 1912.

TAYLOR, C. S. A., GENERAL RICHARD—*Destruction and Reconstruction.*

UNDERWOOD, REV. J. L.—*The Women of the Confederacy.* New York, 1905.

Washington Star, The.

WILLIAMSON, JAMES J.—*Reminiscences of the Civil War.*

NOTES

(1) Charles Gayarre, the famous and favorite historian of Louisiana who relates this tale of the Savage Maid, had a habit now and then of stepping out of character. When the mood and the place conspired to please him, he would doff his serious air of chronicling the evolution of his native state from the first French explorer upward, and spin a good yarn. These he told without attempting to "document" them, give them support of chapter or verse set down in cryptic symbols and footnote abbreviations, as is the custom of most learned historians. Evidently, when Gayarre felt romantic, he dipped into the writings of that *Munchausen* of early Louisiana Colonial history—Pennicaut.

Only part of Gayarre's story of the Savage Maid can be authenticated—the first part. But even here he departs from existing documents. In his version of the story the expedition is headed by the local French commandant, with whom the Savage Maid is desperately smitten. When they reach France, he marries the woman of his choice and the Savage Maid, "on the rebound" and for good official reasons, is married off to Dubois. The "Jesuit Relations," the letters of the missionaries of the time, state that Fr. Beaubois headed this traveling show. Dubois is not mentioned in them, and further than stating the fact of the expedition to France, no details are given. The details are found in a newspaper report of the times. According to Gayarre their squaws accompanied the chiefs to France; the newspaper mentions only the Indian Maid. Her departure and murderous return to the fort seem to be nowhere chronicled. That she went to France and had her crowded hour of glory there, we are assured, however, by contemporary documents.

(2) Apropos of this habit the young Frenchmen had of going into the woods for their wives, we find that during the early days of the Dutch in New York the Rev. Dr. Douglas proposed that young missionaries marry the daughters of the Indian sachems. "Their progeny," he believed, "will forever be a certain cement between us and the Indians."

(3) These lines are quoted from "Quabi, or the Virtues of Nature," an Indian Tale in Four Cantos. By Philenia (Mrs. Sarah Wentworth Apthorp Morton), Boston, 1790.

(4) One hundred years after this first Indian visit to France, another band of six Osage Indians went to that country from St. Louis and were accorded a lively reception. So generous was the hospitality at Havre that one of the chiefs mixed his drinks, with disastrous results. On the occasion of their going to the theatre, the crowd was so great that they were almost crushed and smothered. As one of them remarked, "We will go to no more spectacles! If we have braved the dangers of the sea, it was not to be suffocated on the other side of the great lake."

A striking coincidence about this visit was that "the great grandfather of the chief of these Indians visited France under Louis XV; and much flattered by the welcome he received at the court, and in all parts of the Kingdom he visited, he gave an account of his travels to his assembled nation when he returned to the shores of the Missouri. At this recital, the present chief, then a child, cried out, 'And I also, I will visit France if the Master of Life allows me to become a man.'"

(5) The peaceful penetration of Indian lands by William Penn and his followers was greatly assisted by gifts. "Large sums of money were raised annually and spent by the trustees of the Friendly Association in presents for the Indians." Israel Pemberton, an influential and wealthy Quaker, once saved a desperate situation at Fort Duquesne, where Pittsburgh is now, by dispatching a messenger with £2000 worth of presents, which had been contributed largely from his own pocket. For further data on this see the "Life of William Savery" by F. R. Taylor.

It is also interesting to note that the Indians with whom Penn had to deal immediately on his arrival were cowed tribes who had been badly beaten up by their enemies and had made a public acknowledgment to the fact that they were less than the dust. To prove their ineptitude as men at arms, the chiefs were obliged to wear squaws' clothes for a time. What a delightful way to serve an enemy! How strange the Germans would have appeared, for instance, if, following the Treaty of Versailles, the French had obliged Teutonic manhood to squeeze itself into the "slim silhouette" gowns considered so *chic* by the French couturiers at the time!

(6) Charleston had its first theatre in 1736, Philadelphia in 1749. Prior to the Revolution Charleston had enjoyed theatrical seasons in 1734-5, 1736-7, 1763-4, and 1773-4. The Council Chamber was first used for concerts, plays, and balls. To see Otway's, "The Orphans" in this building in 1734 Charlestonians paid the prodigious sum of forty shillings a seat.

Its second theatre, the Dock Street, opened in 1735-6 with Farquhar's "The Recruiting Officer," the epilogue being especially composed for the occasion by Thomas Dale, an Associate Justice of the Province of South Carolina.

Under Douglass's supervision, and ably assisted by local Masons, Charleston's third theatre, the Queen Street, was erected and became a centre of public amusement. It was larger than the Southwark of Philadelphia or the John Street of New York.

Lindsay and Wall gave permanence to the stage in Baltimore. They played as "The Baltimore Comedians." In their company were a Mr. and Mrs. Denis Ryan who, in 1783, succeeded to the management. This troupe played a short season in New York, returned to Baltimore in 1784 and came to Charleston for a brief run of repertoire in 1785. Ryan died the next year in Baltimore.

(7) For further details of the early antagonism against the theatre and all forms of amusement, see my "Hawkers and Walkers in Early America."

(8) John Henry's choice of a British uniform as the proper costume for *Othello* may be quite in the modern taste but we can rest assured that he did it from necessity not from any meticulous or advanced notions of costuming. The costumes of these early American actors were whatever they could scrape together.

So far as we know, it was Coleman the elder who, in 1762, first conceived the idea of presenting Shakespeare in the habit of the periods in which plays were set. Macklin produced "Macbeth" at Covent Garden in 1773 "in the old Caledonian habit," and although Garrick had played "Macbeth" in a laced scarlet coat, he later made an effort to attain accuracy in costume and setting, for in 1776 he produced "King Lear," in what he considered to be the dress of the time that play represented.

(9) Tracing this apostolic succession of the New York Theatre a little further, we find that in 1796 William Dunlap joins the managerial firm. Hallam sells out and the company becomes Hodgkinson & Dunlap. On Jan. 13, 1798, under the direction of these two, the John Street Theatre saw its last performance. Its next role was as a carriage factory. Then it was demolished. The Southwark Theatre of Philadelphia ended its worthy career as a brewery!

(10) In his day, Joseph Corre was quite a figure of New York. A cook by trade, he served in that capacity during the Revolution at Perth Amboy where the British were stationed. After the war he became proprietor of the City Tavern. Later he established the famous Columbia Garden facing the Battery, and in the summer of 1800 managed another popular resort known as the Mount Vernon Garden located north of Leonard Street on Broadway. Some of the old Hallam Company actors appeared here, among them Mr. and Mrs. John Hodgkinson.

(11) The visit of Indian chieftains to Paris in 1725, as told in the first chapter, was duplicated almost exactly in the expedition of Tomochichi and his fellow warriors and their squaws to England in 1734. They went over at Oglethorpe's suggestion and under his chaperonage. During their four months' stay they were royally entertained, saw all the important people from the King and the Archbishop of Canterbury down to a great concourse of the commonalty which gathered whenever they appeared. At the Court presentation in Kensington Palace, Tomochichi and his squaw were garbed in scarlet and gold. Their gift to the king was a bundle of eight rare eagle feathers. When they left for Savannah in October 1734, they carried back with them over £2000's worth of gifts, in addition to assurances of the good will of the English. During this stay John Wesley doubtless saw them and Tomochichi's plea for missionaries to be sent to his people struck a spark in the great soul of Wesley, which accounts not only for his visit to the Indians on first landing but his misconception of the work intended for him to follow in Georgia.

(12) The forming of this society at Savannah was the second manifestation of Methodism. The first was at Oxford when

four men formed the Holy Club; the second at Savannah in April 1730, when twenty to thirty met at Wesley's parsonage; the third at London when 400 to 500 people agreed to meet together every Wednesday evening, to talk about religious matters, a meeting begun and ended with singing and prayer. The general rules for this society were drawn up by John and Charles Wesley in 1743, but even then there was no intention that people should leave the Church of England. A third Wesley brother, Samuel, was in Orders, and, like his brother Charles, he lived and died a minister of the Anglican Church.

It is interesting to find that in these embryonic days of Methodism, Charles Wesley was the first to form a conception of it, just as, in later years, George Whitefield conceived the idea of itinerant preaching before John Wesley adopted it.

Since in this chapter we are concerned merely with what happened to the Wesleys in Georgia, it is only just to observe that John Wesley's real conversion came after his return to England. Methodism, as he conceived it, was to be a revival of Apostolic Christianity, within the Anglican Church, and his most stimulating experience, which urged him on to his great work, came while he was associating with Lutherans and Moravians in England and Germany.

The accomplishments of John Wesley's life are almost incredible. On his preaching tours he is estimated to have traveled 225,000 miles, delivered over 40,000 sermons, some of them to open air congregations of 20,000; and he wrote upwards of 200 books.

(13) It seems inevitable that heroes who take to religion or later become national figures must suffer being splashed with whitewash by their pious and patriotic biographers. John Wesley was no exception. We have to wash off several coats of saccharine and pious alibis before we come to the real man. This affair with Sophia Hopkey is variously termed by his early biographers as an act of God, a demonstration of the wisdom of Providence and such, and John is said to have been a brand snatched from the burning. Since 1862, when his shorthand notes were deciphered, we have been able to see how utterly silly are these maudlin sentiments. Neither God nor Providence should have to take the blame for his weakness in the presence of women. The cold fact is that John Wesley lacked the wisdom

of the serpent, as his brother Charles said; he seemed to lose all perspective once his thoughts turned on some woman.

Four distinct women played parts in his life:

1. Betty Kirkham, known as "Veranese," from the way she signed her letters. He kept up a correspondence with her for four years, until 1731, from his 24th to his 28th year. It is indicative of the mind of the man that while this lively correspondence was going on, he was stating that he considered it unlawful for a priest to marry—and he was in Orders at the time! The affair was broken off and she married in 1731 and died the following year.

2. Sophia Augustiana Hopkey.

3. Grace Murray, a widow of 33, who after a frivolous girlhood became an ardent follower of Wesley. When Wesley and John Bennett, one of his preachers, were sick in Newcastle, she nursed both of them—Bennett for 26 weeks and Wesley for a shorter time. Both fell under her spell and with both of them she was apparently in love for six months—professed love for Wesley and the same day would sit down and write love letters to Bennett. Finally in 1749, when she was 46, she told John that her mind and heart were settled on him. John was panic-stricken. He temporized and shilly-shallied, so Grace changed her mind and in a few days she married Bennett.

4. Molly Vazielle, likewise a widow (it is too bad John Wesley lived before the day of Sam Weller's advice regarding "vidders"!) and his nurse. Indeed Wesley could not resist a woman who nursed him. Sophia Hopkey saw him through that bout of fever after he had eaten meat and drunk wine at General Oglethorpe's dinner party; Grace Murray saw him through a bilious siege which, of course, wasn't so romantic; and now Molly Vazielle takes him in hand after he has slipped on the ice in London. They had a nine days' brisk courtship, at the end of which John Wesley, now 48, hobbled up to the altar on a crutch and solemnized his undying devotion for Molly.

But Mrs. Vazielle was the last person in the world John Wesley should have married. She badgered the life out of him, picked on him, abused him at every turn. Finally, when she had poured out the vials of her wrath for twenty-nine long years, this *Xantippe* left him—and he made no effort to get her back. She carried with her all his papers and journals. Wesley was

77 at the time. She finally died in 1781, leaving him ten more years of life in which to find tranquillity. Fortunately they had no children.

In the end, this brand that was snatched from the burning in Savannah, was wholly consumed in an even hotter fire! Well, that sort of circumstance makes either a great saint, or a great sinner. In this case the phoenix that arose from the ashes was a saint.

(14) The unrevealed Amazon has fought in all wars. At Waterloo and other European battlefields women in men's clothes were found dead. Our Amazon of the Mexican War was a Mrs. Coolidge, a native of Missouri, who there married a Mexican trader. Evidently they had a parting of the ways, for when the United States declared war on Mexico, she dressed in men's clothes and enlisted under the name of James Brown. She marched to Sante Fe and later became bearer of dispatches. In addition to being in numerous Indian fights, she was in the assault on Mexico City.

In the Civil War three women we know fought as men until their sex was revealed, viz.; Louisa Wellman of Iowa, who enlisted in a state regiment, took part in the storming of Fort Donelson, and, at the Battle of Pittsburgh Landing was wounded. Her sex being discovered by a surgeon, she became a nurse. Two others were Sarah Stover and Maria Seelye, who joined the Federal Army in '63 and fought at Chancellorsville. In this battle Miss Stover was reported missing and her friend deserted and finally discovered her in a Confederate prison. She helped her escape, and brought her back to the Union lines, where they joined their regiment until discharged. It is said that their sex was never revealed.

The avowed Amazons are aplenty. In the Great War Russia had its female Battalion of Death, and Serbian women and girls fought openly in the ranks of that army. Among the Serbians fought Flora Sandes, once a nurse, who donned men's clothes and for her services rose to the rank of captain. She was badly wounded, shared all the hardships of the men and made an enviable record for herself. Her story is told in the "Autobiography of a Woman Soldier," London, 1927. Another quaint female belligerent is recorded in Kirby's "Wonderful and Eccentric Museum or Magazine of Remarkable Characters,"

London, 1803–5. She was Mary Ann Talbot, otherwise John Taylor, a footboy, drummer, powder monkey, sailor, and prisoner. She was wounded at the Battle of Valenciennes and in 1795 came to New York and Providence. She always worked in men's clothes.

De Foe, also, is remembered for his life and adventures of Mrs. Christian Daires, commonly called "Mother Ross," who served as foot-soldier and dragoon in several campaigns under King William and the Duke of Marlborough in the habit of a man. Then there was Mary Katie Irwing 1678–1721, who sailed the Spanish Main as a pirate dressed in men's clothes, and who came to a sordid end on the gallows at Port Royal, Jamaica.

Perhaps our earliest record of women in warfare is recorded by Aeneas of Stymphalus, a general of the Arcadian League of 367 B. C. and mentioned by Xenophon. When the people of Sinope ran short of men, "they disguised and armed the fittest of their women, so as to make them look as like men as they could, gave them jars and such like implements of brass to represent armour and helmets and marched them round the walls in full view of the enemy. They did not allow them to throw missiles; *for you can tell a woman a long way off by the way she throws.*"—Vide "Aeneas on Siegecraft," edited S. S. A. Hanford, Oxford 1927.

(15) In addition to the opening up of the Western Reserve to Revolutionary veterans, a large area of central New York State offered an opportunity to them which constituted payment due them in 1782. This land was set apart as a gratuity by the New York State Senate and Assembly, March 27, 1783, in accordance with the resolution by Congress of September 16, 1776, which called for eight-eight battalions from the thirteen colonies, four to be enlisted in New York State and paid from United States lands.

On July 3, 1790, Governor George Clinton presided at a meeting of the Commissioners of the Land Office of the State of New York held in New York City and with a committee accepted a survey of twenty-eight townships set apart for Revolutionary soldiers. Each township was divided into 100 lots of 600 acres each. And the land was to be awarded as follows: to a Major General, 5,500 acres; to a Brigadier General,

4,250 acres; to a Colonel, 2,500 acres; to a Lieutenant Colonel, 2,250 acres; to a Major, 2,000 acres; to a Captain and Regimental Surgeon, each 1,500 acres; to every subaltern and surgeon's mate, 1,000 acres; to every non-commissioned officer and private, 500 acres.

At this meeting the board designated the townships by the following names: Lysander, Hannibal, Cato, Brutus, Camillus, Cicero, Manlius, Aurelius, Marcellus, Pompey, Romulus, Scipio, Sempronius, Tully, Fabius, Ovid, Milton, Locke, Homer, Solon, Hector, Ulysses, Dryden, Virgil, Cincinnatus, Junius, subsequently adding the towns of Galen and Sterling.

And this was the way the towns and cities in central New York that bear classical names first were assigned them.

P. S.   This subject of the classical names for towns has caused considerable discussion, and many differing views have been expressed.   The above theory has the advantage of being a matter of record in the archives of New York.

(16) These devastating anti-Catholic riots of the 50's echoed in both their form and their virulence the Gordon Riots of 1780 when, for seven days and nights, a vast rabble held London at its mercy, a drunken mob that surged through the city howling "No Popery!" and burnt Catholic churches and homes.   Over $5,000,000 worth of property was destroyed. When soldiers came into action over 600 people were killed. Twenty-one were executed.   This terror was started by Lord George Gordon, leader of the Protestant Association and member of Parliament, who fought the Catholic Relief Act.   He was tried for treason and acquitted.

(17) "The Angel Gabriel," Sanders McSwich, was a native of the Isle of Skye.   He changed his name to Orr.   His stepfather, by whom he was reared, was an itinerant Baptist preacher who relinquished the meadow pulpit for the more alluring life of the circus.   Under his tutelage young Orr became an acrobat.   Soon he eloped with the daughter of a Liverpool liquor dealer.   We encounter him next in Wales, where he was a Methodist preacher.   Here he adopted, and evidently found successful, the ballyhoo methods of the "Big Top."   Overnight he and his horn disappeared.   He next shows up in Jamaica where he is an ardent Baptist.   Thence he came to the United States, where he served successively as a dancing master,

convert to Mormonism, circus performer, temperance lecturer, tin peddler, and editor of a Nativist paper in Philadelphia. His next step was to New York where he acquired a brass trumpet and went into street-preaching again. Finally he departed for British Guiana. There he became ring leader in anti-Creole and anti-Catholic riots. He was arrested for sedition against the Crown and sentenced to Demerara, where he died. His age was then thirty-five. A pretty crowded career for thirty-five years!

(18) The last of the Maria Monk type of books appeared in 1871, "The Trials and Persecutions of Miss Edith O'Gorman," otherwise Sister Theresa de Chantal of St. Joseph's Convent, Hudson City, N. J. Her experiences and biography are much more interesting and more intelligently presented than the experiences of the earlier convent-jumping ladies. She became a friend of Emerson and the Alcotts.

(19) Legend says that William Newport was an illegitimate son of the uncle of Lord Baltimore and that he was paid an annuity. This would bring to Anne, through bars sinister, Calvert and Stuart blood. Sarah Porter, author of "The Life and Times of Anne Royall" remarks that there were "startling mental resemblances" between him and Sophia Dorothea, Electress of Hanover and mother of George II. The legend is further supported by the fact that William Newport's removal from the comfort and safety of Maryland to the frontier of Pennsylvania coincided with the cessation of the paying of the annuity.

(20) Mrs. Royall's "spice" was not restricted to personalities. Many of her anecdotes and adventures have quite a racy tang. She tells a story well. As witness the houseboat story in "Letters from Alabama." Close by a town on one of the southern rivers were moored some arks or houseboats which were used for rendezvous by gentlemen of the town and ladies of purchasable virtue. A prominent citizen is seen boarding one of these. His friends wait until the night is well along, then cut the mooring cable. The next morning the two awake to find themselves drifting down stream. With difficulty the boat is steered into shore, and the leading citizen flees, leaving his *amorata* to get back to town as best she can. Mrs. Royall

expands the story to three pages, and tells it as an evidence of her sympathy for women who are misused by men.

(21) At one time the question of whether or not the mail should be transported on Sunday occupied the attention of the nation. The Blue Sunday advocates opposed it as unnecessary labor and put up a long and stiff fight before they were finally voted down by a more liberal-minded majority.

(22) In the Colonial days of America there were no fashion papers and very little intelligence, in the ordinary press, of changes in the mode. But from this it must not be surmised that our great-great-grandmothers were ignorant of style changes or lacked interest in them. The style information was circulated by means of dolls dressed in the latest mode. Thus, in New England in the eighteenth century there was advertised the arrival from London of the latest model doll. The charge to see it was two shillings, but if you took it home and kept it to copy the style, the charge was seven shillings. Even in those days women were willing to pay steep prices for their fashion news!

(23) Perhaps the two earliest feminists we can boast were Anne Hutchinson of Salem and Lady Deborah Moody. The strivings of the former lady with the unyielding Puritan theocracy, her banishment and tragic end, are too well known to recount here. Lady Deborah Moody, on the other hand, has received no such extended notice from historians.

The widow of Sir Henry Moody of Garesden, Wiltshire, and herself a descendant of the famous Fighting Dunches of Berkshire, she first came into public notice in England by clashing with the court of the Star Chamber in 1635. Five years later she came to America with her young son, accepted a 400-acre grant near Lynn, Mass., and the following year bought "Swampscot," the farm of Deputy-Governor John Humphrey. She also had a house in Salem and belonged to the Salem Church. Scarcely had she gotten the farm stocked, than she ran afoul of the local authorities because she differed with them on the subject of infant baptism. They invited her to leave the colony, and so this contumacious virago sold her place and stamped the dust of Massachusetts off her feet. She then went to Rhode Island, where her advanced views did not altogether coincide with Roger Williams's; thence to Hartford and New

Haven, in each of which places she saw that she could not live unmolested, and finally she came to the country of the Dutch. Thanks to their generosity she was given a grant of land which included the whole of present-day Gravesend, Sheepshead Bay, and Coney Island. There she built her house, stocked her farm and reigned over her fellow settlers with a rod of iron. A willful, strong-headed woman, she made a record for herself in the annals of New Amsterdam as a termagant, managing to roil the placid Dutch at every turn. Indeed, she was Coney Island's first queen!

Her story is told in detail in "Lady Deborah Moody" by James W. Gerard, New York Historical Society Publications, 1880; Nathaniel S. Prime's, "History of Long Island," and in H. D. Eberlein's "Manor Houses of Long Island."

(24) Another of these female genius editors was Ann Sophia Stephens, who founded the *Portland Magazine* at Portland, Maine in 1835 and edited it for two years. Thence went to New York where she edited, *The Ladies Companion* for four years, wrote for *Graham's Magazine* and *Peterson's* and in 1843 founded *The Ladies' World* and, three years later, *The Illustrated News Monthly*. She was also author of many novels successful in their day.

(25) For the greater part of its career Godey's was called *Godey's Lady's Book*, but toward the end this was changed to *Godey's Magazine*. Mr. Godey sold it in December 1877 to a Philadelphia company, which in turn sold it to Frank A. Munsey, that unrivaled mortician of American magazines. After coming into Mr. Munsey's hands it suffered the fate of so many others over which he gained control—it disappeared. Meantime he had founded a boys' and girls' paper called *The Argosy*. He then bought *Peterson's*, another old Philadelphia publication, and *Godey's* and the two were amalgamated into the new property. For a few issues *Peterson's* appeared on the title page as *The Golden Argosy and Peterson's*, but the latter was eventually dropped as also was the word "Golden." The Godey name seems never to have been used. *The Argosy* issued its first number on December 2, 1882. This first issue, by the way, appeared just two months and nine days after Frank A. Munsey landed in New York from Augusta, Maine, a lad with great publishing ambitions.

Mrs. Hale's half century of editing *Godey's* is well-nigh equalled by Matthew White, Jr., who for forty-two years has been editor of *The Argosy*. In that time Mr. White has "discovered" many of the fiction writers now famous in America. As dean of the Corps of New York magazine editors, Matthew White, Jr. occupies an honored and beloved place.

(26) The careers of the Claflin Sisters were brought to mind as recently as 1927 when Victoria died. She was born in 1838. Her matrimonial vagaries were many. Shortly after coming to New York she divorced Woodhull and thus permanently removed him from her life. The poor fellow was said to have died of delirium tremens eventually. Her next conquest was Col. James H. Blood, commander of the 6th Missouri Regiment and President of a Spiritualistic society in St. Louis. Col. Blood was stowed safely away by being given a job as sub-editor on the Weekly. Her third husband was John Biddulph Martin and his name she bore until her death in 1927 in London. Meantime her sister Tennie acquired a title and became Lady Cook. Victoria's speeches and writings were voluminous. A woman capable of great quantities of work, a striking figure, she was among the feminist curiosities of the latter half of the last century.